Population Decline and the Remaking of
GREAT POWER
POLITICS

Population Decline and the Remaking of

GREAT POWER
POLITICS

Edited by **SUSAN YOSHIHARA** and **DOUGLAS A. SYLVA**

Foreword by **NICHOLAS EBERSTADT**

POTOMAC BOOKS
WASHINGTON, D.C.

Library of Congress Cataloging-in-Publication Data
Population decline and the remaking of great power politics / edited by
Susan Yoshihara and Douglas A. Sylva ; foreword by Nicholas Eberstadt.—
1st ed.
   p. cm.
 Includes bibliographical references and index.
 ISBN 978-1-59797-550-6 (hardcover : alk. paper)
 ISBN 978-1-61234-112-5 (electronic edition)
 1. Demographic transition—Political aspects. 2. Population—Political aspects. 3. Balance of power. 4. Security, International. I. Yoshihara, Susan. II. Sylva, Douglas A. III. Title.

 HB887.P659 2012
 327.1'12—dc23

                       2011023385

Potomac Books
22841 Quicksilver Drive
Dulles, Virginia 20166

First Edition

10 9 8 7 6 5 4 3 2 1

*To my parents, George and Joyce Fink,
with love and deepest gratitude*
—Susan

*To my dear wife, Susan Sylva, and our children: Antonia,
Damien, Eliana, Lucia, and Josefina*
—Doug

CONTENTS

FOREWORD

Nicholas Eberstadt

This welcome book sheds new light on the topic of human numbers and international power, which has been discussed, as far as we can tell, for very nearly as long as states themselves have been in existence. It is a subject, moreover, that is just as current to the modern reader as it was to the literati of the early Chinese dynasties and the citizens of ancient Greece and Rome. Today, as in antiquity, almost everyone with an interest in the question can agree that human numbers definitely have a bearing on the friendly—and sometimes unfriendly—interactions between countries in the world arena. So far, so good: but exactly what are these patterns, tendencies, and/or rules and how exactly does the aggregation of human beings, with their myriad individual qualities, end up shaping the tenor and outcomes of international power arrangements? All of a sudden the seeming consensus breaks down into a fracas of contending assertions and stubbornly held but mutually inconsistent contentions.

Everybody, it would seem, "knows" that population matters to the course of international relations—but what people profess to know differs remarkably among persons, places, and historical settings, and furthermore can at times be manifestly at variance with easily established facts. This is the dilemma immediately encountered by every scholar and researcher who endeavors to undertake serious study of the complex, subtle, far-reaching, and sometimes surprising interplay between the shifting international population profiles and changes in the balance of power and in international security.

Looming over so much of the modern era's discourse on the population factor in international affairs is the premise that there is "strength in numbers":

a point upon which thinkers as otherwise estranged from one another as, say, V. I. Lenin and Henry A. Kissinger could commonly concur. As this volume reminds us, it should come as no surprise. After all, more or less since the beginning of recorded history, and with remarkably few obvious exceptions up until the era that commenced with decolonizations in the wake of World War II, population growth was the handmaiden of political ascendance the world over; conversely, population decline (whether absolute or relative) was the lot of regions whose political fortunes were waning. Apprehension of this seemingly universal historical truth, as it happens, was instrumental in the birth of the very discipline of population studies. "Demography" may be a word with Greek roots, but it was not coined until the second half of the nineteenth century, and then in French, as *la démografie*. French intellectuals, statesmen, and patriots were all too well aware of the direction in which the Franco-Prussian struggle for mastery of Continental Europe was heading at the time—and they laid blame for France's flagging strategic prospects very largely on the country's comparatively low birthrate and its relatively sluggish tempo of population growth. As originally conceived (so to speak), demography was to be the study—possibly even the science—that would permit France to revitalize its fertility; bolster a youthful, growing, confident national population; and thereby help in eventually turning the tide in the long contest against rival Germany.

The Franco-Prussian experience is a template that has informed, if not framed, what might be called "strategic demography" for at least four generations (and longer in the Francophone world). But should it? In historical hindsight, we now know that Germany was definitely successful both in out-peopling and out-soldiering France over the course of the "long century" that extended from 1789 to 1914. The actual contribution of Germany's more rapid pace of population growth, however, to Berlin's ultimate ascendance over Paris in that age of power politics is much less certain. History can never be re-run, of course, but we know that a number of other critical factors essentially non-demographic in nature played a major role in this story: among these, the revolutions in nineteenth-century German science, chemical and heavy industries, and finance; the advent of the now-famous Prussian General Staff with new approaches to the strategy and doctrine of war-fighting; and not least important, German unification. Given these and other important advantages, it might seem entirely possible that Germany should have overtaken France as the continent's prime power even without a differential edge in population growth.

Current headline-rating developments demonstrate plainly by themselves that we must be ready to qualify carefully any number of prevailing assumptions about the connections between people and power. Strength may indeed lie in numbers—but that precept *simplicatur* cannot explain the rise of China during the post-Mao era. During the decades since the big policy shift under Deng Xiaoping, by the estimate of the economic historian Angus Maddison, China's share of world economic power jumped from something like 4 percent to something like 17 percent of world global economic output (economic potential being a requisite of international power these days); but over the same period, China's share of world population decidedly declined—from about 22 percent of the global total to under 20 percent. Over those same years, by contrast, the continent of Africa's population waxed from an estimated 11 percent to almost 15 percent of humanity—yet Africa's share of planetary output remained unchanged over that interim, at just over a mere 3 percent of the global aggregate, and the African states likewise remained relegated to the margins of international power politics.

Other big generalizations about population and world affairs must be handled just as carefully. The great demographer Alfred Sauvy, for example, warned that population aging would result in the risk of societies where "old men sit in old houses ruminating about old ideas." Perhaps so. But at the same time, we must punctiliously note the Adolf Hitler's Germany—not exactly a paragon of risk-averse state behavior—was in fact one of the "grayest" countries of its day, and that the Serbia of the 1990s, the state that enforced a savage and violent "ethnic cleansing" on a neighboring victim—pieces of what had once been Yugoslavia—encompassed one of the most elderly populations of any country in Europe, or in fact the world, at that juncture. Demography may be destiny, as the great polymath and socialist Auguste Comte is reported to have declared in the 1800s—but in the here and now its impact on global affairs has to be studied with great caution, and indeed hesitant scrupulousness. The breathtaking explosion in human potential over the past century—and the simultaneous increase in the complexity of both domestic and international political processes—can only mean that generalizations about the impact of population on power and plenty require an ever more solid grounding in empirics. (As evidence accumulates to suggest that man may be altering both global climate and local ecosystem capacities, the need for such care is only reaffirmed.)

At the dawn of the twenty-first century, it is apparent that we have entered a very different demographic world from the one that our immediate predecessors took for granted. In the twentieth century, human numbers exploded—world population nearly quadrupled, thanks to a tremendous increase in worldwide life expectancies (all of that population growth was due to improved mortality—and then some). On the whole—some gruesome exceptions noted—further steady improvements in health look to be in the cards around the world for as far as the demographer's eye can see. But at the same time, an unprecedented and sustained transformation of childbearing patterns has pressed long-term fertility prospects for the world's major powers (and also presumptive rising powers like China) down below the level needed for long-term population stability in the absence of compensatory immigration. In Europe as a whole, according to estimates of the United Nations Population Division, fertility levels have been below replacement rates overall since the late 1970s; in Japan, subreplacement fertility has been the rule (with few annual exceptions) since the mid-1950s: that is to say, for well over half a century.

Despite immigration inflows, these fertility trends mean that quite a few of these so-called developed countries in question now seem on a path that must lead in coming decades to a peaking and decline of the conventionally defined working-age population; to a subsequent peaking and decline of national population totals; and to a pervasive and pronounced aging of national population profiles. At this writing, statistical authorities in three of the G-7 countries—Germany, Italy, and Japan—report national population total to be in decline; the G-8 member Russia is also a net-mortality society, and has been for almost two decades. China is also on track, by current U.S. Census Bureau projections, to be a net-mortality society a generation hence (in the year 2027).

It is by no means certain that subreplacement fertility should be the fate of affluent Western societies for the indefinite future. This much should be clearly understood. Population studies have never offered any reliable scientific method for long-range fertility forecasts (much less predicting the birthrates of the then-unborn). Consequently, we cannot be sure that the recent past decades of subreplacement fertility in today's affluent and powerful Western societies should lead inexorably to net-mortality regimens, or net-population-decline regimens, in the generations ahead. (For that matter, we can have no great confidence in the projected trajectories for today's high-fertility societies.) But there are reasons to anticipate that pressures for low fertility will be increasing, rather than receding, in the decades immediately ahead. Perhaps more important than any of the other portents for future childbearing is what has been termed by demographic specialists "the flight from marriage": the modern global tidal wave away from early stable lifelong conjugal unions. This phenomenon, we should note, is not simply a "European thing." On current trajectories, by some Japanese estimates, today's young Japanese women as a cohort are on track to end up 25 percent unmarried—and 38 percent childless. Given such prospective family formation patterns, the outlook for attaining above-replacement fertility regimens in today's Western societies may be increasingly problematic.

Given today's differential fertility rates among countries, and the attendant population growth rates therefrom, it is all but certain that today's rich countries in general will experience a gradual decline in their relative global demographic share over the next several decades. (The United States may be a fascinating exception to this generalization—but this is another story altogether.) Given prolonged subreplacement fertility, moreover, pronounced population aging is an inescapable reality the world over—even for countries with low average income levels today. And there is a political economy problem embedded in all these prospective trends: will demographic realities constrain the ability of contemporary societies (including not only affluent countries but also some so-called emerging economies) to augment their potential for extending their influence abroad, given political claims on the public fisc for social spending rather than defense allocations? Do changes in domestic population profiles, finally, presage changes in political sentiment, or more specifically in the disposition of electorates to support investment in capabilities, or international application of those capabilities, in any reliable and predictable fashion?

These are profound and as yet unanswered questions. With more studies such as this one, however, we may hope that the inquiry into them will be ably under way.

ACKNOWLEDGMENTS

Underlying the age-old debate about population and power is a moral question of ends and means. This study is based upon the belief that people are not the means to the ends that are national power and international security. To the contrary, power and security are the means to preserving and protecting national populations, that is, individuals living together as families, communities, cities, and countries. For that reason, we strived to explore and respect the various normative, cultural, and social causes and consequences of population decline while pursuing the ultimate question of the future of international stability.

We are grateful to the many people who helped us realize this project. Most of all, we thank our contributors for their fine work, promptness, and forbearance with our editorial queries. The book initially took shape in 2006 and gained steam with some encouragement from Nicholas Eberstadt when he came at the request of our institute to give a talk at the United Nations General Assembly's Third Committee in New York, "The War Against Baby Girls." After his presentation, a veteran European delegate turned to Susan and said, "That was the first time I have heard something genuinely new at the UN." Recently, the global crisis of sex-selective infanticide and abortion has achieved more public awareness, but it was in no small part Nick's impeccable and persistent research that made it possible. Phil Longman accepted with alacrity our invitation to preside over a panel discussion at the March 2008 International Studies Association meeting in San Francisco where four authors presented their first drafts. His course correction, especially his now-vindicated pessimism about the U.S. housing market and financial stability, were invaluable in setting the tone of the book. We are grateful to our interlocutors during that discussion, including Richard Cincotta, for their unvarnished and expert feedback. We thank Nick Eberstadt and the offices of the American Enterprise Institute in Washington for hosting our second discussion in the summer of 2010, where we honed our thinking about wild cards, counterfactuals, and knowledge production. We owe Murray Feshbach special thanks for his work on the Russian military—the culmination of some five decades of research, writing, and teaching. A generation of scholars is indebted to the content and quality of his research and the scholarly standards he has set for all of us.

The project would not have been possible without the support and personal encouragement of Austin Ruse. Austin's faith in it witnesses to his dedication to fostering quality research. We thank our colleagues at the institute for their encouragement and understanding during the most intense periods of the project and are indebted to Sean Fieler and the Chiaroscuro Foundation for their generous support of the project. Special thanks are due to Hilary Claggett at Potomac Books for her enthusiasm in the topic and guidance on the path to publication, and Julie Gutin for her expert copyediting. We are grateful to those who took time to talk with us, reviewed iterations of the prospectus, or read initial chapters, including Richard Jackson, Don Jacobs, the late Fr. Richard John Neuhaus, Piero Tozzi, David Yost, and three anonymous reviewers. While many people deserve credit for the book's merits, these interlocutors bear no responsibility for its content, and we heartily accept credit for any flaws in conceptualization or conclusions. We hope the book will continue to foster a robust and diverse conversation.

Susan is grateful to her husband, Toshi, without whose encouragement this book would not have come to be. The editors have been blessed along the way with unfailing help and good cheer from their spouses and children.

INTRODUCTION

Susan Yoshihara and Douglas A. Sylva

There is a revolution taking place right now, one with implications for the future of world order. But despite this revolution's importance, it is taking place quietly, with a whisper rather than a shout. Barely anyone seems to be noticing; hardly any scholars seem to be assessing the geopolitical ramifications of this revolution, or whether any policies may be enacted now in order to mitigate the worst potential outcomes. And that is because this is not a political revolution at all; it is a demographic revolution. Across the globe, nations are now in the midst of a profound set of changes: fertility is falling at the same time that life expectancy is rising, and both changes are so deep and sustained as to be entirely new experiences in human history.

There is no doubt now that, in the next few decades, many nations will have older, smaller populations. In some cases, this demographic decline may be so steep as to raise doubts about a nation's ability to achieve economic growth, to afford social-welfare costs, to maintain adequate defense, and to meet international security obligations. While truly a worldwide phenomenon, the extent and timing of the decline shows enough variation—nation by nation, and region by region—to raise serious questions about the balance of power and the stability of the current world order.

The conventional belief through much of human history concerning the relationship between population and power is as unsurprising as it is simple: *more is better*. In this view, more people means more soldiers for the field of battle and more citizens for the tax collector. For every monarch who has desired a larger purse to pursue his aims, and for every general who has looked across the front line longing for reinforcements, more has been better. All things being equal, more people has meant more power.

It was Thucydides, writing in the fifth century B.C., who first raised a voice counter to this conventional view. According to Thucydides, smaller numbers of soldier-citizens may be more powerful than hordes of soldier-slaves. Under some circumstances, *less can be better*. Of course, for there to be free men, and imaginative generals to lead them, there would need to be the requisite social organization—the educational, political, and cultural institutions—to create such citizens. And so Thucydides suggested that population was not an uncontrolled or uncontrollable fact of nature; choices would need to be made at the most profound levels: just what type of civilization, producing what type and number of citizens, should be the aim of sovereigns interested in maintaining or increasing strategic power?

To answer these questions, historical and geographical contexts appear paramount. The strategic setting of ancient Peloponnesian Greece is a world apart from the context of England at the start of the industrial revolution, when Thomas Malthus took up this same question about the interplay between population and power, thereby framing the new conventional wisdom that, to a certain degree, still dominates the field of study. According to Malthus, there is a point at which population growth outpaces the physical resources necessary to maintain that population, resulting in potentially massive levels of human suffering and political destabilization. In a phrase, according to Malthus, *too many will be catastrophic*.

The resilience of this theory has continued, despite the evidence against it. Malthusian and neo-Malthusian thought have served as guiding principles of population and development programs throughout the twentieth century and into the current one, especially as it relates to the bilateral and multilateral aid efforts designed for the developing world. According to this logic, poor countries cannot emerge from their circumstances because population growth rates have already reached catastrophic levels, with base numbers of people overwhelming all attempts at health and education reform. This stunted development, in turn, fosters cultural and political unrest; unchecked population growth renders instability almost a certainty.

But now, the context appears to be changing again. Perhaps in part because of the population alarmism instituted by Malthus, the last few decades of the

FIGURE 1-1
Annual World Population Change (1950–2050)

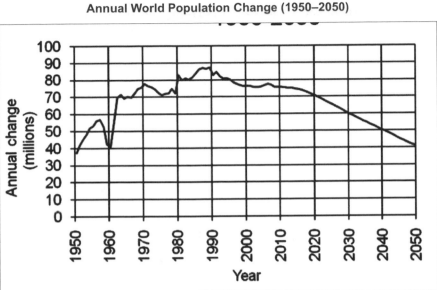

U.S. Census Bureau, International Data Base (December 2010 update)

twentieth century saw worldwide population decline as fertility rates fell dramatically (though unevenly), from an average of seven children per woman at the start of the century to fewer than three at the end of the century.[1] This fact alone, coupled with projections of continued fertility decline, would call for new assessments of the relationship between population and power. The new questions turn the old on their heads. While most studies of international security and national power continue to focus on the issue of population growth, if they consider population at all, demographic trends would suggest different questions, and different concerns.

This study will explore the new demographic reality that is now locked into the next few decades of the human experience, and assess whether and to what extent population decline in the key world powers—characterized first by fertility decline and population aging, then by actual population decrease—affects global stability. From a geopolitical standpoint, *is less better or worse than more?*

To answer this question, the authors of this study have assessed a number of variables. For instance, just what is the true nature of power in the modern world? Is the hard power of military and economic might still paramount, as

TABLE 1-1

**Fertility Rates, Population 1950–2050 (in Thousands),
and Onset of Population Decline**

	Fertility rate	Population in 1950	Population in 2010	Population in 2050 (projected)	Onset of population decline
China	1.77	550,771	1,341,335	1,303,424	2029
France	1.89	41,832	62,787	71,348	2050
Germany	1.32	68,376	82,302	68,560	2006
India	2.76	371,857	1,224,614	2,019,849	–
Japan	1.27	82,824	126,536	99,689	2008
Russia	1.37	102,702	142,958	114,125	1992
United Kingdom	1.84	50,616	62,036	70,425	2050
United States	2.09	157,813	310,384	402,072	–

United Nations, World Population Prospects: The 2010 Revision. *Constant fertility variant.*

realists assert? Or is multilateral dialogue and the soft power of attraction by normative appeals replacing or reducing the hard-power nature of relations between states, as internationalists might contend? Is conventional war between major powers becoming outmoded, and with it the need for large standing armies? If traditional measurements of power are obsolete, then population decline may not matter, but if nations continue to pursue their interests and back that pursuit with large economies and military force, then global aging will determine the winners and losers of the future.

Regarding economics, do new, service-based economies still require growing populations of workers and consumers in order to achieve growth? What is the real interplay between population and development? Will there be "demographic dividends" for all of those countries that successfully slowed their demographic growth, or will inertia and stagnation set in?

To what extent is the rise of China and India the result of abundant labor? Traditionally, increases in worker productivity require improvements in capital, technology, and labor. If technology trumps or replaces manpower, or if fewer elderly workers can be even more productive than abundant young labor, then the coming demographic changes may be irrelevant. If nations cannot make such sweeping change in the near term, however, then there is no way to avoid cataclysmic effects of aging on national economies.

Overall, what are the relative effects of population decline on the great powers? What are the effects on individual economies and defense budgets, as well as on unquantifiable qualities, like entrepreneurship, knowledge production, thirst for innovation, outward spirit, optimism, military strength, and willingness to engage in military operations? Each of the major nations will experience, or already experiences, demographic decline and aging in diverse ways that are potentially significant for the assessment of the changes in their geopolitical positions. As these relative effects take hold, how will they influence regional and international alliances? What regional powers will become global ones? What global powers will see their influence fade? Finally, how will all of these variables interact to impact global stability? If alliances are no longer based upon hard security arrangements, or if a normative power has replaced standing armies, then the retreat of European nations from NATO or the United States from the Pacific Rim may not spark conflict. But if realists are right, then tensions within alliances and reordering of regional powers will have reverberations on global stability.

To understand these general points, some specific issues will be addressed in detail. Are U.S. political and military planners poised to take advantage of American demographic exceptionalism to exploit significant political and economic advantages over a declining European Union and an emerging Asia? Can the European Union show the world the way forward for managing demographic decline in a way that allows it to maintain a significant presence on the world stage? In other words, can it buck the conventional geopolitical wisdom concerning the need for a robust population to maintain geopolitical influence, and pull the world toward a locus of multilateralism and soft power? Can Russia's remnant reserve of great power qualities compensate for its demographic decline in order to maintain a place as a world power? Is Japan fated to economic and geopolitical demise, or can technology and engagement in international institutions underwrite continued world leadership? Which rising Asian giant, China or India, is better positioned to exploit population as a boost to its aspirations of regional and global power? Will global aging hasten the coming of an

Asian century, or cause destabilizing trends between China and its neighbors? Finally, how will Islam, with fertility relatively higher than most of the rest of the world (but falling quickly) influence world stability?

As these many issues are explored, we propose an answer, however tentative, to the question of whether demographic decline will usher in a new age of tranquillity and cooperation between nations or a new era of instability and conflict. We believe that, while some say demographics is destiny, it is not necessarily *geopolitical* destiny. Many qualities of national power figure into the equation: regime type, culture, and technology, such as whether a country possesses nuclear weapons, all matter. While difficult choices need to be made, the most competitive nations can adopt policies to blunt some of the worst outcomes of demographic decline.

Demographic Peace or Turbulent Twenties?

The United Nations calls the 60 percent drop in fertility in the last five decades "dramatic" and simultaneous twenty-year increase in life expectancy "unprecedented." The number of old people, sixty years or more, increased 3.5 times

TABLE 1-2
**Percentage of Population Over 65 and 80 Years of Age,
Median Age, and Life Expectancy**

	Percentage of population over 65 years old		Percentage of population over 80 years old		Median age	Life expectancy
	2010	(2050)	2010	(2050)		
China	8.2	(25.4)	1.4	(7.5)	34.4	72.7
France	16.8	(25.3)	5.4	(10.2)	39.9	81.0
Germany	20.4	(33.7)	5.1	(14.7)	44.3	79.8
India	4.9	(11.3)	0.7	(2.2)	25.1	64.2
Japan	22.7	(38.7)	6.3	(15.9)	44.7	82.7
Russia	12.8	(25.6)	2.9	(6.6)	37.9	67.7
United Kingdom	16.6	(24.4)	4.6	(9.3)	39.8	79.6
United States	13.1	(21.3)	3.8	(7.9)	36.9	78.0

United Nations, World Population Prospects: The 2010 Revision. *Constant fertility variant.*

TABLE 1-3

Change from Year 2010 to 2050 in Working-age Population (15–64 Years) and Workers per Dependent Old Person (65+ Years)

	Working-age population (year 2010)	Working-age population (year 2050)	Percent change	Worker per dependent old person (year 2010)	Worker per dependent old person (year 2050)
China	970,532	790,010	–2	8.8	2.4
France	40,713	41,633	–2	3.9	2.3
Germany	54,435	40,839	–25	3.2	1.8
India	789,750	1,143,065	+45	13.1	5.0
Japan	80,926	55,446	–31	2.8	1.4
Russia	103,161	75,705	–27	5.6	2.6
United Kingdom	40,973	43,090	+5	4.0	2.5
United States	207,534	241,725	+16	5.1	2.8

United Nations, World Population Prospects: The 2008 Revision.

(from 205 million in three countries to 705 million in eleven countries). That number is expected to reach 2 billion in thirty-two countries by 2050, comprising 22 percent of the world's population.[2] Further, the cohort of people over eighty is the fastest growing segment of the older population (see Table 1-2). The very old accounted for one in fifteen elderly in 1950, one in eight by 2007, and are expected to be one in five elderly by 2050.[3] Half of them live in just five countries: China, the United States, India, Japan, and Germany. This has shifted the dependency ratio—the number of workers per dependent—significantly toward the aged. In the last fifty years, the ratio of workers (people fifteen to sixty four) to older dependents (persons sixty-four and older) fell globally by 25 percent. The drop was nearly 50 percent in developed countries. It is expected to fall by another 55 percent by 2050 (see Table 1-3).[4]

According to the United Nations, the primary cause of global aging is fertility decline, because people of reproductive age are having fewer children relative to those of older generations.[5] For years demographers assumed that there would be a fertility convergence, whereby all nations' fertility fell to replacement level, about 2.1 children per woman. In reality, fertility rates have continued to fall and no one knows how low they will go. The divergence in worldwide fertility rates has implications for the security environment that the major powers will face in the coming decades. The fact that Palestinian women have nearly twice the number of children neighboring Israeli women bear has already changed security dynamics in the Middle East, and this situation is replicated from sub-Saharan Africa to the cities of Europe.

In some countries, fertility rates have remained at three or more children on average and this has slowed their rate of aging. Columbia University historian Matthew Connelly has demonstrated how, in the developing world, fertility rates have been indifferent to whether a country had population programs to suppress birthrates.[6] Harvard political scientist Lant Pritchett has shown that, no matter how many children governments promote as "ideal," the ultimate driver of family size is the preference of parents.[7] An emerging consensus, even among population control proponents, is that cultural and religious norms have much to do with how low a nation's fertility rate will go.[8]

What is certain is that national leaders cannot change the demographic future; they can only assess its ramifications upon the future security environment and prepare for it. So what do these trends portend? Population experts have proposed that as long as the developing world completes the "demographic transition"—a shift to lower fertility and mortality rates—they will also enter a "security demographic," whereby they will be more stable and peaceable.[9] The corollary to the security demographic is the "demographic peace" thesis, which assumes rapidly growing societies are apt to be poorer, more violent, and more of a burden on the environment, while older societies tend to be prosperous and stable.

The security advantages of having fewer people in the developing world has informed international social policy for half a century, and provided the intellectual foundation of the U.S. Agency for International Development (USAID), the world's largest donor to population programs. U.S. Army general William Draper was the godfather of population assistance programs,[10] and the founders of USAID were veterans of the Vietnam War who transferred the counterinsurgency tactic of "population control" to create the agency's international fertility reduction program by the same name.[11] The appeal of the notion that it is better to prevent the birth of an enemy combatant than to face him on the battlefield has endured. Since the Cold War, the idea of a security demographic has been promoted in top U.S. intelligence and military circles.

In last few years, as the crisis of population decline has drawn closer, promoting an uncritical version of the demographic transition theory and the security demographic has become more difficult. In their landmark study on population and geopolitics, Richard Jackson and Neil Howe question demographic transition theory and refute the demographic peace thesis. They argue that instead of tranquillity, nations that are well into the demographic transition will be the cause of a very turbulent and sometimes violent period throughout the 2020s.[12] Jackson and Howe conclude, "Just because the present-day developed countries, which have completed the demographic transition, are relatively peaceful and democratic does *not* mean that today's developing countries, en route to completion, will become steadily more peaceful and democratic."[13] The past is not prologue.

Proponents of demographic transition theory point to the success of the East Asian Tigers in the 1990s, but in fact the Asian miracle has failed to materialize beyond the Tigers. Jackson and Howe call them the exception that proved the rule. What helped East Asia was not just fertility decline and a smaller dependency ratios, but stable and effective governments, sound macroeconomic policies, pro-business tax and regulatory regimes, public confidence in the rule of law, massive public investments in human capital, and cultural values that emphasize hard work, filial piety, and social order.[14] Latin America, the Arab world, non-Arab Muslim Asia, and South Asia have experienced large drops in their dependency ratios on par with the East Asian Tigers, but they have not reaped the same economic growth rates and have failed to close the income gap. The gap in living standards in these countries is actually larger today than it was in 1975, before many of them went through their demographic transitions.

The rapid fertility decline of the last few decades will also lead to destabilizing "echo booms" in pivotal states like Iran in the years ahead. Despite the fact that women today give birth to fewer children than their mothers, the fact that there are a large number of women means they will have a large cohort of children. This cohort will come of age in the 2020s and 2030s. If governments cannot fulfill raised expectations for social services during these years, political unrest in countries like Iran will result. In general, developing nations do not have the advantage of Europe and Japan, which had social safety nets in place before fertility and population decline set in. As Nicholas Eberstadt has pointed out, developing societies—even China, with its tremendous size and growth rate—are getting old before they get rich, which already causes serious internal social instability.[15]

The conventional wisdom surrounding "demographic peace" also focuses too narrowly on chaotic state failure while ignoring more globally destabilizing threats such as neo-authoritarianism, Jackson and Howe conclude. Conventional wisdom also ignores the fact that many violent societies are in fact well into the demographic transition and are not poor, high-fertility states. Jack Goldstone further argues that demographic factors are only a part of the complex causal forces behind violent conflicts. For decades, experts have argued that population growth leads to violence due to competition for scarce resources, but as Goldstone points out, environmental degradation is not the cause of major international wars. Furthermore, small wars are often the result of other factors, such as elite behavior or popular resistance to elite attempts at conflict moderation.[16]

In other words, there is no conclusive evidence that current development programs aimed at suppressing the fertility rate in the developing world will make those countries more prosperous and peaceful. To the contrary, the cases of China, Russia, and India in this study provide cautionary tales about the economic and security perils for developing nations who cannot pay the high costs of aging.

Finally, an underlying assumption in the demographic peace thesis pertaining to the powers is that all of them would respond the same way to the aging crisis. Experts have crafted a one-size-fits-all approach to demographics and security analysis. It is not at all clear that China and Russia will respond the same way as Germany and Japan to the aging crisis, however.[17] In fact, the authors in this study have found wide-ranging responses among the powers.

Logic of the Study

The focus of this book is on great powers: the developed nations of Europe, Japan, and the United States, and countries at various other stages of economic and political development, namely China, India, and Russia. While the dynamics of demographics and security in places such as sub-Saharan Africa are important, they do not affect geopolitics or international stability per se. A greater concern is the threat of great power war, the diminished ability of affluent Western nations to fulfill their international security obligations, and whether large, developing nuclear-powered states will rise peacefully or cause regional and international conflict. Thus, this book concentrates its analysis on the great powers of today and the contenders for tomorrow. In 1950, the developed world accounted for most of the world's populous nations. Today, three remain so, but by 2050 only the United States will remain in that category (see Table 1-4).

The fate of America's most important alliances hang in the balance, and in this study we examine more narrowly and more deeply the way that demographic decline may jeopardize inter-state relations even further. We propose that in order to understand national power, it is essential to first appreciate mili-

TABLE 1-4
Decline of the Powers: Change in Largest Countries by Population Size

Rank	1950	2005	2050
1	China	China	India
2	India	India	China
3	United States	United States	United States
4	Russia	Indonesia	Indonesia
5	Japan	Brazil	Pakistan
6	Indonesia	Pakistan	Ethiopia
7	Germany	Bangladesh	Nigeria
8	Brazil	Nigeria	Brazil
9	United Kingdom	Russia	Bangladesh
10	Italy	Japan	Philippines
11	Bangladesh	Mexico	Mexico
12	France	Philippines	D. R. Congo
		Germany (15)	Russia (16)
		France (21)	Japan (20)
		United Kingdom (22)	Germany (21)
		Italy (23)	United Kingdom (22)
			France (24)
			Italy (28)

U.S. Census Bureau (December 2010 update), http://sasweb.ssd.census.gov/idb/ranks.html.

tary and strategic power, and that previous studies have not dealt sufficiently with this nexus. As Ashley Tellis put it, one must not only have a "meticulous detailing of visible military assets," but must also scrutinize broader capabilities "embodied in such variables as the aptitude for innovation, the soundness of social institutions, and the quality of the knowledge base—all of which may bear upon a country's capacity to produce the one element still fundamental to international politics: effective military power."[18] To assess military power, the contributors to this study take account of crosscutting normative, technological, social, and political drivers that will influence the remaking of great power politics in the decades ahead.

Reordering of global power is destabilizing. As nations rise or fall, they historically have caused other major powers to change military and strategic postures, alliances, and even engage in military adventurism. It is not possible to determine how today's powers will react to the coming shift without also understanding the purpose for which those nations wield their power. National character shapes the way a country assumes its new rank. In turn, the new status—and the path to attaining it—shape national purpose. The contemporary case of Japan is telling. With its population shrinking in absolute terms, Japan was overtaken by China as the world's second largest economy in 2010. Many Japanese welcomed the news with more relief than regret. At the same time, Japan's foreign-policy makers are far from signaling retreat. Just the opposite, Japan is expanding its international commitments in order to maintain its rank as a global player. Yet it has done so despite insufficient military assets to fulfill those obligations. Demographic change can prevent a nation from fulfilling its national purpose and international role, or force it to modify or abandon them altogether.

Since Japan is leading in global aging, the way depopulation affects its global stature will serve as a model for Europe in the years ahead. Will Japan's reputation as an international team player—its support for the UN, engagement in international legal regimes, reliability as an economic and military ally—be enough to maintain its rank as its population contracts? One litmus test might be whether it is afforded a seat on the UN Security Council as part of that body's reform in the coming years. As a non-nuclear state, this prospect seems unlikely, and if India becomes the second Asian nation on the Security Council, it would only serve to underscore Japan's decline.

Russia's abysmal fertility rate, shockingly high mortality, and stagnant immigration have also led to absolute population decline. The nation transformed rapidly from global superpower to economic basket case in 1991. Russia's return to authoritarian political and economic policies in the last decade has been aimed not just at restoring order, but also at regaining international prestige. It has wielded its veto on the UN Security Council and chosen key battles with its former American peer in order to leverage remnant great-power prerogative until it can rebuild its military and economy. But the nation's demographic ill health is a dark cloud hanging over its ambitious military modernization plans. Those plans are funded largely by Russia's vast oil and natural gas reserves, which are dependent upon the international market. While the market is now in a downturn, it could surge again and enable enough force transformation to allow Russia to maintain its status as a great power, but given its demographics, Russia will not field forces like those that won World War II and challenged NATO.[19] Given the severe health crisis in its armed forces, it will have trouble maintaining its status among the powers.

Both Japan and Russia are counting in part on their current or future leadership roles through international organizations. The future prominence of these organizations is not guaranteed, however, especially since global aging will reinforce the role of the sovereign state at their expense in the decades ahead.[20] Europe has the most to lose if and when this happens. Its native population in relative decline due to low birthrates and immigration, Europe is constrained by the high price of social democracy. At the same time, Europe has based its security policy explicitly on United Nations' goals, and has aligned its military policy in a significant way toward peacekeeping in order to fulfill this aim.[21] More important, Europe's idea of itself—and its projection of power—has included "civilian power" since the end of the World War II. Today, civilian power is a way to offset the dearth of soldiers and cost of hard power by replacing it with human rights and other normative aspects of soft power centered at international and European institutions.

Demographics is not destiny, but it sets the boundaries of the possible. India's and China's populations have allowed them a large domestic market and plenty of cheap labor to bolster their export markets. Yet while China and India are the world's most populous nations, they face a host of economic, social, and ecological challenges in the decades ahead that may slow or forestall their rise to the top. Chief among China's problems is an increasingly restive population whose appetite for democratic and economic liberalization has been whetted by Beijing due to political necessity, but which will never be satisfied by the current regime. Successive Chinese regimes have sought to bolster then quash the people's fertility rate through coercive means. Whatever demographic benefits these efforts provided have now been spent, and the Chinese workforce and number of recruitable youths will be in decline for several decades to come.

India instituted harsh population control policies in the 1960s and 1970s, which failed to significantly suppress the fertility of poor Hindus and Muslims. Conversely, cultural norms shifted toward smaller families among more affluent Hindus, leaving India with a bifurcated fertility rate favoring the less educated Northern population. India's relatively high overall fertility rate will lead to its surpassing China as the world's most populous country. In order to convert its demographic advantage into military and economic power, however, New Delhi must overcome high social hurdles to increase productivity and man an information-age military.

The example of the United States is the most illustrative in the question of population-as-power. At just over 300 million people, it is one third the size of India and China, yet its economy is nearly four times the size of China's and more than ten times larger than India's. American military forces are generally younger and more educated than the U.S. population at large. They are the most technologically proficient—and since the Iraq and Afghanistan wars the most combat-experienced—forces in the world. Experts credit the U.S. military's high caliber to the thirty-five-year-old All-Volunteer Force (AVF), which is both successful and expensive to maintain. Since the 2008 economic downturn, the defense budget has become a primary target, and while many decision makers fail to fully realize it, the fiscal decisions made today will have strategic ramifications for decades to come.

Chapter Summaries

Part 1 of this book addresses geopolitics and demographics: prospective scenarios for the global future, precedents in classical history, and the principles of population in the study of geopolitics. The cases in part 2 on the West and part 3 on Asia are arranged to first address the countries on the leading edge of aging and population decline: Russia and Japan. Next, they treat the countries in flux: a declining Europe and a rising China. Finally, they examine the exceptions to the global aging rule: the United States and India. Each of the chapters addresses one or more aspects of the conventional wisdom about population, power, and international security.[22]

Phillip Longman sets the backdrop in part 1 by establishing basic demographic and economic projections. Longman proposes three possible scenarios for the future. In the short term, the best outcome could be a vindication of the prevailing belief in a global demographic dividend, with rising prosperity caused by the rise in the proportion of the working-age population to dependents. The worst short-term outcome could be greater economic uncertainty and stagnation, if population growth proves necessary for economic growth and the regimes of the developing world find it difficult to foster the growth of a middle-class base of consumers. The best long-term outcome would be demographic change fostering a new era of geopolitical stability, growing prosperity, and cultural and political maturity. The worst long-term outcome could be a new sort of dark age, ushered in by the fact that only "fundamentalists"—people at odds with the assumptions and institutions of the modern world—will continue to reproduce at relatively high levels.

James Holmes looks to classical history to examine whether nations respond to demographic shocks in violent or peaceful ways. In his case studies from the ancient world—Athens and Sparta—Holmes shows how the nature of the regime in question, the nature of the larger society, and the nature and timing of the demographic shock all contribute to whether the regime will adopt risk-averse or risk-taking policies. Sparta's oligarchic leadership followed its already inherent conservative tendencies, while democratic Athens decided to gamble on foreign military adventures. According to Holmes, the case of Athens shows that democratic regimes, like India today, may be more likely to respond effectively to demographic shock than authoritarian regimes like Sparta's, or like China today. On the other hand, the case of Athens shows that democratic states can also react more violently.

Francis Sempa shows that, despite the fact that contemporary scholarship often ignores traditional geopolitical frameworks, these models are highly relevant in an era of massive demographic shifts. Sempa establishes theoretical links between demographic and geopolitical influence—in other words, links between people and power. Sempa finds that there is no fixed formula for great power status, and population is only one important variable among many others. Throughout history, however, states have often failed to gain dominance because of insufficient manpower. Failure to build national institutions that harness population momentum is a key reason for these missed opportunities. Historical precedent shows that nations with large and growing populations tend to seek to expand their geographical control. For that reason, Sempa foresees the expanding influence of Islam and believes the next major threat to the global order will emerge from Asia. If European and Japanese geopolitical decline follows their demographic decline, much of the burden of maintaining the current global order will fall to the United States.

Part 2 examines the United States, Europe, and Russia. Like Japan in the Asia-Pacific region, Russia is on the leading edge of the crisis. While the Japanese have the lowest fertility rate and are the oldest among the powers, the onset of Russian population decline came more than a decade before Japan's. Further, the average Russian dies a full two decades younger than his or her American, French, German, or Japanese counterpart (refer back to Table 1-2). A stunning 50 percent drop in births between 1987 and 1999 will slash by one-third the pool of recruit-age youth by the early 2020s. Additionally, a rapid rise in HIV and tuberculosis has shrunk the number of those youth who are service-eligible from more than 50 percent in 1988 to less than 10 percent today. Mental disorders, malnutrition, muscular-skeletal and spinal disorders—results of Russia's poor maternal and child health, and public health more generally—are top reasons for rejection from service. At the same time, poor pay has made draft dodging among eligible youth commonplace. Some 200,000 young Russians avoided military service in 2010. As a result, youngsters have been unceremoniously taken from classrooms and pressed into service. Murray Feshbach's analysis calls into question the effectiveness of Russia's recent military modernization plans.

Douglas Sylva focuses on normative drivers and repercussions of aging and demographic decline in Europe. In particular, Sylva examines the likelihood that the nations of Europe will be able to manage their ongoing demographic decline in order to maintain the continent's geopolitical influence. He finds that deeply held values and beliefs among the European people do not seem compatible with reversing fertility decline or fostering large families. Thus, policy efforts to this end will likely fail. In fact, it is even possible that Europe may not have reached the lowest point of its fertility decline, since it may be the case that these normative ideals become self-reinforcing over time. Most important, the effort to boost fertility by closing the gap between real and ideal family size will prove ineffective, since ideal family size itself is beginning to shrink. Sylva recommends a fundamental shift in European social policy and concludes that European nations are likely to continue to place foreign policy emphasis upon soft power and multilateralism in place of military power in the international arena.

Susan Yoshihara examines the conventional wisdom about how the great powers will cut defense spending to pay for an aging society. She finds that the American demographic advantage could be turned into prolonged American primacy if policymakers do not delay important decisions about health care and social security, and if cuts in major systems and personnel are made according to strategic interests and not as political reaction to fiscal constraints. Relatively robust fertility and immigration can help the United States avoid the near-term economic crisis that demographic decline will visit upon the rest of the West. Its enviable demographic situation has led to a peerless military based upon the All-Volunteer Force. While costly, the AVF is economical given the fact that it has been able to overcome the recruiting and retention challenges of fighting two wars during an economic downturn. However, the AVF will soon be in jeopardy if policymakers do not resolve lackluster coordination and prioritization of national and military strategy, meteoric increases in entitlement spending, and cost escalation for military assets that outpaces inflation. If careful policy choices are made in time, the United States will continue to enjoy the fruits of its demographic advantages.

In part 3, the book turns to Asia and the three regional giants: Japan, China, and India. Toshi Yoshihara examines the implications of Japan's population decline on defense planning and Japan's strategic prospects. He challenges the conventional wisdom about "demographic peace," showing that long after completing the demographic transition, population issues may cause an aging nation to pursue regionally destabilizing behavior. According to Yoshihara, Japan is an "unfolding experiment" in demographic aging, due to its low fertility, high life expectancy, and negligible immigration. Yoshihara considers two geopolitical scenarios caused by demographic decline: first, the creation of a power differential so severe that China goes to war with Japan, and second, a manpower shortage that dramatically reduces Japan's strategic options. Yoshihara considers the first scenario unlikely for a number of reasons, including the basic fact that Japan is protected by the United States' nuclear arsenal. But Yoshihara does consider the second alternative plausible, based upon a set of demographic outcomes: the gradual decrease in the size and quality of the military recruitment pool, limited funds for military spending as the cost of social programs grows, and the creation of a culture of risk aversion. Yoshihara questions the Japanese government's decision to expand its regional and global security obligations, as well as its faith that technology will allow it to meet these obligations, despite the demographic challenges. Instead, Yoshihara argues that Japan will need to prioritize its obligations based upon a clear understanding of its resource limitations.

Gordon Chang then considers the geopolitical consequences of China's tumultuous demographic situation, challenging the notion of a "geriatric peace," whereby the great powers will be too old to fight one another. Chang contends that demographic decline will create a series of "closing windows" on important foreign policy objectives, potentially causing Chinese leaders to act sooner rather than later on issues like war over Taiwan. Demographic demise will delay and may even thwart China's rise, but will inevitably make it less stable. To Chang, the cause of this demographic decline is self-inflicted: after the imposition of the coercive one-child policy in the late 1970s, the Chinese fertility rate fell from 2.9 to 1.54, and it will take decades to correct the demographic problems stemming from this decline, most notably the vast sex imbalance that has produced far more boys than girls in the last thirty years. Considering the likely continuation of this policy into the future, Chang explores the various geopolitical scenarios. For instance, it is possible that an aging, shrinking population will result in a more pacific culture, a culture in which a nation of only sons moves toward an aversion to potential casualties in wartime. More likely, however, is that large numbers of unmarriageable males will result in a more aggressive, crime-ridden culture. The regime may then respond with greater repression at home and greater risk-taking abroad.

In her chapter on India, Lisa Curtis demonstrates that diverging fertility trends within a country can cause internal security crises that may distract a government's attention from external security commitments, thus making a region less stable. India is on the cusp of an enormous demographic dividend, a period in which the increased proportion of workers to dependents will allow for both dramatic economic growth and a rise in India's geopolitical influence. Curtis identifies a number of problems that Indian policy-makers must overcome in order to achieve these outcomes. Education must be improved, literacy rates must be increased, labor must have more flexibility, the multiple challenges of increased urbanization must be met, and internal strife—including the Maoist-Naxalite problem and increasing Hindu-Muslim tensions—must be addressed. As in China, the growing sex imbalance caused by selective abortion of baby girls has already given rise to human trafficking and may cause further social unrest. It is projected that India's population will surpass China's by about 2025. In fact, India will be enjoying its demographic dividend at the same time that China will be facing the problems caused by a rapidly aging population. If India can mitigate these problems, Curtis believes that India will emerge as the democratic counterweight to Chinese influence, resulting in greater regional stability.

The imminent demographic revolution is like so many drops of water cutting crevices in solid rock: the aggregate of millions of individual choices not to bear another child, to delay starting a family, or to forgo childbearing altogether. Those choices, informed by many social and cultural changes over just a few decades, have created a global fertility freefall that has defied prediction by the world's top demographers. But while policymakers cannot reverse the causes of global aging, they may be able to affect the consequences.

PART I.
PROSPECTS, PRECEDENT, AND PRINCIPLES

1

THE GEOPOLITICAL IMPLICATIONS
OF GLOBAL AGING

Phillip Longman

Introduction

In both hemispheres, in nations rich and poor, and under all forms of government, one broad social trend holds constant at the beginning of the twenty-
first century: the world is undergoing a demographic transformation of historic
and unprecedented dimensions. Two major countries, Japan and Russia, are
already experiencing absolute population decline. Due to a fall in birthrates,
the working-age population of all developed countries except the United States
will stop growing within five years. Thirty years ago, every developed country
produced enough children to maintain a stable population from one generation to the next. Today, among developed countries, only the United States and
France come close to producing the average 2.1 children per woman necessary
to sustain population over time.

As births decline, life expectancy is also increasing, causing the population
as a whole to age rapidly. Today in the developed word, persons sixty-five and
older comprise 16 percent of the population. According to projections from the
United Nations Population Division, the elderly share is expected to rise to 23
percent by 2030, and to 26 percent by 2050.[1]

Yet the steepest drops in fertility, and the most rapid rates of population
aging, are now occurring in the developing world, where many nations are
now growing old before they get rich. Iran, under the tight rule of a militantly
Islamic clergy, has slashed its fertility level by fully two-thirds (from 6.6 children per adult to 2.1) and now produces barely enough children to sustain its
population over time. Four Islamic countries—Iran, Turkey, Morocco, and

23

Lebanon—now are at or below replacement-level fertility. The one major exception to the worldwide trend is Pakistan, where, although birthrates have fallen by one-third since the middle of the last century, they still hover at 3.79 children per woman. India, by contrast, has a fertility rate of just 2.8 percent, with its southern states already reproducing at below replacement rates. India's drop in fertility means that its population will be aging at three times the rate of the U.S. population over the next half-century.

China's low fertility, brought on in part by its one-family/one-child policy, will lead to shrinking in the labor supply by 2015. In twenty years, its population as a whole will be in decline even as the number of elderly increases more than two-fold. Because of falling fertility, Brazil, Chile, and Mexico may have older populations than the United States by mid-century. All told, some fifty-nine countries, comprising roughly 44 percent of the world's total population, are currently not producing enough children to avoid population decline, and the phenomenon continues to spread. By 2050, according to the latest United Nations projections, 75 percent of all countries, even those in underdeveloped regions, will be reproducing at below replacement levels.

How will the global distribution of power and geopolitical relations change, given current trends in fertility and population aging? In the following sections I offer three scenarios each for both the short and the long term.

Best Case Scenario (2010–2020)

Slower world population growth, to be sure, can offer many benefits, some of which have already been realized. Many economists believe, for example, that falling birthrates made possible the great economic boom that occurred first in Japan, and then in many other East Asian nations beginning in the 1960s. As the relative number of children declined, so did the burden of their dependency, thereby freeing up more resources for investment and adult consumption. In East Asia, the working-age population grew nearly four times faster than its dependent population between 1965 and 1990, freeing up a huge reserve of female labor and other social resources that would otherwise have been committed to raising children. Today, China's rapid industrialization is aided by a dramatic decline in the share of dependent children in the population.

Over the next decade or so, the Middle East could benefit from a similar "demographic dividend." In every country of the Middle East, birthrates fell, often dramatically, throughout the last two decades. The resulting "middle aging" of the Middle East will ease the overall dependency ratio, thereby freeing up more resources for infrastructure and industrial development, all else being equal. With young adults accounting for a declining share of the population, the appeal of radicalism may also diminish, as Middle Eastern societies become increasingly dominated by middle-age people concerned with such practical issues as health care and retirement savings. Because of population momentum from the past, there will still be considerable strains on water and other natural resources in the region, but much less than if the rate of population growth was not declining. It is also important to remember that the rate of population aging will be much faster in the Middle East and other developing regions than that seen in any other time or place in recorded history.

The population and GDP of the developed world as a whole will steadily shrink as a share of the world's total, causing the global influence of the developed world to decline. At the same time, however, the population and GDP of the United States will steadily expand as a share of the developed world's total, which should strengthen the influence of the United States within the currently developed world.

The three greatest strategic threats to the United States are its unsustainably high cost of health care, its energy dependence, and its under-regulated and oversized financial sector. In the context of current domestic politics in the United States, all three problems may seem intractable, but all can also be fixed through relatively minor changes in policy and technology. The examples of other developed countries show, for example, that the United States could cut its per capita health care spending in half (thereby eliminating its fiscal deficits) without incurring any adverse effect on population health. Switzerland enjoys 70 percent higher per capita GDP than the United States, and does so using half the United States' per capita energy consumption, primarily by heavy use of an energy-efficient nineteenth-century technology: railroads. The essential solvability of the United States' major problems is no small difference when compared to those of other Great Powers, such as Russia, Japan, and the European Union, which face demographic decline for which there is no obvious policy solution or self-correcting mechanism.

Theoretically, a highly efficient global financial market could ease the challenges of population aging. Japanese and European pension funds, for example, may be able to earn the high returns they need to cover their long-term deficits by investing in the emerging markets of comparatively youthful countries. These countries, in turn, may thereby be able to develop quickly enough to afford the coming cost of their own very rapid increase in the number of dependent elders. By running persistent trade surpluses with the developed world, countries such as India and China may be able to acquire sizable foreign assets. This scenario requires continuing globalization and integration of world financial markets, as well as underlying sustainable balances of trade—trends that cannot necessarily be relied on to continue at the pace seen in the last two decades, due to such factors as resurgent protectionism, high energy costs, and fears of terrorism.[2]

Similarly, high rates of immigration from the developing to the developed world may help to smooth out existing imbalances in the age structures of the different regions of the globe. The United States, for example, has been able to avoid any prospect of population decline due primarily to its success in attracting and assimilating immigrants—a model that Europe and Japan may be able to emulate. Yet here, too, openness to great flows of immigrants may be reduced due to concerns with security and political backlash. On paper, aging populations could benefit from higher infusions of youthful immigrants, but in practice, aging societies also seem prone to increased nativism as their majorities lose cultural self-confidence.

In developed countries, the challenge of population aging may also be eased by increased workforce participation among women and older citizens. Currently in the European Union, only 50 percent of men and 40 percent of women aged sixty are still in the labor market. The European Commission forecasts that participation rates for the fifteen to sixty-four age group will increase in the EU-25 (the group of twenty-five nations in a proposed expansion to the European Union), rising from 65.5 percent in 2007 to 69 percent in 2020, due primarily to increased participation by women. If these targets are achieved, it will be possible for the European workforce to continue growing, albeit ever more slowly, through 2019. At the same time, policies designed to ease the tensions between work and family life, such as family allowances and more flexible work arrangements, have had modest success in Scandinavia and France in maintaining fertility even as working mothers become the norm.

Baseline Scenario (2010–2020)

Many countries—notably Sweden, Germany, the United Kingdom, and Japan—have already made large prospective cuts in their pension promises to future retirees. However, enacting or following through on plans to reduce spending on the elderly will be politically difficult and often detrimental to social stability, due to a combination of factors threatening elderly populations around the globe.

In the United States, inadequate retirement savings, excessive consumer borrowing, poorly performing private pension plans, rising health care costs, and lost home equity will cause many members of the post–World War II "baby boom" generation to face severely reduced circumstances as they age. According to a survey by Barclays Global Investors released in April 2009, an astounding 58 percent of American baby boomers with retirement savings say they expect to work until they die.

In the United States and increasingly throughout the world, the ability of delayed or cancelled retirement to solve the global aging crisis is increasingly undermined by trends in public health. Life expectancy at older ages is generally still rising among the nonpoor. But so are rates of chronic illness and disability. Just between 1995 and 2000, for example, the number of obese adults increased worldwide from two hundred million to three hundred million, with 115 million of these living in developing countries. Over a billion people worldwide are now estimated to be overweight, creating a global pandemic of chronic conditions from heart disease to diabetes.[3] At the same time, we see a massive spread of "Western" diets high in fat and unhealthy processed foods. The techniques of modern medicine have also proved to be remarkably ineffective in improving the health and productivity of older populations even when, as in the United States, they are widely available.

These trends are inconsistent with predictions of a coming golden era of "productive aging." So too are trends in technology that make many job skills become rapidly obsolete. We will continue to see increasing examples of individuals who make useful contributions through advanced old age, but based on current trends they will constitute a small minority of their generation.

High rates of childlessness will also present elders with many challenges. In the United States, about 17 percent of those now approaching retirement age never had children. In many European countries, the number is (or will soon be) between one in five and one in four. Even in countries with robust welfare states, tasks like navigating the health care system or arranging for long-term nursing home care can be daunting without the aid of family. In countries lacking formal provision for the elderly, the costs of childlessness are often more extreme: at the start of this decade, elders living in urban China had an average of three grown children to share the burden of their care; by 2025, they will have just 1.3.

Throughout the 1990s and until the world economic crisis that began in 2008, the conventional wisdom at the World Bank and other leading global institutions held that financial provision for old age could best be accomplished through increased individual saving and investment in integrated capital markets. So called "pay-as-you-go" public pension plans, in which younger taxpayers support older retirees, it was pointed out, can offer individual participants generous rates of return only so long as population growth remains strong. In the absence of population growth, returns are limited to underlying increases in productivity (or its usual proxy: wage growth). In contrast, returns on capital, it was argued, could more than make up for the declining numbers of workers available to support each retiree.

Around the world, this thinking led to rollbacks in conventional social security programs, and the implementation of so-called "individual accounts" in which workers attempt to pre-fund their own retirements with matching contributions from their employers or sometimes their governments. The United Kingdom, Australia, and Sweden were leaders in this approach. Other countries such as Canada have tried a hybrid approach in which government pension funds invest in the private economy.[4]

In theory, it makes perfect sense in an aging society for each generation to pre-fund the cost of its own retirement through investment in capital markets that ultimately raise each new generation's overall productivity. In practice, however, we have seen vast amounts of retirement savings wiped out by the global economic downturn. World financial markets engaged in what was clearly excessive risk taking. Moreover, rather than making investments that might improve the productivity of the next generation, the global financial system diverted much of the world's savings into current consumption, by lowering lending standards on home mortgages and credit cards, for example. Though it is still too early know how this crisis will play out over the next ten years, a few trends can be confidently predicted:

- Banking and financial markets will become subject to much tighter regulation.
- Credit-financed consumption, particularly by Western consumers, will play a much reduced role as an engine of world economic growth.
- Populations around the globe will look to government for more protection from financial risk and job loss.
- Stagnant or declining working-age populations will retard economic growth in the absence of "game changing" technological developments.
- The promise of unfettered capitalism and globalism will seem diminished, even as the limits of socialism and communism remain well remembered.

Worst Case Scenario (2010–2020)

During the 1930s, many key observers of the Great Depression—notably John Maynard Keynes and his American counterpart, Alvin Hansen—attributed its root cause to the falling fertility rates of the Western world at that time. Population growth creates more supply of the labor capitalists buy (so the logic went), and more demand for the products and services capitalists sell, making it perhaps essential to keeping up the animal spirits of investors. John Hicks, in his famous review of Keynes's General Theory, went so far as to remark:

> Expectation of a continually expanding market, made possible by increasing population, is a fine thing for keeping up the spirits of entrepreneurs. With increasing population investment can go roaring ahead, even if invention is rather stupid; increasing population is therefore actually favourable to employment. . . . One cannot repress the thought that perhaps the whole Industrial Revolution of the last two hundred years has been nothing else but a vast secular boom, largely induced by the unparalleled rise in population.[5]

Today, analysis of the world economic downturn has so far concentrated on financial architecture: the growth of a shadow banking system, the complexity and synthetic nature of new financial instruments, problems with moral hazard, too much leverage, etc. Yet, stepping back from these details, one cannot repress the thought that the excess risk that infected the system had a root cause: it was ultimately driven by a quest to retain high returns on capital at a time when truly productive opportunities were diminishing, due at least in part to slackening population growth.

Japan's economic stagnation began in the late 1980s, just as its growth in its working aged population slacked. Slow population growth in the Western world is arguably a root cause of the excess capacity now found in nations dependent on it for export trade. For a long while, expanded consumer credit (financed by recycled foreign capital and asset inflation) could sustain high consumer demand in the United States and most of Europe, but in the face of decelerating population growth the trend becomes unsustainable due to exhausted consumer balance sheets and sheer satiety. There are only so many iPods and high-definition televisions any given household needs.

If this analysis is correct, then averting a second Great Depression depends critically on raising effective consumer demand in areas of the world where population is still growing and consumer needs are great. One might expect this to happen automatically, and it may well in the long run, but not before wrenching changes that cause economic and social turmoil. Africa, Russia, and much of the Middle East face problems of governance, from corruption to ethnic strife, that seem to stand intractably in the way of an expanded middle class. India, China, and other export-driven countries must restructure their economies to stimulate domestic consumption. Yet they must somehow do so without causing a spike in global energy and food prices and without cutting off the United States from the credit it needs to continue as a strong export market, all the while providing for domestic populations that are themselves aging rapidly. The challenge of fostering a sustainable, world-wide middle class are even more daunting if one takes seriously the asserted relationship between increased greenhouse gas emission and climate change.

The Challenge of the 2020s

As challenging as the remaining years of this new decade may be, it is the 2020s when the maximum effects of demographic change are likely to occur. During that decade the giant baby boom generations around much of the world will begin to experience en masse the infirmities of old age. At the same time, there are reasons to worry about a return of "youth bulges" in different regions of the Middle East. Birthrates there, to be sure, have been consistently falling. Yet because of the large numbers of people of childbearing age, even a declining average number of children per woman can still create a so-called echo boom. In the Arab world, for example, the growth rate in youth age fifteen to twenty-four is currently slowing, from 2.6 percent per year between 1990 and 2005 to 0.9 percent between 2005 and 2020. But then a subsequent echo boom will occur when the population of young adults will again accelerate to 1.9 percent per year between 2020 and 2035.

Further, as geopolitical strategists Neil Howe and Richard Jackson of the Center for Strategic and International Studies point out: "The echo booms of the 2020s will be largest in precisely those countries where fertility has fallen the fastest over the past twenty to twenty-five years and youth populations are now declining most rapidly." In Iran, where the fertility rate plunged from 6.6 children per adult in 1980 to 2.1 in 2005, the number of people aged fifteen to twenty-four will shrink by 34 percent between 2005 and 2020. Between 2020 and 2035, however, the number will again swell by 34 percent. Many other Muslim countries, from Libya to Pakistan, will also experience huge oscillations in their youth populations."[6]

Most of the former Soviet republics in Central Asia will also face large echo booms in the 2020s. Long a battlefield for larger powers, from the Mongols and Persians to the Russians and British, this region of newly independent states is once again the object of geopolitical competition due to huge natural gas and oil reserves. The same is true of two of Latin America's most volatile countries, Peru and Venezuela, which will face large echo booms in the 2020s.

The 2020s will also see the consequences of today's imbalanced sex ratios in many parts of the world. In a normal population, there are roughly 105 baby boys born for every 100 girls. In India there are 110 boys born for every 100 girls, and in China there are 117. These exaggerated gender imbalances have ominous implications. Today's "missing girls," as they are called in China, will become tomorrow's missing brides. China is projected to have a surplus of some thirty million men of marriageable age by 2020, and the numbers in India are similar.

By the 2020s military manpower shortages, along with fiscal constraints caused by population aging, are also likely to play a large role in determining how and whether wars are fought, and by whom. The United States is the last remaining nation with enough manpower and hardware to deploy large, permanent military forces beyond its immediate boundaries. By the 2020s, however, the numbers of Americans fit for military service will likely be substantially reduced, while the "graying" of the U.S. federal budget will put pressure on military hardware spending. It may be that national power today is much less dependent than before on the ability to raise large armies and navies. Yet the technologies the United States currently uses to project its power—laser-guided weapons, stealth aircraft, navigation assisted by the space-based Global Positioning System, nuclear aircraft carriers—are all the product of massive and ongoing investments that the United States will not be able to afford if the cost of pensions and health care continues on its current course.

The same point applies to the United States' ability to sustain or increase its levels of foreign aid. If the war of terrorism is indeed a "generational struggle," as some have warned, then the United States will have a very difficult time sustaining its financing. Even within the U.S. military budget, the competition between guns and canes is already becoming extreme. The Pentagon today spends eighty-four cents on pensions for every dollar it spends on basic pay. Other nations that might challenge the United States for military supremacy, such as China, are of course facing even more dramatic population aging, so the United States' relative position may remain unchanged or even improve.

Viewed from afar, India's demographics present a mixed picture. Driven by momentum from the past, India is poised to become the most populous nation on earth, eclipsing China for the first time in history. Falling fertility in the south is causing the country to age, but not with such rapid speed as can be seen in China. India's population age sixty-five and older is expected to increase from 60 million today to 221 million in 2050. More than 40 percent of India's remaining population growth will come from increases in the ranks of the elderly. This is a substantial rise, but it still leaves only 13.7 percent of the population older than sixty-five by mid-century, which is a smaller fraction than what Japan and European countries face today.

At the same time, India exhibits a wide differential in fertility rates among different segments of the population. This pattern is commonly seen in the Western world, but not in Asia. Specifically, there are pervasive Muslim-Hindu fertility differences in India that remain evident even after adjustment to such possibly confounding factors as socio-economic status. According to the latest available 2001 census data, Muslim fertility in India was 3.06 children per woman, as compared to 2.47 percent for Hindus.[7] Also, we see wide differences in reproductive behavior between educated and illiterate women, and between city dwellers and those living in the country. An urban Indian woman with a graduate degree has only 1.6 children over her lifetime, while an illiterate Indian woman living in the countryside has, on average, 4.1.[8]

Medium- to Long-term Scenarios (Twenty to Fifty Years)

BEST CASE SCENARIO

Properly managed, the vast demographic transition now affecting nearly every corner of the world could lead to a new era of stability, prosperity, as well as cultural and political maturity, particularly in regions where birthrates are falling, yet the labor force is still growing. The sub-replacement fertility rates now evident in nearly all developed nations may prove to be a temporary phenomenon, as societies take measures to reduce the cost of children to their parents, and to ease the tensions between work and family life. In the United States and in every European nation, for example, women aged forty in 2000 were coming to the end of their reproductive years having produced fewer children than they intended, according to surveys. American women born in 1960, for instance, desired an average of 2.3 children, but wound up producing 12 percent fewer. In Europe, the gap is even greater between the number of children women of this generation wanted and the number they actually produced. Indeed, if European women now in their forties had been able to produce their ideal number of children, the continent would face no prospect of population loss.

Continuing improvements in technology may so improve productivity that even the oldest nations will enjoy ample surpluses. Societies may spend a greater and greater percentage of their wealth on health care, but improving efficiency in the provision of everything else will make the burden easier to bear. Today, for example, a typical American must work 260 hours to earn enough money to secure his or her annual food supply. Yet as economic historian Robert Fogel points out, "If agriculture productivity grows at just two-thirds of its recent rates, then by 2040 a family's annual food supply may be purchased with about 160 hours of labor."[9]

Meanwhile, a slowdown, or absolute decline, in world population growth, combined with the disappearance of destabilizing "youth bulges" in different parts of the world, could lead to less competition for natural resources, a cleaner environment, and to a generally more peaceful and prosperous world. Some strategists believe that population aging around the world will lead to a "geriatric peace." In a world of single-child families, popular resistance to military conscription will grow, as tolerance of military casualties will fall.

BASELINE SCENARIO

If Europe's current fertility rate of around 1.5 births per woman persists until 2020, this will result in 88 million fewer Europeans by the end of the century. If European fertility rates remain unchanged, the only European countries that will avoid population loss by 2050, according to UN projections, are France, the United Kingdom, Ireland, and Luxembourg, and even these countries will face rapidly aging populations. Without an increase in its fertility rate, France's working-age population (ages fifteen to sixty-four) will decline by more than 9 percent by 2050, while its elderly population will increase by 79 percent.

By 2050, based on present demographic trends, there will be seventy-five retirees in Europe for every hundred workers; in Spain and Italy, the ratio of retirees to workers is projected to be one to one. By mid-century, if current trends continue, Europe will be a society in which most adults have few biological relatives. In Italy, almost three-fifths of the nation's children will have no siblings, cousins, aunts, or uncles—only parents, grandparents, and perhaps great-grandparents. Even among immigrants, families with more than one child are becoming increasingly rare throughout Europe.

If the United States is able to maintain its current birth and immigration rates, America will vastly increase in size, and most likely in geopolitical power, relative to Europe and Japan. However, current trend lines suggest that the fertility rates in United States may well converge with those of other developed nations. Among major ethnic and racial groups, only Hispanics are reproducing above replacement levels, and that is primarily because of the comparatively high fertility of recent arrivals, who are themselves having decreasing numbers of children.

Meanwhile, it is unclear how long the United States can sustain even current rates of immigration. One reason, of course, is the heightened security concerns about terrorism. Another is the prospect of a cultural backlash against immigrants, the chances of which increase as native birthrates decline. A final reason is the prospect of a decreasing "supply" of immigrants. Some Mexican demographers say, for example, that the country's fertility rate, which is officially measured at 2.5 children per woman, has already dropped below replacement levels. Puerto Rico, with a fertility rate well below replacement level and a median age of 31.8 years, no longer provides a net flow of immigrants to the U.S. mainland, despite an open border and a lower standard of living. Generally, fertility rates are dropping throughout Latin America and the West Indies, and are already below replacement rate in many major countries of the region, including Brazil, Chile, and Cuba.

If current rates of economic growth continue, the output of the Chinese economy could rival that of the United States by 2020. Yet before China can emerge as a true economic powerhouse, it must contend with a demographic challenge that it so far shows few signs of addressing. Even after assuming a substantial increase in future fertility rates, the United Nations projects that by 2050 nearly one in four Chinese citizens will be elderly. Other estimates, based on an assumption that future fertility rates will increase less substantially, show that by 2050, there may be as few as two working-age citizens available to support each retiree.

For the world as a whole, forecasts by the United Nations and others show world population growth could well turn negative during the lifetime of people now in their forties and fifties, and is very likely to do so before today's children reach retirement age. A study by researchers at Austria's highly regarded International Institute for Applied Systems Analysis, published in the prestigious journal *Nature*, predicts that world population will most likely peak before 2070 and then trail off rapidly.[10] Under such a scenario, most of the remaining growth in human population would come from increases in the number of people over sixty.

WORST CASE SCENARIO

Some biologists now speculate that modern humans have created an environment in which the fittest or most successful individuals are precisely those who have few, if any, children. As more and more of the human race finds itself living under urban conditions in which children no longer provide any economic benefit to their individual parents, but are instead rather costly impediments to material success, people who are well adapted to this new environment will tend not to reproduce. Many others who are not so successful will imitate them.

"The great range of conditions under which fertility has begun to fall all over the developing world," notes Alaka Malwade Basu of the Harvard Center for Population and Development Studies, "and the most potent correlates of such decline—education, exposure to the mass media, exposure to the ideologies (rather than the material trappings) of modernization—strongly suggest that the urge to control fertility and to have fewer children than one's parents comes largely from wanting to do what others do."[11]

So where will the children of the future come from? They may well come disproportionately from people who are at odds with the modern environment—from people who "don't get" the new rules of the game that make large families an economic and social liability, or who, out of fundamentalist or chauvinistic conviction, reject the game altogether. If so, the future may belong to fundamentalism.

2

STRATEGIC EFFECTS OF DEMOGRAPHIC SHOCKS

THE CLASSICAL PRECEDENT

James R. Holmes

James Holmes is an associate professor of strategy at the Naval War College. The views voiced here are his alone.

Introduction

Why do demographic shocks produce disparate effects on the behaviors of different nations? I conscript history to investigate the impact of demographic shocks on the chief antagonists in one of history's greatest conflicts, the Peloponnesian War. Declining manpower encouraged the ultra-conservative Spartan leadership to avoid risk, as might be expected, but it gave free vent to boldness, if not recklessness, in Athens. Why?

A simple equation from Carl von Clausewitz's *On War* furnishes a platform from which to appraise Athenian and Spartan conduct. National strength, writes Clausewitz, is a product of force and will.[1] How did demographic decline affect the force available to these warring city-states, and how did it affect their will to use it? The analysis presented here considers the nature of the contending regimes; the nature of the larger societies, including the resources available to each; and the nature of the demographic shock to each society. With any luck, considering the classical precedent will help contemporary students and practitioners ask the right questions about the relation between demographics and great-power politics—and may point the way to plausible answers that inform policy-making in the contemporary world.

Grinding a Clausewitzian Lens

Many societies today are experiencing gradual demographic decline owing to diminishing fertility. Because human capital forms one of the sinews of national strength—historian Alfred Thayer Mahan lists "number of population" among his six determinants of sea power—demographics has clear implications for foreign policy and strategy.[2] Societies with too few people, either in raw numbers or in certain sectors, find their policy options fettered. By exploring the cases of classical Athens and Sparta, analysts can identify factors and trends at work in the contemporary world, schooling their judgment.

These two superpowers of antiquity fought a protracted war from 431 to 404 B.C. Sparta's triumph left it atop the Greek international order. The warring societies could hardly have been more different. Sparta strictly regulated the makeup of the populace to supply the Spartan infantry, which was considered nearly invincible, with the finest genetic stock. The practice of discarding imperfect infants imposed limits on the expansion of the Spartan citizenry even in normal times. But this selectivity left Sparta vulnerable—a natural disaster compounded the dilemma created by artificially low manpower, setting Spartan demographics on a downslope and disrupting the city-state's social and economic system. An earthquake demolished the city in 464 B.C., magnifying Sparta's manpower woes while touching off a slave revolt and disrupting the labor supply on which the state relied. The leadership, however, chose to adapt incrementally rather than act decisively to widen the pool of potential military recruits. Skittish about innovation, Spartans found themselves fretting constantly about battlefield losses during the protracted struggle with Athens. Minor combat losses generated major strategic effects in ruling circles, constraining both the means and ambitions of the Spartans.

Archrival Athens endured demographic travails of its own during the Peloponnesian War. While the Athenian assembly limited full citizenship to people of Athenian descent, Athenian law imposed no eugenics regimen comparable to the one in Sparta. At the behest of "first citizen" Pericles, the assembly ordered residents of the countryside to move inside the city walls. Taking shelter when the Spartan army invaded Attica, the populace was thus shielded from Spartan ravages while sparing Athens the burden of land defense. But Pericles' policy also exposed Athenians to misery, moral collapse, and death when plague broke out within the city's cramped confines. Pestilence and repeated military setbacks sharply reduced the corps of experienced rowers and steersmen for Athens, the preeminent sea power of the age. Manpower constraints compelled the assembly to modify the navy's policy on recruitment during the latter stages of the war, liberalizing citizenship requirements to increase the manpower available to crew Athenian triremes (their triple-decker rowed warships). Despite their famous propensity to innovate, however, the Athenians ultimately lost the war.

Whereas demographic decline bred caution among Spartan leaders, it did not deter Athenian adventurism. Indeed, Athens hurled itself into reckless military enterprises despite its growing shortfall of manpower. Clearly, then, there is no predictable, linear relationship between demographics and strategy. This basic insight should inform strategists' understanding of the contemporary world. Why, then, do downward demographic pressures exert disparate influences on the behavior of different states? It appears self-evident that a blow to available manpower should engender risk aversion among national leaders. Sensible leaders craft policies to achieve important goals at the least cost to finite resources. Such a conservative outlook ought to be especially pronounced in the decision for and conduct of war, an undertaking pervaded by chance, uncertainty, and dark passions like fear and spite. War is a matter of national survival. By venturing as little as possible, a state avoids losing everything. It husbands its resources. The state that sees its populace depleted yet dares all could lose all. Sobriety, then, would seem to be the best outlook for the rulers of any state beset with demographic woes.

Judging from the Peloponnesian War, some states that find themselves short on manpower defy this straightforward logic. Why? To bring history to bear on this puzzle, I consult Thucydides' acclaimed *History of the Peloponnesian War*, a work the author immodestly but justly calls "a possession for all time." His writings represent the primary source of historical data about the conflict.[3] The acknowledged "father of history," Thucydides is also considered to be the forefather of the "realist" school of international relations. Accordingly, his *History* sheds light on enduring themes in diplomacy and warfare while hinting at how demographics influence foreign policy and strategy. I supplement Thucydides' observations with insights from the few other contemporaries whose works have survived, notably Herodotus and Xenophon, and from secondary commentators old and new.

A simple equation from Carl von Clausewitz's *On War* furnishes a gauge for measuring the impact of demographic blows on the two belligerents. Clausewitz writes that strength is a product of force and will.[4] Some action, event, or trend that directly amplifies or degrades force or will imposes strategic effects. How did demographic decline affect the material strength commanded by the two antagonists and their resolve to wield the sword? Clausewitz's formula suffices for Sparta, a poor agrarian state whose national power rested on a force of infantrymen unmatched in fifth century B.C. Greece. Disaster sapped Spartan resources without transforming deeply conservative Spartan institutions.

If Spartans dominated land warfare in classical Greece, Athens ruled the sea. Thucydides defines sea power as a product of wealth and naval strength.[5] A thriving sea power accumulates wealth from seaborne commerce and expends wealth on maintaining a navy and merchant marine. To examine Athenian power, accordingly, I define strength as a product of wealth, naval power, and will. Athenian leadership frittered away maritime resources in peripheral ventures, falling to Sparta despite distinct material superiority.

Athens and Sparta can be compared by applying three broad metrics and hypotheses. The analysis starts with Sparta to establish a baseline for comparison, and then inquires into conditions in Athens:

1. *Nature of the contending regimes.* An entering hypothesis is that the nature of the regime shapes how a society responds to demographic change. Athens was a direct democracy, whereas Sparta was an oligarchy dependent on slave labor. Demographic shocks seemingly reinforced native Spartan caution and conservatism while giving free rein to Athenian enterprise. It's important to ascertain why the earthquake and slave revolt encouraged Spartan prudence while the plague prompted Athenians to redouble their war effort.

2. *Nature of the larger societies.* Land warfare was Sparta's element and the key to Spartan ambitions in the Greek world. Spartan society, consequently, was geared to fielding dominant military might. This gave rise to a deeply conservative polity that revered the constitution, laws, and institutions. By contrast, Athenian society was founded on seagoing trade and commercial and naval fleets. Sea power thrives on risk-taking and experimentation, both pronounced Athenian traits embedded in the city's laws and institu-

tions. Continental and maritime nations, it appears, may respond differently to natural disasters like earthquakes and epidemics.

3. *Nature and timing of demographic shocks.* An earthquake delivers a sudden, devastating jolt to a state and society. The Spartan earthquake initiated a downward trend in the number of Spartan infantrymen while refocusing oligarchic leaders' attention on internal security and regime maintenance. The earthquake, moreover, took place three decades before the outbreak of the Peloponnesian War, during a period of relative tranquillity. Athens underwent its demographic trauma over the course of several years and amid repeated invasions of the homeland. The Spartan leadership responded conservatively to demographic stress, while the rising generation of Athenian leaders reacted by departing from the defensive strategy prescribed by Pericles. It appears, therefore, that the Spartan earthquake was the relatively "easy" disaster to overcome.

Precise numbers about population trends in antiquity are elusive, given the dearth of systematic recordkeeping. Mogens Herman Hansen, a specialist in classical Athenian demographics, jokes: "I would happily sacrifice a tragedy by Euripides—not one of the best, of course—if, instead, we could get access to the data to be found in a statistical yearbook. But such a source will never be found because it never existed." The guesswork quotient is considerable even in figures proffered by contemporaries like Thucydides and Aristotle.[6] Nevertheless, examining the classical precedent through a Clausewitzian lens will help contemporary students and practitioners of power politics ask the right questions about the relationship between demographics and great-power politics.

Sparta: Disaster Reinforces Conservatism

Thucydides ascribes the protracted bloodletting between leading Greek city-states to the "growth of the power of Athens, and the alarm which this inspired in Sparta." This "true cause" of the rivalry, he writes, "made war inevitable."[7] Hegemons like Sparta do not lightly surrender their supremacy to ascending powers, especially revolutionary powers like democratic Athens. Signs of enmity began appearing not long after 480 B.C., when the two powers joined forces to repel Persian hosts that had assaulted Greece by land and by sea.[8] Coalition unity did not long survive the defeat of Persia at battles like Salamis, Thermopylae, and Plataea. After the Persian Wars, notes Donald Kagan, the Spartans "simply were not yet prepared to share hegemony with Athens, nor were the Athenians prepared to accept Spartan checks on their ambitions." While Kagan concedes that "no complex human event can be thought of as inevitable," he nonetheless takes rank with Thucydides, proclaiming that conflict and war are natural consequences of swift, drastic change to the established order.[9]

For Thucydides and other realists, then, international politics is primarily a matter of power. How did Sparta measure up? The city's population seems to have grown steadily prior to the earthquake, allowing the city the luxury of bidding for leadership within the Greek world.[10] According to historian Thomas Figueira,

> Sparta appears similar to most other Greek cities in the late archaic period [to 500 B.C.], despite its social and constitutional peculiarities. Spartan population grew during the sixth century. Growing manpower both permitted and perhaps stimulated an aggressive foreign policy by a government prepared to risk losses.[11]

On the other hand, Sparta never seems to have fully tapped available resources or fielded as many troops as it might. The number of elite troops trended downward throughout the fifth century B.C., degrading the quality of Spartan arms over time. Aristotle estimates that Sparta's entire territory, Laconia, produced enough people to support fifteen hundred cavalrymen and thirty thousand heavily armed infantrymen. Sparta had also conquered neighboring Messenia during its archaic period, using Messenians as a source of *helot*, or slave labor. Figueira calculates that Messenia could support sixty thousand helots at bare subsistence levels.[12]

Aristotle reports secondhand that "they say there were once ten thousand Spartiates," the elite class of infantrymen on whom Spartan military prowess—and in turn Sparta's claim to great power—was founded.[13] Spartiates manned the front ranks of the phalanx, the dominant combat formation in Greek warfare. To qualify as a Spartiate, notes classicist G. L. Cawkwell, a Spartan must both have "been through the *agoge*, the education system, and . . . make one's contribution to the common messes, the *syssitia*."[14] To pay his mess dues, a Spartiate depended on the productivity of his *klêros*, a plot of land allotted to him by the city and worked by helots. The proceeds from agricultural produce yielded by the klêros went to pay his living expenses. This arrangement spared Spartiates the burden of earning a living, freeing them for full-time combat training in peacetime and full-time campaigning in wartime.

The number of elite troops may already have peaked by the onset of the Peloponnesian War. Herodotus pegs total Spartiate manpower at around eight thousand on the eve of the climactic Battle of Thermopylae (480 B.C.), when Spartan power reached its apex.[15] Of these, five thousand fought at the Battle of Plataea a year later, which effectively ended the threat of Persian conquest.[16] From this disparity, it seems that the leadership may already have started holding some of the city's military-age youth in reserve, despite the mortal threat confronting the city and Greece itself.

Such figures suggest that Spartan law and policy prevented the city from tapping more than a fraction of its military potential. Aristotle faults Spartan governing arrangements and the leadership for encouraging population growth while at the same time implementing policies that kept most citizens poor. He condemns the "law concerning procreation" for encouraging childbearing while failing to adequately support the young men thus produced. "For the legislator, wishing there to be as many Spartiates as possible, encourages the citizens to have as many children as possible; for there is a law that one who has fathered three sons is exempted from garrison duty, and one with four is exempted from all taxes." And Spartan society provided similar childrearing arrangements for rich and poor children.[17] Aristotle lavishes praise on the city for this: "They most of all pay serious attention to their children, and do so in common, viewing the young less as individuals than as common possessions of the polity."[18]

"Yet it is evident," continues the philosopher, "that if many are born and the territory remains divided as it is, many of them will be poor."[19] Spartan law initially assigned one klêros to each Spartiate, providing ample sustenance.[20] But Spartan law increasingly permitted Spartiates to amass multiple klêroi through inheritance. As a result, some lived well while others could barely meet their basic needs from single plots, if at all. The entire system depended on how well the helots worked the land. A loss or diversion of helot labor exposed the Spartiates, and in turn the Spartan economic and political system, to decay and eventual ruin. A "leveling of possessions" among the military class was imperative according to Aristotle.[21] Yet meaningful land reform eluded the Spartan leadership.

By the fourth century B.C., according to Aristotle, it became obvious "how poor [the Spartans'] condition was as a result of this arrangement; for the city could not bear up under a single blow, but was ruined through its lack of man-power."[22] The philosopher may have meant to say there were too few Spartiates within the army to bring victory at the Battle of Leuktra (371 B.C.), when the Spartan army fell to a Theban force. This is the usual interpretation of his commentary. And indeed, only seven hundred Spartiates fought at Leuktra.[23] Lesser warriors such as the *perioeci*—free noncitizen soldiers—filled in the front ranks of the Spartan phalanx, arguably diminishing the army's aggregate combat effectiveness. An alternative, equally appealing view of Aristotle's words holds that the decline of Spartan manpower kept the city from regenerating combat power after a serious defeat. Either way, demographics contributed decisively to the fall of Sparta in the fourth century—especially as foes innovated in military tactics and began to match Spartan valor and skill on the battlefield.[24] It was increasingly difficult to overcome quantity with quality in a trial of arms.

As the foundations of Spartan power started to erode, the demands on Spartan power started to mount. By Thucydides' inexorable logic of power, reducing Athenian power and influence ranked higher and higher on the scale of Spartan strategic priorities. This was where things stood on the eve of the earthquake and the helot revolt. In 464 B.C. the Spartan leadership agreed to a secret entreaty from the city-state of Thasos. Thasos was a charter member of the Athenian-led Delian League but had quarreled with Athens over matters such as control of gold mines. Furthermore, Thasians resented the Athenians' plans to found a new colony near Thasos that would extend their reach into Thrace.[25] An Athenian army invaded their city—prompting them to plead with the Spartans to invade Attica, the seat of Athenian power, and lift the siege of Thasos by asymmetric means.

Sparta had no treaty obligation to the Thasians, but "as leader of the Spartan Alliance," observes historian N. G. L. Hammond, "she had good reason to fear that Athens' power and ambition might some day threaten the maritime members of her Alliance."[26] The Spartan assembly never publicly debated the Thasian appeal, but the leadership secretly consented to it. Before the assembly's decision could be put into effect, however, disaster struck. The Spartan intervention halted before it could commence. As Plutarch recounts it, in the summer of 464 the country suffered the most terrible earthquake in all its history. The earth opened in many places, several of the peaks of Mt. Taygetus were torn away and the whole city of Sparta was destroyed, with the exception of five houses.[27]

The cataclysm claimed the lives of more than twenty thousand Spartan warriors. A sizable proportion of the victims were Spartiates. Figueira estimates the proportion at half of the casualties.[28] Cawkwell calculates that Spartiate numbers fell by 69–73 percent, "doubtless reflecting the effect of the great earthquake of 465 B.C."[29] For Figueira the disaster represents "an exogenous factor of sufficient magnitude to have caused the steep decline in the number of Spartiates" available during the latter stages of the Peloponnesian War and beyond.[30] This is a direct strategic effect of massive proportions. The earthquake undermined the quality of the army, and by extension the foundations of Spartan national power. Nor was the corps of Spartiates easily replenished. An entire rising generation of Spartiates was crushed when the gymnasium where they were training collapsed on them. Slain youth never reproduced. If strength is a product of force and will, per Clausewitz, then Spartan strength suffered a grievous setback in 465–464 B.C.

As noted before, Spartan society relied on helot labor. Servitude freed up military-age Spartan men for military service. Scholar Nigel Guy Wilson points out that the number of slaves remains a matter of conjecture, but the figure was proportionately higher for Sparta than for any fellow Greek city-state.[31] The earthquake thus collapsed the primary strut supporting internal security, imperiling the city's oligarchic regime. A helot rebellion promptly broke out. First the helots from the Eurotas Plain rose up. King Archidamus, one of Sparta's two monarchs, decreed that Spartans must postpone searching the rubble for possessions and family members. They must take up arms to repel the assault. Next the helots of Messenian descent rose, joining Messenian rebels who had been battling the Spartans at Ithome since 469. Rebel forces overran Laconia and menaced Sparta itself.[32] Figueira points out that guerrilla warfare, an unfamiliar mode of combat, further drained Spartiate numbers. Three hundred fell in a single engagement alone, at Stenyklaros Plain.[33] Sparta could scarcely spare this precious manpower.

Sparta dispatched the Spartiate Pericleidas to Athens for help putting down the uprising. The Athenian assembly considered the Spartan request. Radical democrat Ephialtes urged the assembly to stand aside and let the helots strike down Athens' rival. Cimon, a staunch defender of the dual hegemony of Athens and Sparta within the Greek world, "urged them not to let Greece go lame and Athens lose her yoke-fellow." Cimon's arguments won out, and the assembly deployed an army of four thousand hoplites, or heavy infantrymen, to Sparta's aid. According to Hammond, assistance from Athens, Plataea, and other allies "saved Sparta from extinction."[34] By 463 the Spartans had recovered sufficiently to take the offensive against the rebellion. Once the momentum had shifted, writes Paul Cartledge, Sparta sent the Athenian contingent "packing," fearful that Athenian soldiers would spread democratic ideas and subvert the Spartan political system. Spartans "simply did not want several thousands of democratically minded citizen-soldiers running loose among their Greek servile underclass in their tightly controlled territory."[35] Athenians reverted from saviors to an external threat.

While historical accounts vary, it appears the fighting dragged on for at least four years before Spartan forces subdued the Messenians.[36] The strategic effects of the earthquake were pervasive and long-lasting. The disaster shook Sparta to its core, both literally and philosophically. The twin misfortunes reduced the proportion of elite warriors within the army and, by upsetting the ratio between slaves and citizens, made helot rebellion a perpetual worry for the city's rulers.[37] In Clausewitzian terms, Spartan strength depended inexorably on manpower. Natural disaster cost the Spartans a sizable portion of their material strength and set in motion a long-term decline in the population of military-age recruits. In 425 B.C. an Athenian force surrounded, cut off, and captured a Spartan contingent on the island of Sphacteria. By this time Sparta found it less distasteful to sue for peace than to concede the loss of a mere 292 hoplites—120 of them Spartiates—whom Athenian forces had taken captive.[38]

Nor did the city-state's leaders initiate bold measures to help the population recover. They opted to attempt a gradual recovery through reproduction. This was difficult for a society that discarded infants deemed unfit. Perversely, the earthquake and ensuing guerrilla war foreclosed the possibility of political reform that might have let Sparta compensate adequately for its manpower woes. Fearful of spurring a new helot revolt, the leadership experimented only haltingly with measures to open the army to new warrior classes.[39] The strategic effects of deliberate policy, natural disaster, and the ensuing guerrilla war applied a brake on the resurgence of the Spartan populace and indeed reduced the supply of recruits for the Spartan army, the core of the city's strength.

Sphacteria seemed to humble Spartan arms in the eyes of fellow Greeks. First a contingent of Spartan infantrymen, the finest in the Greek world, surrendered to their presumptive inferiors, lightly armed Athenian troops who used missile weapons like slings. Then the Spartan leadership sought a compromise peace while letting the captives remain in Athens as hostages. "Nothing that happened in the war," reports Thucydides, "surprised the Hellenes so much as this. It was the general opinion that no force or famine could make the Spartans give up their arms, but that they would fight on as they could, and die with them in their hands." The damage to Spartan prestige and claim to international leadership took some time to repair. To add insult to injury, the outcome emboldened the Messenians to conduct raids into Laconia—Spartan home ground.[40]

These events testify amply to the strategic effects of dwindling manpower. The Spartan leadership believed it could no longer afford to risk major army contingents, even to pacify a theater that lay only fifty miles from Sparta—adjoining klêroi that supported Spartiates. Athenians raided Laconia from their fort of Pylos, on the heights above Sphacteria. By ravaging these lands, they undercut agriculture that supported Spartiate livelihoods. By opening this new theater, then, the Athenians indirectly helped impoverish warriors who could no longer pay their dues to the common messes. Many Spartiates were stripped of their lands and the helots who worked them. Manpower losses from Spartan policy were no less costly to the army than battlefield fatalities.

Nor were the strategic effects of demographic shortfalls solely material in nature. During the prewar debate over whether Sparta and its allies should undertake armed conflict with Athens, a Corinthian delegation upbraided the Spartans for failing to avert the rise of Athenian might. "For the true author of the subjugation of a people," proclaim the Corinthian emissaries, "is not so much the immediate agent, as the power which permits it having the means to prevent it; particularly if that power aspires to the glory of being the liberator of Hellas."[41] In today's parlance, the Corinthians accuse the Spartans of letting their native caution interfere with prosecuting an aggressive strategy that preserves their supremacy in the Greek world.

"You, Spartans, of all the Hellenes are alone inactive, and defend yourselves not by doing anything but by looking as if you would do something; you alone wait till the power of an enemy is becoming twice its original size, instead of crushing it in its infancy."[42] In short, say the Corinthians, Spartans are chronically slow, passive, and averse to risk, to the detriment of a successful foreign policy. King Archidamus more or less confesses to these charges while reframing the Spartans' hesitancy as prudent statecraft inspired by noble traditions:

> And the slowness and procrastination, the parts of our character that are most assailed by [the Corinthians'] criticism, need not make you blush. . . . The quality which they condemn is really nothing but a wise moderation; thanks to its possession, we alone do not become insolent in success and give way less than others in misfortune. . . . We are both warlike and wise, and it is our sense of order that makes us so.[43]

Granted, it is somewhat speculative to conclude that the earthquake and helot rebellion implanted certain ways of thinking about peace, war, and diplomacy in the minds of Spartan statesmen. These findings nonetheless stand to reason. By a purely rational calculus of strategy, a blow to manpower *ought* to instill conservatism. With scant manpower and resources to spare for war-making and unrest constantly looming at home, Spartan leaders *should* have mulled over risky enterprises carefully before proceeding. In Clausewitzian parlance, a political object must be valuable indeed to warrant an effort of major magnitude and duration—especially if the effort exposes one's social and political system to internal overthrow. No sane statesman lightly undertakes foreign adventures that might bring down his own regime.

The earthquake and slave revolt of 465–464 B.C., then, brought about three main strategic effects. First, the direct death toll reduced the overall Spartan population, skewing the distribution between the free and servile segments of the populace. Casualties hit the infantrymen—who comprised the hard core of Spartan military might—especially hard, while crushing a generation of soldiers who aspired to become Spartiates.[44] This generational effect compounded the direct strategic effects wrought by the earthquake, costing the city-state much of its capacity for war-making and internal security. In fact, Hammond declares that the earthquake "upset the balance of power in the Greek world." Sparta no longer looked strong enough to oversee the Peloponnesian League or liberate allies of Athens from Athenian tyranny. These states, adds Hammond, "realized that they could no longer look to Sparta for protection, and Athens was tempted to exercise a tighter control over them."[45] The earthquake and ensuing bloodletting upset the balance of power, costing Sparta its credibility. In Thucydides' account, the growing power imbalance created an atmosphere of dread culminating in the outbreak of war.[46]

Second, the cataclysm began to unhinge the Spartan economic (and by extension political) system, further undercutting military manpower.[47] Figueira credits the Spartans for gradually opening up opportunities for social advancement to helots by the closing years of the Peloponnesian War. They attempted to adjust their harsh system. Helots campaigned with Brasidas in Thrace, for example, showing that slaves would fight for Sparta despite their status. A new warrior class, dubbed *neodamodeis*, was created to accommodate freed slaves.[48] Supplying an outlet for talent and ambition allowed the underclass to improve their lot within the existing system, serving as free, though non-citizen, hoplite warriors. Their incentive to rebel diminished commensurately.[49] Despite Spartan forebodings, the helots refrained from rebelling between the post-earthquake revolt and their final uprising, launched when Thebes liberated Messenia from Spartan rule in the fourth century B.C.[50]

On the other hand, permitting helots to leave the klêroi reduced the supply of labor available to support the Spartiates. Many warriors were unable to pay their mess dues and were stripped of their status, lands, and slaves. Disgracing poor warriors imposed additional stress on army manpower. Some six hundred Spartiates were lost to Sparta in the aftermath of Sphacteria, only some of whom fell in battle. "For the Spartan state," remarks Figueira, "losses in Spartiate manpower through political means were as irremediable as deaths."[51] The leadership took certain other steps to reverse the manpower decline. Generally speaking, only first sons of Spartiates were eligible to become Spartiates. In effect younger brothers were disfranchised.[52] Over time, however, the assumption that Spartiates would be replenished by their eldest sons on a one-for-one basis collapsed. In an effort to offset this decline, the city began recruiting younger sons into a new class of "inferiors," or *mothakes*. This class was also open to foreigners from the Peloponnesian League who had undergone Spartan education alongside prospective Spartiates. Sparta, however, proved unable to conscript outsiders in sufficient numbers to make up for the fall in manpower.[53]

Third, the disaster appeared to ratify and reinforce the Spartans' tradition of slow, methodical action informed by reverence for established law and custom. The Spartan political system discouraged change, damping wild oscillations in policy and strategy and encouraging continuity in leadership. Leadership remained static, in stark contrast to Athenian dynamism. Cawkwell observes that despite taking some steps to adapt the Spartan system to war and demographic realities, "The Kings remained the hereditary generals, and although they performed this function as adequately as their predecessors, they were not the men to experiment and innovate."[54] Sparta ultimately found itself overtaken not only by the decline of military manpower, but also by changes to the art of war.

But finally, the earthquake took place during a time of relative calm in the Greek world. Athens remained formally allied to Sparta. These fairly permissive strategic circumstances afforded the Spartan leadership the leisure to put down the helot revolt and mend their political, economic, and military system without undue fear of outsiders' taking advantage of the situation. In short, events did not administer a jolt of sufficient magnitude to challenge time-honored practices or compel innovation and adaptation. Spartans responded to disaster as they habitually responded to such trials: cautiously and conservatively.

Athens: Disaster Encourages Gambling

If the earthquake vindicated and amplified the Spartan tendency to risk aversion, the plague seemingly gave free vent to Athenian adventurism. Herodotus estimates the population of Athens at thirty thousand adult male citizens at the turn from the sixth to the fifth century B.C.[55] Wilson maintains that the population swelled to between fifty and sixty thousand by mid-century as Athens assembled a prosperous thalassocracy, or maritime empire.[56] Prosperity and dominion emboldened Athenians. The Corinthian delegates allude to Athenian daring in their speech imploring the Spartan assembly to declare war. They contrast Spartan lethargy unfavorably with Athenian energy and drive while pointing out that the Athenian way has pitfalls of its own. The Athenians, they say, are "addicted to innovation, and their designs are characterized by swiftness alike in conception and execution."[57] Historian John R. Hale connects this culture to sea power, suggesting that the life of the sea bred in Athenians a revolutionary culture premised on industry, commerce, and brash endeavor, whereas the rigors of land defense demanded constant vigilance and constant preparation for war.[58] The domain in which each society excelled, then, helps account for the cultural gulf between them.

While the Athenians could act with dispatch, however, a slapdash approach to strategic calculations was a byproduct of their democracy. Few institutional checks were built into the system. The assembly, consequently, often authorized strategies with costs and perils out of any proportion to rational political aims. "Again," maintain the Corinthians, Athenians "are adventurous beyond their power, and daring beyond their judgment, and in danger they are sanguine."[59] With no constitution, law, or long-standing traditions to govern the will of the majority, the Athenians were prone to act without deliberating sufficiently about the value of the object and the likely magnitude and duration of proposed enterprises. They scanted the rational calculus of war in their thirst for action.

Events exaggerated this tendency. Thucydides describes the plague in stark terms. All of Attica had crowded within the walls at Pericles' behest. The first citizen had thrust a strategy upon the assembly that called for refusing battle when Spartan forces invaded. Athens would avoid a decisive land engagement while conducting amphibious raids around the Spartan periphery. The symptoms started appearing soon after the Spartan army invaded Attica in 431 B.C., laying waste to the countryside. Inhabitants of Piraeus, the seaport that provided Athens its outlet to the Aegean, were the first to fall ill. This suggests that the pestilence arrived over sea. Thucydides speculates that it originated in Ethiopia and reached Greece via seaports in Egypt and Libya.

Sickness struck physicians "most thickly," reports Thucydides, "as they visited the sick most often." The pestilence struck indiscriminately, and it appeared senseless. Good health was no defense: "The nature of the distemper was such as to baffle all description, and its attacks almost too grievous for human nature to endure." Strong or weak, most victims succumbed within seven or eight days. Carrion-eating birds and beasts shunned their remains.[60]

Classicist Victor Davis Hanson surveys the demographic and moral wreckage left by the plague. Hanson contends that the pestilence did the most damage to Athenian power of any blow the city-state suffered during the Peloponnesian War. In relative terms, the losses endured by Athenian society rivaled bloodlettings like the Thirty Years' War, the Battle of the Somme during World War I, or the Battle of Stalingrad during World War II. The contagion felled between one-quarter and one-third of the Athenian populace.[61] (The ravages of disease and war apparently cost the city fully half its population by the time it surrendered in 404 B.C.[62]) Disease not only brought misery and death to individuals, but also loosened the ties of civilized society. Virtue and ordinary human compassion came to appear suicidal. The healthy refused to render aid to the stricken for fear of falling ill. Notes Thucydides:

> By far the most terrible feature in the malady was the dejection which ensued when anyone felt himself sickening, for the despair into which they instantly fell took away their power of resistance, and left them a much easier prey to the disorder; besides which, there was the awful spectacle of men dying like sheep, through having caught the infection in nursing each other. This caused the greatest mortality.[63]

Nor did entreating the gods help. "Supplications in the temples, divinations, and so forth were found equally futile, till the overwhelming nature of the disaster at last put a stop to them altogether."[64] People abandoned religion and such comforts as it supplied. Sacred places, reports Thucydides,

> were full of corpses of persons that had died there, just as they were; for as the disaster passed all bounds, men, not knowing what was to become of them, became utterly careless of everything, whether sacred or profane. All the burial rites before in use were entirely upset. . . . Many from want of the proper appliances through so many of their friends having died already, had recourse to the most shameless modes of burial.[65]

Athens was a devout society that vested enormous importance in proper disposal of the departed. For Thucydides, abandonment of burial rites offered a parable for the city's moral collapse. His account of the plague is especially poignant, coming as it does immediately after Pericles' Funeral Oration, a moving tribute to soldiers who fell during the first year of war.[66]

Neither medical science nor divine succor, then, furnished any relief from anguish. According to Thucydides, despondency helps explain the "lawless extravagance" that prevailed amid the epidemic. "Men now did just what they pleased, coolly venturing on what they formerly had done only in a corner. Citizens squandered their fortunes on pleasure, "regarding their lives and riches as alike things of a day." Honor "was popular with none." Thucydides' verdict:

Fear of gods or law of man there was none to restrain them. As for the first, they judged it to be just the same whether they worshipped them or not, as they saw all alike perishing; and for the last, no one expected to live to be brought to trial for his offenses, but each felt that a far severer sentence had been already passed upon them all and hung ever over their heads.[67]

Concludes Hanson, "A threshold had been crossed: once the Athenians had been reduced to such straits, it was nearly impossible to recover their moral bearings in subsequent years. Criminality and savagery became accustomed, or rather institutionalized, behaviors, almost as if the Athenians, once freed from decades of civilizing influences, could not shake off the newfound habits of brutality."[68] A new, wantonly abusive, self-defeating culture was in the making.[69]

Nor did the city soon rebound from the effects of plague, despite the resiliency for which its democracy was famed. Hanson attributes to the plague the assembly's seemingly inexplicable decision to sentence to death the generals who commanded an Athenian fleet in victorious battle at Arginusae, late in the war. Bad weather compelled the victors to abandon the search for survivors of the action, but the generals' failure to recover the bodies of the slain conjured up memories of corpses strewn about during the plague without proper burial. Etched in their collective consciousness, this memory goaded Athenians into ordaining the execution of successful commanders. They ordered the generals to drink hemlock.[70] Hale ascribes the decline of Athenian generalship in part to the Arginusae trial.[71] Unsurprisingly, rewarding triumph with death supplied future commanders little incentive to excel. Military effectiveness suffered indirectly from long-ago demographic trauma.

In light of such incidents, Hale maintains that democracy can be as violent, fickle, and unjust as tyranny.[72] The mercurial nature of Athenian democracy was a constant challenge.[73] In stark contrast to Sparta, with its reverence for law and tradition, Athenian behavior knew few restraints. Only the city-state's political culture of deliberation, complemented by the self-restraint of individual citizens, could discourage erratic words and deeds. Once the plague enfeebled the tradition of reasoned deliberation, little remained to quell wild swings in political behavior. The live-for-the-day mentality implanted by disease worked against foresight, a quality Thucydides deemed the cardinal virtue for statesmen. Shortsighted policy and strategy resulted.

The plague, then, exerted lasting, destructive influence on Athenian conduct of the war. For Thucydides, sound democratic governance in Athens
meant rule by the first citizen, Pericles. He was the best man for the state not
only because of his wisdom, but because he could manage popular passions.[74]
Donald Kagan notes that one immediate effect of the contagion was to turn
the populace against Pericles. His defensive strategy fell into disrepute, while
the peace party in the assembly was empowered to sue for peace.[75] Athenians
attributed the miseries of the plague in part to overcrowding within the city
walls, which was a direct consequence of Pericles' strategy of ceding the countryside to the Spartans and avoiding pitched land battles. In his final speech
before the assembly, Pericles prevailed on fellow citizens to ratify his strategy,
rejecting proposals to expand the empire or undertake a head-on clash with
the Spartan army. Given time, he insisted, peripheral raids would exhaust the
Peloponnesian League, which possessed inadequate resources to finance a long,
drawn-out conflict.

But Pericles himself contracted sickness and perished shortly afterward.
His death removed the one flywheel that kept popular sentiment, and thus the
machinery of state, from spinning out of control. An important demographic
result of the plague, then, was to claim the life of a single indispensable statesman. The first citizen's demise accelerated generational change among the Athenian political elite while eliminating a restraining influence on public sentiment.
As the heroic generation that had resisted the massive Persian onslaught in the
early fifth century passed from the scene, the youthful generation sought its
own share of glory.[76] Demagogues like Cleon, whom Thucydides portrays as
the most brutish man in the city, or the adventurer Alcibiades could now deploy
powerful rhetoric to goad the assembly into self-defeating schemes. They vied
with one another to take Pericles' place at the forefront of Athenian society and
politics.

Writes Thucydides, such leaders were constantly "grasping for supremacy."
Their "committing even the conduct of state affairs to the whim of the multitude" resulted in "a host of blunders."[77] Of the unwise policies they advocated,
the disastrous decision to invade Sicily—a debacle that cost Athens the fleet on
which its sea power, unrivaled prosperity, and wealth were founded, along with
the flower of its military-age youth—stands as the most notorious.[78] In Clausewitzian terms, demagoguery subverted the rational calculus of war. Ignorant

of conditions in Sicily, the Athenian assembly had little chance of accurately estimating the value of the political object they were being urged to seek. With little idea even of the size of the theater, let alone of the cultural terrain and the capabilities of their Sicilian allies, they could not foresee the magnitude or the duration of the effort it would take to subdue Syracuse and other Sicilian city-states. Dismal results were apt to follow absent a sober, well-informed appraisal of the situation. And indeed, not one Athenian who had embarked on the Sicilian Expedition returned to Attica. These were strategic effects of the first order, claiming a large share of Athenian military strength and forcing Athenians to pour scarce funds into rebuilding the navy.

According to Hanson, a final lingering strategic effect of the plague was to fan paranoia about imperial maintenance while reinforcing the maritime character of Athenian society, culture, and politics. Conscious of their manpower shortfall, Athenians were even more reluctant to risk land engagements, and they were more inclined to act preventively when an ally showed signs of wanting to defect from the empire. The male population of the island city-state of Melos was put to death, for example, and the women and children enslaved. Before his death, Pericles had warned the Athenians that their empire, originally a consensual league of city-states, had degenerated into a tyranny. The epidemic reinforced its tyrannical character, further interfering with the Athenian assembly's efforts to craft rational policy and strategy amid the stresses of war.

In his speech urging the assembly to declare war, Pericles had prophesied that Athenian blunders were more apt than Spartan prowess to bring down the city.[79] And indeed this appears to have been the case, owing in large measure to demographic pressures applied by the plague.

A Holistic View of Demographic Shocks

This short survey of the impact of demographics in classical Greece militates against assuming that nations undergoing demographic decline will conduct their affairs cautiously. To be sure, in a sense the Athenians probably *did* see themselves as acting prudently. Attacking problems like unrest within the alliance before they could metastasize into full-blown rebellion makes intuitive sense. Quashing restive allies would demand massive, manpower-intensive Athenian naval and military intervention. Preemptive action represented a way to hold down the costs of imperial maintenance and conserve resources. The methods the assembly chose, however, were rash and offensive in character even if inspired by defensive, conservative motives.

In the final analysis, there is little substitute for Clausewitzian net assessment of a given contingency. The Prussian theorist enjoins statesmen and commanders to consider not only the strength and situation of the contending parties but also the value they attach to their political objectives, the capacity of their people, governments, and armed forces, and the sympathies and likely actions of third parties before launching into military ventures.[80] Heeding his wisdom can help analysts glimpse the likely strategic effects of demographics and factor them into strategy.

Look at the Peloponnesian War through a Clausewitzian prism. In the case of the Spartan earthquake and the helot rebellion, a relatively permissive external environment, a sudden demographic blow, and an uprising at home comprised the strategic context. Natural disaster struck, then it was over. A single sharp trauma lacked the agonizing social and cultural effects of the Athenian plague. The revolt drove up the value of the object to its maximum—survival is the paramount goal of any society—while affording Spartans time to rebuild their city and put down the revolt with few worries about third-party military intervention. Recovery took place under the aegis of a constitution and laws of centuries' standing, which muted voices espousing drastic action. In short, the earthquake and its aftermath did little to disturb the Spartan political system and indeed likely ratified the precepts by which Spartans lived.

In the Athenian case a drawn-out epidemic threatened the city's survival amid an ongoing war with a deadly enemy. This entailed disproportionate effects precisely because Athenian democracy lacked political institutions to discourage rash action. Ironically, the statesmanship of a first citizen counted more in the democratic city-state than it did in oligarchic Sparta. Since the pestilence discredited Pericles' defensive strategy and ultimately killed him, the assembly cast about for more offensive-minded strategic alternatives. After the plague subsided, Athenian deliberations were unfettered by the political management of a Pericles, who could help the assembly align ways and means with strategic ends. Demographics imposed heavy strategic effects in both material and cultural terms, prodding the assembly into policies that drained the treasury, sacrificed the navy, and frittered away manpower for little gain.

In short, it is probably true that demographic shocks bias policy and strategy toward caution, but demographics are a less reliable predictor than they might seem. During the Peloponnesian War, different demographic shocks reinforced different characteristics inherent in each regime and society. This worked in favor of Sparta over time. The Spartans prevailed by being less error-prone than their enemies. Major disasters, it seems, entail unforeseen consequences. There is no substitute for thoroughly studying the nature of a disaster, the regime and society on which it acts, and the surrounding context. As statesmen and scholars survey today's strategic environment, they must not assume that established or rising great powers undergoing demographic decline will display restraint in foreign policy. The Peloponnesian War shows that such assumptions cannot bear scrutiny.

What of today? Disasters like the ones that befell Sparta and Athens are by no means uncommon. Look no further than the 2004 tsunami that struck Southeast Asia, claiming some quarter-million lives, or the 2011 earthquake and tsunami in Japan that left nearly twenty thousand dead or missing. Thankfully, there have been no recent epidemics comparable to the Athenian plague. But the Spanish flu outbreak in the closing months of World War I was not so long ago in historical terms, and it claimed roughly as many victims as did the war itself. Recent near encounters with avian and swine flu offer reminders of the potential for disease to strike on a massive scale, as it did in ancient Athens and postwar Europe. Indeed, a globalized world is perhaps even more conducive to such an outbreak than classical Greece. If the plague reached Athens through maritime transport, imagine how readily it could be transmitted through the immense numbers of conveyances that crisscross the seas and skies today. The modern world is not exempt from demographic shocks of this kind.

From the cases of Sparta and Athens, it is tempting to conclude that authoritarian regimes react better than liberal regimes to natural disasters. But this would be too simple. Sparta indeed coped with the earthquake better than Athens coped with the plague, but it did so in peacetime under relatively hospitable conditions. Furthermore, the Spartans fared far more poorly dealing with the long-term effects of the earthquake than they did meeting the immediate challenges of suppressing the helot revolts and rebuilding the city. The earthquake set the city on a path of long-term decline that ultimately cost the Spartans their leadership in the Greek world. For Athens, which had faced the more difficult test, defeat in the Peloponnesian War lasted only a moment. Within a few years the Athenians had cast off the tyranny imposed on them by Sparta at war's end and begun to regain their former eminence. While unruly democracy had spurred the Athenians into unwise actions in wartime, it also equipped them to rebound in peacetime. In the long run, then, Athens proved more resilient than authoritarian Sparta.

Apply these findings to today's Asia, bearing in mind the inexactitude of such a comparison. Some Asia specialists argue that China, an authoritarian country facing demographic decline, is better equipped to handle challenges than India, a freewheeling democracy and a beneficiary of robust population growth. If so, China, like ancient Sparta, would presumably exercise prudence in stressful times, avoiding serious mistakes. India, a rough analogue to Athens, might incline toward rashness. But the example of Sparta reveals that the quality of individual leadership determines how shrewdly an authoritarian regime acts in particular contingencies. Such a regime admits few institutional constraints on leaders' authority. Spartan kings were not feckless, but they did not excel at meeting challenges faced by their city. Gradual decline ensued. Similarly, how well Beijing reacts to natural disasters, war, and other crises depends on the skill and virtue of a Hu Jintao. The example of Athens, by contrast, suggests that a liberal regime accustomed to aggregating the wisdom of many people has better prospects of enduring and bouncing back from disaster. The gifts of a Manmohan Singh are important, but not all-important, to Indian statecraft. If so, the smart bet in times of trouble is on New Delhi, not Beijing.

3

POPULATION IN THE STUDY
OF GEOPOLITICS

Francis P. Sempa

"In the last analysis, the outcome of the struggle will be determined by the fact that Russia, India, and China, etc., constitute
the overwhelming majority of the population of the globe."
—V. I. Lenin (1923)

Demographics and relative global population distribution affect great power
politics, and their impact can best be appreciated within a broader geopolitical
analysis. Saul B. Cohen concisely defined geopolitics as "the relation of international political power to the geographical setting."[1] Geography is the most
important factor in the study of international politics because of its unchanging
nature. The grouping of land masses, seas, and oceans has not changed significantly during most of recorded history, though the impact and strategic meaning of geography has changed due primarily to technological and scientific
advances. The geographic location of a country, therefore, is always an important element of that country's power.

The other significant elements of a nation's power include its character of
government, economy, natural resources, national cohesion, and people. It is
this latter element of a country's power—its people—and the impact of relative
population distribution and organization on the global balance of power that
comprise the subject of this chapter.

Population and geography by themselves do not determine great power
politics. While great powers have often controlled large landmasses and had
large populations (Imperial Russia and the Soviet Union, Imperial Germany

59

and Nazi Germany, the United States), some countries, notably China and India, occupied large land areas with very large populations but were not great powers. Some great powers, on the other hand, have controlled relatively smaller insular land areas with significant but relatively smaller populations (Great Britain and Japan), while other countries, such as Australia, have controlled large insular land areas but lacked sufficient population to attain great power status. There is no fixed formula for great power status. Relative geographical position, as well as population density, organization, age, and education are all important variables.

The relative distribution, organization, growth, and decline of population have always been important factors in assessing the global balance of power. Princeton University's population expert Frank W. Notestein in 1944 noted that "differences in rates of growth of nations have powerful effects on economic life, political climate, and military potential," and that an "analysis of the future military potential requires as careful an evaluation as possible of prospective changes in population."[2] The great classical geopolitical theorists invariably included a demographic analysis in their relative power estimates. Although this chapter will emphasize the demographic factors in relative power estimates, it is important to remember that such factors, by themselves, are strategically meaningless. Relative demographic analyses become strategically meaningful only when they are considered in the context of geography, economics, industrialization (or lack thereof), globalization and the "information" revolution, culture, the nature of government, and other geopolitical factors.

In his seminal 1904 paper "The Geographical Pivot of History," the great British geopolitical theorist Sir Halford Mackinder noted that "the actual balance of political power [in the world] at any given time is . . . the product . . . of geographical conditions, both economic and strategic, and . . . of the relative number, virility, equipment, and organization of the competing peoples."[3] It was in that paper that Mackinder first identified the northern-central core of the Eurasian landmass as the "pivot region" of world politics that could serve as the base of a world empire. In the past, he noted, a series of nomadic peoples emerged from that region to threaten the settled people of the marginal lands of Europe and Asia. The nomadic raiders, however, lacked sufficient manpower and technology to establish a lasting hegemony over Eurasia. Even the ferocious and militarily brilliant Mongols were eventually absorbed by the more populous and settled inhabitants of Russia, China, the Muslim lands of the Middle East, and India.

By the time of Mackinder's article, however, industrialization and scientific-technological innovation had revolutionized land transportation (railroads, motor cars), while population growth in Eastern and Central Europe and Russia provided sufficient manpower to potentially exploit the geographical advantages of the "pivot region." In Mackinder's words,

> Is not the pivot region of the world's politics that vast area of Euro-Asia which is inaccessible to ships, but in antiquity lay open to the horse-riding nomads, and is to-day about to be covered with a network of railways? . . . Russia replaces the Mongol Empire. Her pressure on Finland, on Scandinavia, on Poland, on Turkey, on Persia, on India, and on China replaces the centrifugal raids of the steppe-men. . . .
>
> The oversetting of the balance of power in favor of the pivot state, resulting in its expansion over the marginal lands of Euro-Asia, would permit of the use of vast continental resources for fleet-building, and the empire of the world would then be in sight.[4]

Mackinder suggested that either a Russo-German alliance or a Sino-Japanese combination could provide the sufficient population base to realize a pivot-region-based world empire.

Fifteen years after the paper was published, while the world was convulsed by the tremendous clash of empires in the First World War, Mackinder greatly expanded on its geopolitical ideas in his most famous book, *Democratic Ideals and Reality*. He renamed the pivot region the "Heartland" and redefined and re-characterized the potential base of a world empire from the "great continent" of Eurasia to the larger Eurasian-African "World-Island." He reexamined the historic clashes of land powers and sea powers, and sketched a compelling geopolitical map of the world. And, once again, he emphasized the crucial importance of population distribution and organization to the global balance of power.

Mackinder illustrated the significance of relative population to geopolitical struggles with several historical examples. The ancient Egyptians, he noted, achieved regional supremacy by gaining possession of the Nile Valley, "a more extensive material basis for its man power, and on that basis organized further conquests."[5] The Dorians used the greater manpower resources of the Greek peninsula to conquer insular Crete. The more populous and better-organized Macedonians subsequently conquered the city-states of Greece, then expanded their control of the Eastern Mediterranean by conquest. Rome, having established its control of the Mediterranean Sea and surrounding lands, used its greater population and resources to conquer much of insular Britain.

Historically, Mackinder noted, the Heartland of Eurasia could not be fully exploited as a strategic base because it lacked sufficient population or "manpower." The Muslim Saracens, based in the region we now call the Middle East, advanced northeastward into the Heartland and across North Africa, envisioning an empire "extending from the Straits of Gibraltar to the Straits of Malacca, from the Atlantic gate to the Pacific gate."[6] "This vast Saracen design," Mackinder explained, "was vitiated by one fatal defect; it lacked in its Arabian base the necessary man-power to make it good."[7]

That same defect—the lack of sufficient manpower—undermined the efforts of Heartland-based raiders (Huns, Avars, Tartars, Turks, Magyars, Mongols) to exercise lasting political control over the marginal lands of Eurasia, areas which Mackinder called the Coastlands.

"Not until about a hundred years ago," Mackinder concluded, was there available a base of man-power sufficient to begin to threaten the liberty of the world from within the [Heartland]."[8] Beginning in the mid-nineteenth century, however, the Heartland hosted what Mackinder termed a "vast triple base of man-power" in Prussia, Austria-Hungary, and Russia. It was that fact, coupled with the spread of industrialization, which gave the Heartland concept its full geopolitical potential.

Mackinder understood that the importance of relative population to the balance of power was not merely a matter of numbers alone, although he knew and wrote that "other things being equal, numbers are decisive."[9] For Mackinder, the significance of population was inextricably linked to its social organization—what he called the Going Concern. "Man-power," he wrote, "is . . . in these modern days very greatly dependent on organization, or, in other words, on the Going Concern, the social organism."[10] A country is a Going Concern if its population is organized economically, politically, and militarily in a manner that produces "social momentum."

Writing in 1919, Mackinder noted that both Germany and Russia were Going Concerns, and that "Russia was the first tenant of the Heartland with a really menacing man-power."[11] Moreover, a sufficiently armed and organized Heartland power could gain effective political control over the Eurasian-African World-Island, which Mackinder noted contains "more than fourteen-sixteenths of all humanity."[12] Mackinder explained the geopolitical meaning of these facts in one of the more memorable passages in the book:

> What if the Great Continent, the whole World-Island or a large part of it, were at some future time to become a single and united base of sea-power? Would not the other insular bases be outbuilt as regards ships and out-manned as regards seamen? Their fleets would no doubt fight with all the heroism begotten of their histories, but the end would be fated.[13]

Britain and the United States, Mackinder noted, barely escaped this fate in the war that just ended. "Had Germany elected to stand on the defensive on her short frontier towards France," he wrote, "and had she thrown her main strength against Russia, it is not improbable that the world would be nominally at peace to-day, but overshadowed by a German East Europe in command of all the Heartland. The British and American insular peoples would not have realized the strategical danger until too late."[14]

Twenty-four years later, in the midst of the Second World War and another, even greater, struggle for control of the Heartland by Germany and Russia, Mackinder revisited his geopolitical thesis in "The Round World and the Winning of the Peace," which appeared in the July 1943 issue of *Foreign Affairs*. He foresaw that Soviet Russia would emerge from the war as the greatest land power on the globe, and that the Heartland would be occupied by a population "sufficient both in number and quality."[15] After the war, the British and Americans duly took note of Mackinder's ideas, which formed the basis of their Cold War strategy of "containment."

Mackinder's approach to the study of world politics was in some respects similar to that of the American naval historian and strategist Alfred Thayer Mahan. Beginning in 1890 and continuing until his death in 1914, Mahan wrote numerous books and articles in which he analyzed global politics from an Anglo-American geopolitical perspective. Mahan greatly admired the British empire and its use of sea power to construct and maintain its preeminent position in a maritime world order. He repeatedly urged American statesmen and the American people to emulate the British, and predicted, accurately, that the United States would one day be the successor to the British empire on the world stage.

In the introduction to his classic, *The Influence of Sea Power upon History, 1660-1783*, Mahan identified a country's population as an important element of national power.[16] In subsequent articles and books, Mahan invariably noted the demographic impact on the power equation. For example, in 1893 Mahan urged the United States to annex Hawaii and to push for controlling influence in the northern Pacific Ocean region, because if the United States did not exert such control, the "vast mass of China" would fill the power vacuum.[17] In another article a year later, Mahan warned against the threat to our interests posed by the "teeming multitudes of central and northern Asia."[18] In the 1897 article "A Twentieth Century Outlook," Mahan foresaw a clash with the Asiatic powers of Japan, India, and China that "surrounded and outnumbered" Western nations and would eventually acquire Western scientific and technological knowledge.[19] In *The Problem of Asia*, he noted that it was "difficult to contemplate with equanimity such a vast mass as the four hundred millions of China concentrated into one effective political organization, equipped with modern appliances, and cooped within a territory already narrow for it."[20] Still later, in *The Interest of America in International Conditions*, Mahan noted Germany's growing threat to the European balance of power due, in part, to its ability to draw upon "a population now . . . greater than any one European state west of Russia, and with a rate of increase superior to that of any other."[21]

While Mackinder and Mahan were developing an Anglo-American approach to geopolitics, the German scholar Friedrich Ratzel and the Swedish political scientist Rudolf Kjellen were laying the basis for a continental European approach to geopolitics. Ratzel, considered the father of modern political geography, and Kjellen, who coined the term "geopolitics" in his book *Der Staat als Lebensform* (*The State as a Form of Life*), viewed the state as a living organism which grows, expands, declines, and dies. Both writers envisioned a world power structure dominated by large and growing states engaged in an endless struggle for space and power. Their concepts, significantly, included *Geopolitik* (geography and the state) and *Demopolitik* (population and the state). The inescapable logic of their geopolitical theories was that states with large and growing populations would seek to expand their living space and thereby dominate world politics.

During the inter-war years of the 1920s and 1930s, a group of German geopolitical theorists—led by Karl Haushofer, a retired general and lecturer in geography at the University of Munich—imbibed the theories and concepts of Ratzel, Kjellen, Mackinder, and Mahan to produce a German-centered approach to global geopolitics. Haushofer and his associates (including his son Albrecht, Erich Obst, Otto Maull, Josef Marz, Wulf Siewert, and Hermann Lautensach) established a monthly journal, *Zeitschrift für Geopolitik*, in which they discussed various aspects of German world strategy, including population policy.

The German geopoliticians divided the world into large "pan-regions," and advocated that Germany expand its "space" and increase its population to properly exploit and master that space. "Space mastery" was one of the key concepts promoted by Haushofer and his associates, and it depended to a great extent on the number, organization, and distribution of population. Haushofer predicted that a lack of "space mastery" would lead to the decline of the British Empire, while his colleague, G. Seiffert, praised the "space mastery" of China that resulted from "strong population pressure in already settled territory. . . . Every people has a certain strength to grow," wrote Seiffert, "but none has been able to expand to such an extent, over such long periods of time, and in such uniformity as the Chinese."[22]

Although the German geopoliticians were rightly criticized for the racial aspects of their theories, which matched the racial ideology of the Third Reich, Haushofer and his colleagues understood that world politics would be increasingly dominated by large states with large and well-organized populations. Haushofer himself urged German statesmen to form an alliance with, rather than attempt to conquer, Russia and its vast spaces. That would have produced a Mackinder-esque Heartland-based alliance with a sufficient population, well armed and organized, to bid for world hegemony. Haushofer believed that Mackinder was the author of "the greatest of all geographical world views."

The impact of relative population and its organization and distribution on the global balance of power was also recognized by Nicholas Spykman, the Yale professor who in the early 1940s wrote two classic works on geopolitics, *America's Strategy in World Politics* and *The Geography of the Peace*.[23] Spykman, like Mackinder and Mahan, recognized the overwhelming power potential of the Old World (Eurasia-Africa), but viewed control of the area he called the Eurasian Rimland (Western Europe, the Middle East, and East Asia), rather than the Heartland, as the key to world power.

Population, Spykman wrote, "is in itself an indication of power potential."[24] It is possible, he explained, "to get a certain picture of the relative strength of nations by noting the distribution of population density in the world." Further, "the population density of a region bears a close relation to its strength."[25] Of course, Spykman recognized that population and its distribution alone do not determine relative power, but must be factored into the power equation with industrial production, political organization, national cohesion, natural resources, geographic location, and other relevant matters.

The Old World, Spykman noted, had ten times the population of the New World, and he foresaw that the spread of industrialization and technology would result in India and China, with their vast populations, becoming great powers. The power potential of Eurasia, therefore, was so great that the United States must pursue a strategy that ensured no hostile power or alliance of powers achieved by Eurasian hegemony. This idea, fundamentally consistent with Mackinder's theory, formed the basis of the U.S. post–World War II strategy of "containment."

The intellectual father of containment, George F. Kennan, similarly recognized the importance of population distribution and organization to the global balance of power. Writing in the early 1950s, Kennan explained that in an era of large-scale warfare, sophisticated weapons, and control over huge populations, "military strength on a major scale . . . can be produced only in a limited number of parts of the globe: in those regions where major industrial power, enjoying access to raw materials, is combined with large reserves of educated and technically skilled manpower."[26] Kennan identified five such regions: North America, England, Japan, Germany, and the Soviet Union.

In 1945, Harold and Margaret Sprout in *Foundations of National Power* wrote, "In making an over-all estimate of a nation's international position, one logical starting point is population. . . . The number of people, their age distribution, their health and literacy levels, and other qualities, all have a bearing upon a country's position."[27] The Sprouts expressed the power potential of a nation in an equation: "Manpower plus economic resources plus tools and skills plus organization plus morale equals power potential which . . . can be transmitted into power in being."[28]

The geopolitics of the Cold War that emerged from the ashes of the Second World War was affected by an analysis of demographics. As the quotation that begins this chapter indicates, Soviet leader Lenin believed that the struggle between communism and capitalism would ultimately be decided by the greater population of Asia. Once the geopolitical aspect of the Cold War began in earnest in the mid to late 1940s, population and population trends played a role in the course of the struggle.

The formation of the Sino-Soviet bloc in 1949, which combined the population and industrial power of Soviet Russia and its Eastern European satellites with the immense population of the Chinese mainland, presented the Western powers with the very real prospect of a Eurasian-based world empire. This development prompted the great French strategist Raymond Aron to lament that "Russia has in fact nearly achieved the 'world island' which Mackinder considered the necessary and almost sufficient condition for universal empire."[29] It similarly led one American Cold War strategist, James Burnham, to call for an offensive strategy to "liberate" or roll back the communist empire, because "if the communists succeed in consolidating what they have *already* conquered, then their complete world victory is certain. . . . The present Soviet territorial base, if it is successfully integrated under the control of the monolithic and aggressive regime, is enough to guarantee the ultimate outcome."[30]

The interaction of geopolitics and demographics explains, in part, the logic behind the U.S.-Soviet struggle in the so-called "Third World" nations, many of which experienced significant population growth during the Cold War, as well as President Nixon's successful efforts to fully exploit the Sino-Soviet split to the West's strategic advantage. At its most fundamental level, the U.S. strategy of containment was designed to deny the Soviet Empire further accretions of population and territory.

Before discussing the contemporary interaction between geopolitics and demographics, it will be useful to briefly note their historical interaction. The time period between the sixteenth century and the early twentieth century was the age of European-centered geopolitics. During that era, the European balance of power was repeatedly threatened from within by a single great power or alliance of powers. The Austrian-Spanish Hapsburgs, Louis XIV's France, Revolutionary France, Napoleonic France, the British Empire, and Wilhelmine Germany allied with Austria-Hungary were successively the most powerful empires and had the largest relative aggregate populations.

The age of European-centered geopolitics ended with the First World War, when it took the intervention of the United States, a non-European power, to decide the outcome. The outcome of the Second World War punctuated the end of the European era as the United States and Russia emerged triumphant and dominant in the shadow of a devastated continent and a worn-out British Empire. Europe became a prize, instead of a contestant, in the next great power struggle, the Cold War. By that time, both the United States and Russia had significantly larger populations than any single European power.

The United States and Russia, in fact, had larger populations than the European powers even before the First World War, but the United States deliberately failed to translate its demographic and economic power into permanent military power, and Russia was much slower to industrialize than the European powers—two examples among many where numbers, by themselves, were strategically meaningless.[31]

During the Cold War, the Sino-Soviet bloc initially held a potentially decisive geographical and demographical advantage over the Western powers, but the Sino-Soviet split, the fundamental weakness of the Soviet economy and political system, and the technological advantage of the West in support of what Walter Russell Mead calls "the maritime order" eventually resulted in the West's victory.[32]

In the wake of the Cold War, some observers consigned geopolitics to the ash heap of history. Francis Fukuyama announced the "end of history." Edward Luttwak claimed that "geo-economics" superseded geopolitics. Thomas Friedman declared the triumph of globalization. President George H. W. Bush proclaimed the "new world order." Democratic presidential candidate Bill Clinton's campaign in 1992 disdained the primacy and importance of geopolitics with the remark "It's the economy, stupid."

Meanwhile, forces were gathering and plotting in the Islamic world with the immediate goal of attacking the United States and U.S. interests around the world, and the more distant and broader goal of establishing an Islamic caliphate or world empire. This geopolitical development also had a demographic aspect. As Harvard's Samuel Huntington pointed out in *The Clash of Civilizations and the Remaking of World Order*, the "resurgence of Islam" was fueled by "spectacular rates of population growth." He explained further that "population expansion in Islamic countries . . . has been significantly greater than that in the neighboring countries and in the world generally."[33] Huntington, confirming UN population figures and estimates, noted that while Muslims constituted about 18 percent of the world's population in 1980, they will likely constitute more than 30 percent of the world's population by 2025, and overall the Muslim populations will be disproportionately teenagers and people in their twenties.[34]

Huntington explained the geopolitical significance of this Islamic resurgence, stimulated by population growth:

> Larger populations need more resources, and hence people from societies with dense and/or rapidly growing populations tend to push outward, occupy territory, and exert pressure on other less demographically dynamic peoples. Islamic population growth is thus a major contributing factor to the conflicts along the borders of the Islamic world between Muslims and other peoples. . . . The juxtaposition of a rapidly growing people of one culture and a slowly growing or stagnant people of another culture generates pressures for economic and/or political adjustments in both societies.[35]

Five years before the attacks of September 11, 2001, Huntington foresaw this geopolitical clash—what he called "an intercivilizational quasi war . . . between Islam and the West."[36]

The other significant geopolitical challenge in the post–Cold War world is the shift in resources and power from Europe to Asia. This is the consequence of several factors, including the collapse of the Soviet Empire and the resultant independence of the former satellite countries in Eastern and Central Europe and the former Soviet republics; the end of European great power rivalry and a more "pacific" approach to world politics among the European states; the global spread of Western technology and the information revolution; and the relative population advantage of Asian states.

As already noted, during most of the previous four centuries the focus of the world's geopolitics was Europe. The successive great powers that threatened to upset the global balance of power, as well as the powers that successfully resisted those threats, were European-based. The Austrian and Spanish Hapsburgs, Louis XIV's France, Revolutionary and Napoleonic France, Kaiser Wilhelm's Germany, Hitler's Germany, and the Soviet Union sought to dominate Europe and, in some instances, the world. Coalitions of lesser powers, often led by Great Britain, formed to oppose these repeated attempts at European or world hegemony.

The twenty-first century has witnessed the decline of the European great powers; a decline that began in the twentieth century. Indeed, it was the catastrophe of the First World War that precipitated Europe's geopolitical collapse. The Second World War and the Cold War hammered the remaining nails into the coffin of Europe's geopolitical primacy. The European great powers suffered both physically and psychologically from this century of conflict. The great wars of the twentieth century cost the European powers tens of millions of lives. Simultaneously, the decline of religion, the changing roles of women in society, the rise of widespread affluence, and the increasing availability and acceptability of contraception and abortion, resulted in lower birthrates in much of the continent.

These developments coincided with the retreat from colonialism among the European powers. As James Burnham pointed out in his masterful *Suicide of the West*, a global atlas in 1914 showed the world dominated by Europe. The same atlas in 1964 showed a Europe largely confined to the peninsula at the western end of the Eurasian landmass. The end of European colonialism was a manifestation not of progression and magnanimity, but of retreat. That geopolitical retreat is even more pronounced today.

George Weigel has written that Europe is "systematically depopulating itself" and is in the process of committing "demographic suicide."[37] The prolific British historian Niall Ferguson laments that Europe is undergoing the greatest "sustained reduction in European population since the Black Death of the 14th century."[38] These grim outlooks and projections are supported by UN population statistics. Eighteen of the twenty countries with the lowest birthrates are in Europe. Not one Western European country has a replacement-level birthrate (2.1 children per woman). It is projected that the total European population (including Russia) will decline from 728 million in 2000 to below 600 million in 2050.[39] As Patrick Buchanan writes, if these demographic trends continue, "the cradle of Western Civilization will have become its grave."[40]

A recent study by the Center for Strategic and International Studies notes that overall the population of the developed world was 25 percent of the world's total in 1930, but only 13 percent of the total in 2005. That is projected to decrease to below 10 percent of the total by 2050. Further, in 1950 five of the top twelve largest countries in population were in Europe, while in 2005 only one was in Europe, and it is projected that by 2050 none will be in Europe. The report warns that these European nations with declining and aging populations will have chronic shortages in young-adult manpower that will pose significant challenges to the economic and national security of those nations.[41]

George Weigel points out that "demographic vacuums do not remain unfilled." For nearly forty years, millions of Islamic immigrants have settled in Europe, and they are reproducing at a much greater rate than the Europeans. Weigel warns that these demographic trends, coupled with the increasing spread of radicalized Islam, "could eventually produce . . . a Europe increasingly influenced, and perhaps even dominated, by militant Islamic populations, convinced that their long-delayed triumph in the European heartland is at hand."[42]

The aging and decline of Europe's population coincides with its retreat or withdrawal (with the important exception of Russia) from great-power geopolitical competition. This phenomenon has been brilliantly analyzed by Robert Kagan in his book *Of Paradise and Power: America and Europe in the New World Order*.[43] Kagan describes a modern Europe that has withdrawn from the Hobbesian world of power politics and entered a "post-historical paradise of peace and relative prosperity."[44] This has led to a strategic disconnect between the United States and Europe in that "they do not share the same broad view of how the world should be governed, about the role of international institutions and international law, about the proper balance between the use of force and the use of diplomacy in international affairs."[45] This development has implications for NATO and for the overall global balance of power.

NATO as a defensive security pact cannot long survive an enduring strategic disconnect among its members. As U.S. and European worldviews continue to diverge on important strategic questions and issues, the foundation of the alliance weakens. And yet, this is happening at the same time that NATO has been expanding to include former Soviet satellite countries in Central and Eastern Europe. How, some may ask, can an alliance that is expanding in size be weakening?

The expansion of NATO is due in large part to a desire on the part of the countries of Central and Eastern Europe for a security insurance policy against a revival of Russian expansionist tendencies. These countries view the United States as the ultimate guarantor of their security and independence; the countries of Western Europe, however, no longer do. That security guarantee was the glue that formed and held together the alliance since 1949. With the fall of the Soviet Union, that security guarantee is not as relevant as it once was to Germany, France, Italy, Great Britain, and the other nations of Western Europe.

Over the long term, as Europe's experience confirms, the relative aging and decline of population undermines national power. Europe, once home to all the world's great powers, is now home to none. This fact undoubtedly contributes to the European preference for multilateral approaches to international security problems, as well as efforts to coordinate and, in some cases, subordinate national foreign policies via the European Union.

Those who place sole blame on President George W. Bush and his assertive unilateralism for the strains among the United States and its allies underestimate the extent to which the strains have resulted from fundamentally divergent worldviews. Those fundamental differences in outlook have not changed with the change of administrations in Washington.

Europe's decline coincides with and reinforces Asia's relative rise in power and influence. In Asia, globalization has accelerated the infusion of Western education, technology, and scientific advances to the teeming masses of China and India. This development made relative population disparities between European and Asian powers more significant and geopolitically meaningful. Relative population growth and decline are subject to qualifying factors such as military-age manpower, labor-force manpower, and the potential knowledge production of the population. All other things being equal or near equal, however, numbers do matter.

In the 1940s Nicholas Spykman wrote that the key to world power was control of the Eurasian Rimland, a great arc of territory stretching from Norway to Eastern China. In the twenty-first century, the European part of the Rimland has declined in importance vis-à-vis the Asian Rimland. The strategic focus of the twenty-first century will be the half moon–shaped territory extending from the Turkish peninsula to the Korean peninsula, an area once described by Mahan as the "debatable and debated ground." The Asian Rimland includes the Middle East/Persian Gulf/Southwest Asia region, which is the base of Islamic fundamentalism and terror, where the United States is currently fighting two wars, and hosts potential nuclear antagonists India and Pakistan; the Central Asian region, which includes energy-rich former Soviet Republics; and the East Asia region, where China, Russia, Japan, and the Koreas vie for influence and power.

The Asian Rimland also includes a key maritime highway that stretches from the Red Sea through the Arabian Sea and Indian Ocean, through the Bay of Bengal and China Sea, to the Sea of Japan. That maritime highway is dotted with the still important choke points of Suez, Aden, the Strait of Hormuz, the Strait of Malacca, and the Taiwan Straits.

Henry Kissinger views America's relationship with Asia as "comparable to that of Britain toward the continent of Europe for four centuries." He has written that "a hostile Asian bloc combining the most populous nations of the world and vast resources with some of the most industrious peoples would be incompatible with the American national interest."[46]

Zbigniew Brzezinski, citing UN population figures, notes that by the year 2020, Asia will contain 60 percent of the world's people compared to 9 percent for Europe and 5 percent for North America, and hosts two of the world's rising economic and military powers, China and India. "Global security," he writes, "will unavoidably be affected by how the international scene in the Far East actually evolves."[47]

Robert Kaplan has recently pointed out that China has been impressively expanding its military for nearly two decades; India will soon possess the third-largest navy in the world; Japan's navy is more than three times larger than Britain's; Pakistan and South Korea spend a larger share of their domestic output on defense than either France or Britain. The vitality and energy of the powers in Asia, Kaplan writes, "will take us back to an older world of traditional statecraft, in which we will need to tirelessly leverage allies and seek cooperation from competitors."[48]

Tony Corn, writing in *Policy Review*, sees a "twofold epochal change taking place" in global geopolitics: "the transfer of the center of gravity of the world economy from the Atlantic to the Pacific . . . and the rise of a 'second nuclear age' in Asia and with it, the concomitant end of three centuries of Western military superiority."[49]

The factors of power in international affairs, including population growth and relative population distribution, make it likely that the next major threat to the global order will emerge from Asia. Asia hosts three continent-size powers (China, India, and Russia), two of which have rapidly growing economies and huge populations. China, India, Russia, Pakistan, and Israel have nuclear weapons; Iran and North Korea may soon have them. Crises in Korea or the Taiwan Straits could cause Japan to join the nuclear weapons club. China and India are investing heavily in military power, including naval power and other power-projection capabilities. Islamic terrorists are largely based and supported in Asia. The fast-growing Asian economies and population will demand an increasing share of the world's energy resources.

The new demographic and geopolitical realities noted in this chapter are reflected in the United States' focus on the Asia-Pacific region. U.S. military and diplomatic assets are increasingly invested in Asia and the Pacific because our statesmen recognize that we have more security interests there than in Europe. This new and dramatic shift in resources and focus will likely continue given the demographic, economic, and political trends discussed here.

Relative demographic decline ultimately undermines national power over the long term. Europe, Japan, and Russia, with relatively declining and aging populations, have become geopolitically less relevant than in the recent past. The decline of Europe and Japan, two close allies of the United States in the developed world, will likely mean that the United States will assume an even greater share of the burden of upholding the maritime world order. Europe and Japan may do more peacekeeping and humanitarian interventions, but their roles in supporting the post–Cold War order will continue to diminish. Thus, relative demographic decline weakens the commitments of former great powers to uphold international peace and security in the post–Cold War world.

Russia's relative demographic decline also creates geopolitical opportunities for China. Indeed, this is already occurring in Russia's far eastern territories, where an influx of Chinese has filled the population vacuum. A world power in relative demographic decline situated in geographical proximity to a rising power with more than sufficient population resources can result in conflict as the rising power seeks to exploit the vulnerabilities of the declining one.

The global balance of power is never static and can never be predicted with anything approaching certainty. Few observers, after all, predicted the rise of Japan in the late nineteenth and early twentieth centuries, or the rapid, peaceful collapse of the Soviet Empire in the late 1980s and early 1990s. Geographical and population advantages can be offset to some extent by governmental or societal lethargy and corruption. The designs and intentions of leaders, as well as the nature of governments, can temper or aggravate relative geopolitical conditions. It matters very much whether Germany is led by Bismarck, Hitler, or Helmut Kohl.

Nevertheless, demographics and demographic trends will always weigh heavily in power calculations. Lenin, it seems, was right after all: in the long run, geopolitics cannot escape the impact of relative population trends.

PART II.
THE END OF WESTERN CONSENSUS?

4

POPULATION AND HEALTH CONSTRAINTS ON THE RUSSIAN MILITARY

Murray Feshbach

A version of this chapter was first presented as a paper for a symposium at the Swedish Defence Research Agency, Stockholm, in 2007. The author is indebted to his research assistants, Eugene Zamastsyanin and Bo Anders Knutson, for their research and computer assistance in preparing that paper.

Introduction

Although many believe that health is a less imperative concern for the uniformed services, in the current and future Russian case the conjuncture of population and health will play a very significant role. These dynamics and trends can no longer be ignored and will influence choices made by the Russian government. A number of important steps have already been taken, but while they will help mitigate some of the constraints, it is likely that they will not be sufficient to overcome the population dynamics and the poor health status of the potential military service personnel.

This chapter describes and analyzes basic information on the demographic echoes of the past significant decline in births and the consequences not only for labor supply per se, but also for cohort size of potential conscripts and the importance of their health status. Given major reductions in their number as well as the need for individuals with appropriate physical and mental ability to operate higher-level weapon technologies, the inauspicious nexus of these issues has finally reached the highest levels of the Russian leadership.

Troubling Trends

What alarms Russian leaders is the bleak set of population indicators. The cohort of recruit-age Russian youth has fallen from 21 percent of the population in 1950 to 14.4 percent in 2010, and is expected to reach just 9.5 percent by 2050. This shift is reflected in the median age, which has risen from 25 years of age in 1950, to 37.3 in 2010, and is expected to reach 47.2 by 2050. That age would be even higher if it were not for the fact that Russians' life expectancy, 69 years of age in 2010, is a decade shorter than in the rest of the developed world. In fact, the death rate has risen from 9.5 deaths per 1,000 people in 1950 to 14.1 per 1,000 in 2010, and the rate is expected to increase to 17.1 per 1,000 by 2050. The Russian total fertility rate was 1.44 children per woman in 2010 and has been below replacement levels since the 1960s.[1]

Along with the quantity of recruitable youth, the quality has also declined. The armed forces suffer from a lack of educated conscripts: whereas high school graduates make up more than 97 percent of new recruits in the U.S. Navy, in Russia the percentage is less than half. About 20 percent of conscripts have completed higher education.[2] To mitigate the problem, military officer training is undergoing major changes in scope, number of facilities, length of contract obligation upon completion, and new programs to recruit women for service. If assignments are not followed up by active duty, any individual completing his or her education at one of the new Military Training Centers in the Military Faculties will have to repay the state 300,000 to 700,000 rubles for such education. Depending on the facility and/or program completed, it appears that the term of service could be one, three, or five years. The two-year reserve officer program is being phased out. Reenlistment rates are reportedly improving, but many still decide not to do so. Overall it would appear that the General Staff has resolved to put the military higher education system under stricter supervision, even to the extent of abolishing those institutions that do not provide good-quality training. Opportunities for female officer training have been expanded to six "high-quality" military programs, and there are promises to expand even further in the near term.

In addition to educational attainment levels, another population-related variable impacting upon service levels and military preparedness has been the overall health of the population of potential recruits. The necessity of addressing health issues in this population has been recognized by the government, albeit after costly delays. In 2006, the federal authorities finally took the HIV situation as seriously as required. Also, the tuberculosis epidemic alone and in combination with HIV/AIDS has led to more cooperation with the efforts of the World Health Organization (WHO) to stop the spread of tuberculosis. Russia ranks among the twenty-two high-burden countries for TB incidence, the only one in all of Europe. Reproductive and child health, the determinants of future population size and quality, are also influenced by past, current, and future trends. Thus, the demographic factor also leads to a major shift to a volunteer military, despite its higher costs and requirements. The combination of population and health issues is strong enough to question whether the Russian Federation will find it possible to cope with the manning crisis of the next decades.

Nonetheless, the Russian military is trying to expand its recruitment base. For example, the military decided to begin drafting Chechens, expand officer and combat training for women, as well as create small military units of volunteers from former Soviet Union countries to close the gap. One key factor, beyond the significant decline in cohorts available for possible conscription, is the major increase in the number of full-blown AIDS cases and deaths, and very importantly, whether these trends will continue into the future. Another major concern is that of all AIDS-related deaths, which the Joint United Nations Program on HIV/AIDS (UNAIDS) estimates at between 35,000 and 65,000 per year and rising, nearly half are co-infected with tuberculosis.[3] According to UNAIDS, the number of TB patients testing positive for HIV grew steadily from 2006 through 2009, while at the same time the number of total new and relapsed TB cases also increased.[4] When and if the emerging number of deaths from AIDS increases even further, the consequences may be more negative than the Russian leadership recognizes.

Despite the warnings issued by the Federal AIDS Center and others over a number of years about the need for anti-retroviral therapy (ART) medication, the Russian government was late in allocating funds for manufacturing and/or purchasing such medication; only since 2007 have they begun a serious effort (but are still short of the full requirement of medication).

If the basic active *Mycobacterium tuberculosis* converts into multi-drug-resistant TB (MDR-TB), let alone to extensively drug-resistant TB (XDR-TB), then the potential loss of life can be quite large. Since the core military conscript age group of eighteen to twenty-seven is roughly synchronous with the fifteen-to twenty-nine-year-old age group in which some 80 percent of registered HIV/AIDS cases are found, the ramifications are possibly extremely serious indeed.

In October 2010, the U.S. Administration for International Development (USAID) reported that only 16 percent of Russians living with HIV/AIDS were undergoing ART.[5] Meanwhile, injecting drug use remained the primary means of transmission of HIV in Russia, accounting for 62 percent of new cases in 2009. UNAIDS estimates that between 1.5 and 8 percent of Russian men under thirty have injected drugs.[6]

Adverse health conditions leave open the likelihood that due to the young-age structure of the incidence of HIV in Russia, HIV infection has increased among the draft-age cohorts. Tuberculosis incidence is much higher than official numbers published in Russia. With a new type of tuberculosis beginning to affect Russia, it could also reduce the steadily decreasing pools of eighteen-year-old cohorts needed by the military. Additionally, increases in youth crime have led many conscripts and/or new contract military to spend time in the penal system, where the chances of infection are very high.

Birthrate and Life Expectancy

The major factor in the dynamics of the Russian population is the remarkable 50 percent drop in births during the period 1987–1999. Coincidentally, five years after the beginning of the decline in births, and the first registered HIV case in 1987, mortality began to exceed births (in 1992). Net in-migration was statistically significant only in 1992 and 1993, immediately after the change in regime in late 1991. Until 2007, migration compensated only for some 10 to 15 percent of the net excess mortality over births. By mid-2007, however, net migration increased to a point covering almost 35 percent of excess mortality. But the UN reports that from 1990 through 2010 there has been a steady decline in the net migration rate.[7]

Efforts in the very recent period to produce a pronatalist upsurge and a fight against mortality are serious.[8] Yet it is likely that these efforts will not prove to be highly successful in the medium to long term. In the long term, the number of recruitable youth will continue to plummet, from 1,038,366 in 1980 to 740,138 in 2023 (see table 4-1).

The head of the Russian Federation Comptroller's Office in downplaying this positive trend cited estimates provided by the Federal State Statistics Ser-

TABLE 4-1
Male Births, Infant Male Deaths, and Year at Which
They Attain 18 Years of Age, Russia (1980–2005)

Year	Births	Infant deaths	Net number	Draft year
1980	1,126,666	28,300	1,038,366	1998
1981	1,145,239	28,141	1,117,098	1999
1982	1,192,252	27,528	1,164,724	2000
1983	1,268,820	28,706	1,258,124	2001
1984	1,234,760	29,551	1,205,209	2002
1985	1,217,322	28,993	1,188,329	2003
1986	1,273,213	27,913	1,245,300	2004
1987	1,283,425	28,669	1,254,756	2005
1988	1,204,907	26,309	1,178,590	2006
1989	1,110,602	22,991	1,087,611	2007
1990	1,021,248	20,691	1,000,557	2008
1991	923,319	19,131	904,188	2009
1992	816,757	17,238	799,519	2010
1993	708,689	16,213	692,476	2011
1994	724,818	15,394	709,424	2012
1995	700,191	14,472	685,719	2013
1996	671,430	13,416	658,014	2014
1997	648,195	12,738	635,457	2015
1998	660,842	12,327	648,515	2016
1999	626,149	12,020	614,129	2017
2000	653,146	11,248	641,898	2018
2001	675,750	11,273	664,477	2019
2002	719,511	10,703	703,808	2020
2003	760,934	10,429	750,505	2021
2004	772,973	10,090	762,883	2022
2005	749,554	9,416	740,138	2023

FSGS (Rosstat), Demograficheskiy yezhegodnik Rossii, Ofitsial'noye izdaniye, *Moscow, 2006, 69.*

Note: The net number shown here needs to be further reduced due to deaths during ages one to seventeen (inclusive), which when infant mortality (before one year of age) is included amounts to about 3 percent up to age eighteen. For 2005, a 3 percent cumulative number of deaths in ages zero to seventeen (inclusive) amounts to 22,487 through this period, or an additional 13,071 male deaths in ages one through seventeen (excluding infant deaths prior to age one).

vice (known by its Russian acronym, FSGS) that the population would number 136.2 million by 2020, down from a peak of 148.9 million in 1993. What is more shocking is that the same projections also predict a growth in the birthrate. The Comptroller attributed the decline to the increasing age of the Russian population as a whole. It is estimated that by 2020 the working-age population will have fallen by 13.6 million from 2005 levels.[9] Even assuming better survival rates, any increase in the number of births will not translate to potential male conscripts or female volunteers until they turn eighteen in the year 2025. Projections of the population by both the FSGS and the United Nations Population Division 2010 Revision show parallel declines in the overall population of Russia for 2025. The Russian official projection for the end of 2025 shows a figure of 134,422,300, whereas in 2011 the UN calculation projected 136,031,000.[10]

The increase in births may be both a reflection of the economic incentive offered for second births and the demographic echo of the increase in number of females twenty to twenty-nine years of age—but only until 2013, when it will start a decline from 13 million to 7 million for the next almost four decades.[11]

Average life expectancy at birth of both sexes in Russia is among the lowest in Europe and North America. The United Nations Population Division calculated in 2011 that average life expectancy for Russian males at birth ranks 156 in the world, and the rank order for females is 97. It is not surprising then to read that about 50 percent of sixteen-year-old males in Russia do not survive until age sixty.[12] Projections of average life expectancy among males in 2025, prepared by the FSGS, showed an expected increase from 58.9 in 2005 to 61.9 in 2025, a very small improvement over the twenty-year period.[13] Russian officials, including President Medvedev, have said they think it will be closer to 70, but expectation of such a profound improvement appears to be based more on optimism than realism.

On the positive side, estimates of life expectancy at birth for males made in 2011 by the United Nations showed an improvement to 61.6 years for males and 74 years for females. The disparity in life expectancy between the sexes is still about twelve to thirteen years in Russia, a gap wider than in any other country of Europe or North America.[14]

In addition, the Ministry of Economic Development and Trade has prepared estimates of labor force trends. The net change in the labor force turned negative beginning in 2007. *Rossiyskaya Gazeta* finds that labor productivity is the only means to overcome the drop in the working-age population, but that an increase of 6 to 7 percent per year is necessary to compensate for the decline in the economically active population, a rate that Russia is not expected to achieve.[15]

Health Issues Among Youth

In all, life expectancy, births, deaths, labor productivity, and reproductive and child health, as well as that of the potential military-age cohorts, concurrently depend on the health status of the population.

However, the health status of the population is not good, especially that of the young and among pre-draft males (ages fifteen to seventeen), which is distinctly worsening. Drugs, alcohol, crime, growing illiteracy, and health per se—to include HIV, tuberculosis, hepatitis B and C, as well as psychological disturbances and muscular-skeletal structure and central nervous system problems—are increasing markedly. In 2001, Dr. Olga Sharapova, then a Deputy Minister for Child and Reproductive Health of the Russian Ministry of Health, convinced the *verkhushka* (the top leadership) to conduct a Child Health Census in 2002. The health of the population even became a Russian Security Council topic of discussion.[16] Whether the discussion was directly related to the later changes in the set of reasons for draft deferment or rejection cannot be precisely ascertained, but most likely had an impact.

Results across a multitude of specific nosological illnesses, by age and sex, from the Child Health Census of 2002[17] show a roughly 30 percent higher rate of illness among the population below eighteen years of age compared with those published by the official health statistics of the State Statistical Agency. The special census covered 30.4 out of 31.6 million children ages zero to seventeen (inclusive). Behind these negative numbers are the early health problems of newborn children, as well as those of teenagers and the working-age population.

According to official Russian statistics, at least 80 percent of all pregnant women suffer a serious pathology during their pregnancy. Not surprisingly, only 30 percent of children are "born healthy."

Within the Child Health Census report, data and analyses are given for many illnesses. At one point, it is flatly asserted that the poor health of fifteen- to seventeen-year-olds is a strategic concern. In addition, it should not be forgotten that the full Child Health Census report is an internal document meant for the president and his coterie. It undoubtedly had an influence on the selection of health as a national project, as noted earlier, as well as on many comments of Medvedev, then–deputy president, on the leadership's attention to this issue as contrasted to the past, when it seemed to be given only minimal budgetary allocations and attention.

Challenges to Professionalizing the Military

It is from this unhealthy population that military leaders must sustain their desired million-man military, including voluntary forces, for a newly professionalized military. Authorization for formation of a voluntary, contract-based military force was passed in 1992. While the number of contract troops (*kontraktniki*) rose to 200,000 by the mid-2000s, that number has now fallen off, and in some places local troops have had to fill the gap.[18] As of 2011, only about 20 percent of the army was made up of kontraktniki.[19] Surprisingly, about 30 percent of the soldiers and noncommissioned sergeants among the kontraktniki are female service personnel. Some 60,000-plus are females, leaving 100,000 males available for combat or similar assignments.[20]

Emphasis is now also being placed on combating psychological illnesses and on physical capability for a professional, contract military, as well as among conscripts. Before the fuller implementation of the program to split the Armed Forces into a contract and conscript military, the head of the Military Medical Directorate at the time, Lt. Gen. Ivan Chizh, already noted in June 1999 that psychological illnesses among conscripts had risen in the previous two years by 30 percent, and by 19 percent among officers.[21]

As always, corruption in obtaining false medical certificates concerns the military, but given other evidence this may not be at such a serious level per se that it could significantly reduce the supply of combat-capable personnel for the Armed Forces.[22] False certificates are usually very costly—reportedly as much as $4,000.[23] The most likely "customers" for this type of evasion are arguably young persons (or their families) from big cities who can afford this expense and do not want to "waste a year and a half" serving in the Armed Forces while they could be making good money instead.

Other devices are also utilized by potential conscripts to evade the draft. Moscow city military prosecutor, Maj. Gen. of Justice Vladimir Mulov, called this technique "stretching the rubber band." Thus, the draftee is temporarily taken off the rolls and his file is sent to a different military commissariat. While it is moving around, the current draft period ends—and someone in the military commissariat receives a certain sum of money for this. It is very difficult to track these violations.

Simultaneously, other problems arise from this modality because commissariats are still required to "supply" a certain number of conscripts to the Russian armed forces. Finding these missing conscripts leads to frequent violations of the law. Cases of the so-called "quick draft" are reported wherein young people are literally grabbed off the street or from their college dormitories. They are not given any chance to present their deferment papers or even to go through a full medical examination. Exact numbers of these cases are not available, but the fact that the military prosecutor of Moscow described this in detail makes it more likely that the possible scope of these "activities" is significant.[24]

Government directive no. 123, issued February 25, 2003, redefined those who are "healthy, partially healthy but can be drafted with limited assignment possibilities" and "those who are not acceptable at all."[25] The follow-up Ministry of Defense listing of "new" diseases, which went into effect on July 1, 2003, exempted certain potential conscripts from being drafted. These included: "drug addicts, drug users, alcoholics and persons who have tested positive for HIV," as well as "men of non-traditional sexual orientation."[26] After going into effect, those found to suffer from any of these conditions, whether acquired prior to being called up for service or since beginning active duty, were to be discharged. Currently, any person found to be ill with tuberculosis is added to the list as a cause for non-acceptability for military service.

Reductions in the list of twenty-five causes for deferments to sixteen may later be adjusted even further, perhaps to nine. Keir Giles of the British Conflict Research Studies Institute estimates in his detailed analysis of the exclusion of five allowable deferments and modification of four others that this will provide an additional 90,000 persons per year.[27] However, as Giles clearly demonstrates, even this addition to the cohorts available will not be sufficient to cover the demand of the military for 700,000 troops per year under a twelve-month term of service and the demographic reality of declining cohorts. According to an article in *Komsomol'skaya Pravda*, the local "registration and enlistment offices recruit more and more contract servicemen" who are "alcoholics, drug addicts, people with previous imprisonment and sometimes people with AIDS."[28] Some

64 percent of conscripts on duty are not medically qualified to join operational units, according to a 2011 study from the Strategic Studies Institute: "Between 2000 and 2008, no one with a criminal record could be conscripted. This restriction has now been relaxed and of the 305,000 called up, for instance, in the spring of 2009, 170,000 had some sort of criminal record."[29]

For a number of years, outright rejection of potential conscripts for health reasons has been about 30 percent, with about 50 percent or more of those actually conscripted serving with "limitations on assignment." The rules have recently been changed to bar these "limited" conscripts from serving in the parachute troops, the navy, and the internal troops.[30] When combined with other deferments, draft evasion, and changing illness patterns, only some 10 percent of the cohort are drafted or enter contract service. However, while the rejection rate has stayed the same over the last decade, the draft pool itself is shrinking (see table 4-2).[31] Meanwhile, the percentage of youth rejected for medical reasons jumped dramatically in the two decades following the end of the Cold War.[32] In just one ominous example, malnutrition has accounted for more than 150,000 rejections for service in Moscow City and Moscow Oblast in a single year.[33]

The HIV/AIDS Challenge to the Military

"Official" registered prevalence numbers for HIV/AIDS in Russia understate the problem of the epidemic. Russian figures are less than half what the UN estimates, which is between 840,000 and 1.2 million in 2009.[34] Some officials, such as the Federal AIDS Center and the Ministry of Health, agree with the UN figures. Given the difficulty in determining a correct number for the total population, it is not surprising that the number affected by HIV/AIDS on active duty in the Ministry of Defense and in other formations, such as Security Services and Interior Ministry, is not readily ascertainable, in addition to the usual secrecy applied to these formations. However, the overall increases, combined with the spread to the female population whereby almost 50 percent of new cases are diagnosed among heterosexual women, would seem to indicate that the problem associated with HIV in the military could be transmitted to the troops of all ranks and become a major threat again—if it ever ceased to be one. In 1996 there were a total of 1,513 new registered cases of HIV/AIDS per 100,000 persons. In 2001 that number jumped to 87,671 and by 2006 had lev-

TABLE 4-2
Actual Percentage of Males Drafted

Year	Percentage drafted
1988	54.6
1994	27.5
1998	17.4
1999	13.0
2000	12.0
2001	12.0
2002	11.2
spring 2004	9.5
2005	9.1
2006	9.7

Giles, Where Have All the Soldiers Gone, *October 12, 2006, 2, 8; V. Kozhukhovskiy, "Vzyatochnichestvo v voyenkomatakh—ne glavnaya problema prizyva,"* Nezavisimoye voyennoye obozreniye, *no. 15 (April 23, 2004): 1, http://dlib.eastview.com/searchresults/article .jsp?art=2&id=6179641 (accessed May 21, 2007).*

eled at 39,988 of new cases registered. According to UNAIDS, the total number of new infections, all ages, spiked at around 200,000 in 2001 and now hovers near 100,000 per annum.[35]

All conscript soldiers and noncommissioned officers who have HIV are discharged. Officers are not. In addition, these numbers are restricted to Ministry of Defense troops and do not include those in other power structures (Security Service, Interior Ministry, Presidential Guard, etc.). In only one instance are details openly published for the numbers of HIV-positive persons in other uniformed services, and that is from the period between 1989 and 1999—more than a decade ago. According to Oleg Yelenskiy (*Independent Military Review*), the number of service personnel who have AIDS (or HIV) in the *siloviye struktury* (regime forces) is "closed," i.e. secret. Nonetheless, Yelenskiy states that about 15 percent of these personnel who were found to be HIV-positive were discharged prior to the end of their normal period of service. An alternative distribution of the percentage of HIV-positive cases, by branch of service, is found in the report by U.S. Colonel Jeffrey Holachek for the Atlantic Council. For the period 1989 to 2002, almost half of the cases found were in the Ground Forces (44.4 percent), the next largest in the Navy (16.8 percent), then Units Under Centralized Subordination (10.6 percent), the Air Force (9.1 percent), Strategic Rocket Forces (7.4 percent), and the remaining 11.7 percent scattered among other branches. While the Centralized Subordination grouping seems high, the others seem to correspond to the size of the various branches.[36]

Officers are treated in military hospitals for the illness. Lower-rank contract troops who are ill are discharged. Whatever the official numbers may be, Russian military officials assert that they are far from complete. The draft pool includes eighteen- to twenty-seven-year-olds (as well as the fact that pre-draft medical examinations were or are not allowed to check for HIV, drug addiction, and hepatitis). As already mentioned, some 80 percent of all recorded cases of HIV/AIDS are among the fifteen- to twenty-nine-year cohort, which is roughly analogous to the recruiting pool. For these reasons, many who are ill with these afflictions may be drafted and not diagnosed while on active duty, if ever. Despite the extensive child health survey of all pre-draft males and females, the then Air Force Chief General Mikhaylov surprisingly claimed that many conscripts from rural areas had never seen a doctor prior to being called up for service. This seems to contradict the Child Health Census assertion that coverage was over 95 percent and therefore should have included a very high proportion of the rural pre-conscription-age males.[37] When the Ministry of Defense petitioned the Ministry of Finance to allocate funds for provision of equipment to examine potential conscripts for these illnesses, the petition was rejected (as it was by the Ministry of Health). The cost for provision of equipment has almost doubled since the original request.[38]

This provision has been altered to test for drug usage and polygraphs are being used to test for mental problems. More likely, however, is that the availability of the appropriate equipment and reagents to all pre-draft medical facilities is not yet universal, and many might be drafted who should not be. The true numbers of these illnesses, as well as others, remain unknown.

The key question about the number of people with HIV/AIDS in the military is whether the authorities do or do not test, or do they test selectively? There is a non-testing rule, but there also seem to be widespread exceptions to it. On one hand, military officials have said that military medicine does not perform HIV diagnostics[39] and federal legislation does not require it (although it has been authorized in some places such as Moscow).[40] On the other hand, they report that thousands of troops have been dismissed because they carried HIV.

Will mandatory testing be expanded nationwide, particularly as the number of HIV cases has resumed an upward trajectory? Years later, nothing more has been written about this possibility.

Tuberculosis: The Undiagnosed Problem

One of the main illnesses not listed, or even rarely discussed, is tuberculosis among potential conscripts, and especially among the active duty military. For the country as a whole, the tuberculosis rate (measured per 100,000 persons) is two to three times the rate determined by the WHO as qualifying for epidemic status. Given methodological issues described earlier, the official rate of 83.8 per 100,000 population in 2008 is adjusted by the WHO to 150 to 170 for the same year.[41] It is no surprise, therefore, that annually about three thousand young males are rejected for active military duty because of this dangerous illness.[42]

Complicating the entire issue of health and sanitation in crowded barracks or on ships, as well as in Russian prisons in particular, there is a high potential for outbreaks of drug-resistant tuberculosis. Military troops, conscripted from a youth cohort increasingly prone to crime, may accelerate the spread of disease to the military and to the general population if they are infected while incarcerated and then transferred or returned home. In prisons, it is clear that the danger exists as many HIV-positive prisoners are also resistant to first-line anti-TB medication.[43] Given that about half of ex-prisoners with tuberculosis (and HIV) do not continue treatment when released from incarceration, they can spread the disease among the population, including youths of pre-conscription age.[44] Tuberculosis cases diagnosed among active-duty servicemen has increased by about 10 percent per year since 1993.[45]

These serving troops with TB are usually found to be infected with TB in their first month of service. Many women in uniform have been found to be infected as well. Given a pattern of increasing tuberculosis among all service personnel, it is not surprising that three thousand are rejected every year—or rather, it is surprising that more aren't rejected for this reason. If the medical and General Staff are not as worried about tuberculosis as about other medical issues, they should be; it is a threat equivalent to HIV/AIDS.

Until very recently in the Russian Federation, the phenomenon of XDR-TB was hardly addressed. According to the WHO, Russia is among the top twenty-seven high-burden countries for XDR-TB, with the third highest number of cases, a total of thirty-one thousand, behind India and China. Of these cases, only about eight thousand are enrolled in treatment and the WHO does not report that Russia has an infection control plan or national guidelines.[46] Because their TB situation is very difficult, it will add to the burden of disease due to lack of proper food supplies and/or consumption, that is, due to poverty and alcoholism. As part of its effort to determine the cost of an expanded effort to deal with MDR-TB and XDR-TB, the WHO Stop TB unit has calculated the estimated numbers of each type of TB expected to be under treatment in the coming years. For the Russian Federation, the numbers for MDR-TB are 16,393 and 19,975 in 2007 and 2008, respectively, the latest period for which WHO has figures. It is important to understand that these are not the total number diagnosed, which was 34,055 in 2007, or slightly more than double the number on treatment. (No other estimates of estimated actual new incidence numbers are provided in this report, nor any of the likely "real" total numbers.) The numbers of persons with XDR-TB under treatment in the Russian Federation are calculated as growing by over 20 percent. How many, or what proportion of these figures, are on active duty in the uniformed services is not detailed in this report, or even whether they are included or not.[47]

Conclusions

It is clear that there are many more cases of HIV/AIDS, tuberculosis, hepatitis, and drug addiction in the Russian armed forces than reported. Whether the number is 2,200 or 5,000 or double that is far from certain, but is likely to be on the higher side, in part because rural recruits are infrequently examined by local military commissariats (*voyenkomaty*). Whether this will lead to weakened combat capability until and if a successful (i.e. well-trained, equipped, and all healthy) contract military is in place remains moot. Achieving these goals will be made more difficult by the overall poor health among fifteen- to seventeen-year-olds.

We are now more than a decade past the officially registered explosion in the late 1990s of persons becoming HIV-positive. Yet there has been a severe lack of provision of anti-retroviral therapy to those who have needed it, and so we can expect the HIV-positive number to climb rapidly.

It is not only HIV/AIDS that impacts the potential of recruits for active duty, but also the array of tuberculosis, drug addiction, alcohol, mental disorders, and other illnesses and disabilities. With only 10 percent of the diminishing cohorts actually conscripted and only 30 percent of these conscripts qualified for full service in all components of the military, the situation is taut enough at present.

The Russian government's attention to the health sector is recently much improved, yet this improvement comes quite late, and is still remiss for allowing anti-retroviral therapy medication to be so inadequate and irregular, and by failing to recognize the potential danger of tuberculosis in all forms to combine with HIV/AIDS. Frequent reference can be found to the "national security" of the state being threatened by health and demographic factors. Other commentators dismiss this "threat," while neo-Malthusians are not bothered by such deaths, blaming risky lifestyles for the affliction. Sergey Stepashin, the then Comptroller General (Chief Auditor) of Russia, wrote that the predicted "reduction in the size of the population and the reduction of population density to a level three times below the world average will create the danger of weakening of Russia' s political, economic and military influence in the world."[48]

In other words, this can be cut down to the simple formula: "the fewer the people, the less sovereignty." If Stepashin is correct, Russia is a country with major ambitions and very low possibilities to realize these ambitions, but, simultaneously, in possession of a huge military arsenal.

The elimination of deferments for full-time students may provide more quantity for the military, but the loss of human capital formation if they do not return to their studies after service could be a loss of quality for the society as a whole. The pronatalist policies of Putin and Medvedev may well also draw down the number of women who might continue their education.

The bottom line, as Harvard University's Dmitry Gorenberg put it, is that "while the military leadership continues to go back and forth on the question of conscription versus professionalization, it has been largely ignoring the simple fact that there simply aren't enough 18 year olds in Russia to staff the military at current levels given the current one year term for conscription."[49] The Russian military's desired million-man army is to include some 150,000–220,000 officers and another 150,000–170,000 contract soldiers, resulting in a needed 610,000–700,000 conscripts per year. The problem is that there are only about 700,000 men reaching the age of eighteen, and only about 400,000 are now draft-eligible due to health and other deferments. The total number of eighteen-year-olds will decline by 40 percent by 2013, leaving fewer than 300,000 draft-eligible recruits per year. This leaves a deficit of recruit-aged youth of about 300,000 per year in the decades ahead, all things remaining the same.[50]

As this chapter has argued, the health constraints in the youth population not only limit recruitment, but also retention and combat-readiness of troops due to apparent high prevalence of disease and slow detection and treatment measures. The possible, or even likely, widespread co-infection of HIV and TB will be an additional heavy burden for the country. The overall combination of population decline and likely increase in mortality will lead to a more tenuous situation in Russian society, including the military, than the economic dimension would portend.

5

EUROPE'S STRATEGIC FUTURE AND THE NEED FOR LARGE-FAMILY PRONATALISM

A NORMATIVE STUDY OF DEMOGRAPHIC DECLINE

Douglas A. Sylva

The nations of Europe are undergoing a dramatic and prolonged decline in fertility, a decline so pronounced that it has been called unprecedented in human history.[1] Recognition of this fact is by now commonplace, as is the recognition—and analysis—of the economic ramifications of this decline.[2] Of greatest concern has been whether the social welfare states of Europe can remain solvent as the elderly population expands and the working-age population contracts.

But other essential aspects of this situation have remained, to date, underexamined. Most important, how will demographic decline alter the strategic and military standing of the nations of the Europe? How will demographic decline change Europe's geopolitical power and influence? This chapter is an attempt to address this gap in the literature. To do this, we will need to go beyond basic numbers and statistics, the realm of demography proper; in fact, this chapter will provide what can be called a normative study of demographic decline.

What if some of the most cherished values of post–World War II Europe run counter to the reproduction of the population of the state? What if depopulation, in a manner of speaking, is bred in the bone? It will become apparent that Europe is not culturally or philosophically prepared to address its own demographic decline. Many of the normative ideals, even those said to encourage greater fertility, run counter to it, and may even depress it further. In this regard, the dominant ideologies of Europe play a significant role in determining

how European nations view and address the problem. What is more, these ideologies close off policy options that could result in substantial gains in fertility.

Thus, the leaders of Europe are left to plan for, facilitate, and hope for profound shifts in geopolitics—the taming of geopolitics through multilateralism,
even the coming obsolescence of conventional war itself—that would render
population level much less important in determining global power. While perhaps admirable, such aspirations are, of course, far from certain, the human
condition being what it is. Without such shifts, Europe's approaching loss of
global influence appears all but assured.

Demographic Situation

The basic demographic facts are startling. The United Nations Population Division provides four possible demographic scenarios for the coming decades:
high, medium, constant, and low fertility scenarios. The high variant posits
that, by 2050, fertility on the continent will recover from a current level of 1.5
children per woman to the robust level of 2.41 (fertility last seen in Europe in
the early 1960s). The medium variant assumes that fertility will recover to 1.91
children per woman. The constant-fertility variant assumes that fertility will
still rise slightly, from the current 1.51 to 1.55, while the low fertility variant
assumes that the trend of fertility decline will continue, with fertility sliding
further to 1.41 children per woman by 2050.[3]

Which variant is most likely is not mere academic speculation. The severity
of the population problem facing Europe will be largely determined by which
fertility projection proves most prescient. For instance, if fertility rebounds to
2.41, the population will continue to grow (although it will still age slightly).
But if fertility were to remain constant, or even to decline further, the Population Division foresees drastic implications. If fertility remains the same as it
is now, by 2050 the median age would rise to 48.6, and the population would
shrink by about 67 million people. If fertility continues to decline, by 2050 the
median age would be 51.1, and the population would shrink by about 106 million people, 14 percent of its current level. By 2050, the European population
would be losing close to five million people per year.[4]

So which is it? The simple answer is that no one knows. As the United
Nations Population Division puts it, "There exists no compelling and quanti-
fiable theory of reproductive behavior in low fertility societies."[5] As many of

the low fertility nations of Europe have now descended into "lowest-low fertility," demographers have lost relevant points of comparison, since there are no similar experiences to study.[6] Most important, as one low fertility "record" after another has been broken, demographers have come to abandon assumptions about the existence of some sort of demographic floor, a level below which fertility simply could not fall: "Here it is sufficient to conclude that there does not seem to be any 'natural law' that would stop fertility from falling further, should preferences and norms change accordingly."[7]

The recent revisions of World Population Prospects have seen the United Nations abandon one such assumption after another, but some still remain.[8] The Medium Variant, generally regarded as the most likely scenario, still assumes that fertility will recover significantly, to 1.91 children per woman. But, as Lutz et al. argue,

> In trend analysis, one would need to come up with a very strong and convincing reason to justify such a deviation from the pervasive trend of the past 50 years of cohort experience. . . . Furthermore, none of these population projections provide the users with a clear theoretical reasoning for why, in the case of fertility, the declining trend is assumed to reverse[9]

A case could be made, therefore, that the most likely scenarios are also the most dire: the constant-fertility variant (if nothing changes) and the low fertility variant (if the five-decade trend of fertility decline continues). And, as we shall see, the Low Fertility Trap Hypothesis offers a plausible theoretical explanation of just why this fertility decline may continue.

According to the European Parliament, by 2050 the average resident of Europe will be forty-nine years of age.[10] Former head of the UN Population Division, Joseph Chamie, estimates that without immense increases in immigration, the population of Europe will drop by around 20 percent, from a current level of 730 million to "well below 600 million by mid-century."[11] In both cases, these projections illustrate at least the suspicion that the constant or low fertility variants may come to pass. It appears highly likely that the future of the continent will witness continued population aging, declining support ratios, declining youth populations, and a shrinking of the absolute population of most European nations.

Military and Geopolitical Implications

Observers are beginning to assess the implications of such demographic decline. Most of the analysis to date has focused on whether or not the governments of Europe will be able to maintain the continent's social democratic model in the face of this decline.[12] But there are important strategic and military implications, as well. To name a few: a decline in general military spending; a decline in military spending on weapons platforms so as to cover other priorities, such as military pensions or military wages; a decline in the vigor of the military, as the military population itself ages; a decline in the absolute number of troops a nation could field; and a decline in the number of troops that a nation could afford to lose in battle, before it sues for peace.

The first major issue is a simple one. After another few decades of fertility decline, will there be money left for guns? A number of scholars, including Mark Haas, have argued that the mushrooming expenses of caring for an aging population will lead to a significant reduction in discretionary spending, including military spending.[13] This contraction in European military budgets is apparently already under way. To save money, the French and British navies will now share the use of an aircraft carrier. According to the *Los Angeles Times*,

> Britain, Washington's closest ally, is determined to shrink its defense budget by 8 percent in real terms during the next four years as part of a sweeping public austerity plan. . . . France intends to cut $1.3 billion, or 3 percent, from its defense budget for next year and eliminate 54,000 defense jobs by 2014. Italy recently canceled an order of jet fighters to save more than $2 billion.[14]

Germany and the Netherlands are likewise reducing military spending.

But it should be noted that this reduction in military spending is not automatic. In fact, the sum of European governments' social welfare obligations to their aging populations will be so many times current military spending levels that cutting this spending, even eliminating it outright, will not solve the financial problems of the social welfare state.[15] Perhaps counterintuitively, therefore, it is quite possible that some level of military spending can be maintained, if a sense of necessity and the requisite political will exists.

A more serious problem concerns military staffing. As the median age of the population of Europe continues its inexorable climb, the trend in military-age manpower will continue to decline. Who will man the guns? According to the European Defense Agency, "the aging of Europe's people will lead to fierce competition for young and skilled workers. The Armed Forces recruitment pool (ages sixteen to thirty) will fall by more than 15 percent by 2025."[16] According to Jeffrey Simon, "What this means is that the Europeans' declining military service cohort could affect their ability to meet planned force levels. . . . Some European allies may have to face the question of whether they will be able to maintain a viable military."[17]

Related to this question of base numbers is a more intangible, even psychological concern: will the soldiers who can be fielded by the nations of Europe be too dear to sacrifice in battle? According to Gunnar Heinsohn, military effectiveness may not solely be determined by the total number of troops, but by the number of troops that are expendable (in the case of war). In this regard, even a relatively even fight will be lost if European nations send an army of "only sons" against an army of brothers: "The strength of a nation's military is affected by the size of a nation's families. Falling birth rates in Western countries mean that even light casualties in Iraq and Afghanistan bring cries of pain in Europe and America."[18] Such concern may artificially constrain military leaders with unrealistic rules of engagement. At a more general level, the result may be a society so risk-averse and cautious as to make military engagements almost impossible to win; in this regard, the European Defence Agency is actively preparing for "societies increasingly cautious about interventionary operations, concerned with issues of legitimacy in the use of force, and inclined to favor 'security' over 'defense' spending."[19]

Finally, it should be noted that there are additional geopolitical implications based upon the fact that Europe's demographic decline is a *relative* decline. As Europe ages, it is still surrounded by nations with higher fertility rates and the corresponding "youth bulges" that go along with it. And as Europe's support ratio declines, those nations with better ratios—whether potential adversaries like China or longtime allies like the United States—will be able to invest at a comparatively higher level in either larger standing armies or more expensive weapons platforms, or both. So we can expect these geopolitical implications to grow in importance in the next few decades, rather than recede.

Role of Ideology in Current Efforts

Looking forward, we will examine the responses of European governments to these potential implications, both mitigation strategies (raising fertility and increasing immigration) and an adaptation strategy (transforming the reality of international relations). As we shall see, Europe's mitigation strategies are hopelessly compromised; in fact, demographic decline could be exacerbated by the existence of strongly held, almost consensus-level values (what I am calling "ideologies").

The presence of such ideologies is readily apparent. For instance, even when discussing the predicament of below-replacement rate fertility, the European Parliament cannot help but celebrate the very cultural changes that have propelled it. The Parliament "recalls first of all that the two chief causes of demographic change—a drop in the birth rate and the ageing of the population—are the result of progress. . . . Women's control over their reproductive lives is the result of their emancipation and goes hand-in-hand with higher levels of education for girls and women's participation in active life and public responsibilities; [the Parliament] considers that this should be regarded as an irreversible benefit to humanity."[20] These changes should be considered "irreversible," meaning presumably that they should not be questioned, no matter how low fertility may fall.

There are a host of general philosophical principles ensconced in European elite opinions, policies, and legislation that would appear to be incompatible with the recovery of robust population growth rates. For instance, European environmentalism has at times posited population growth as inimical to environmental protection. In fact, European environmentalists, including government officials, have called for a reduction in the human population, in order to protect the environment.[21] Multiculturalism, codified into law in many European nations, has made it difficult to gather basic demographic data along racial, ethnic, or religious grounds, thereby making it close to impossible to assess relative fertility rates amongst native-born and immigrant populations. The impact on social cohesion of large-scale immigration (the easiest and to date almost universal European reaction to fertility decline) therefore becomes much more difficult to gauge. Secular humanism, and the establishment of an explicitly post-Christian society, has left many observers unwilling to explore whether or why there may be a link between higher fertility rates and higher rates of traditional religious observance.[22] Similar to this, a belief in the rectitude of redefining marriage, or of expanding the number and type of legally recognized alternative relationships, has rendered many observers unwilling to assess whether or why there may be higher fertility rates among those couples linked together in stable, covenant relationships of traditional marriage.[23] Finally, feminism may be the most powerful ideology creating the lenses through which Europeans view fertility decline. Some of the core tenets of feminism that may impact fertility include the equality, even interchangeability, of the sexes; the encouragement of women to pursue careers outside of the home; and the control of female reproduction through contraception and abortion (which appear to be obvious and direct dampers on fertility).

Tony Fahey and Zsolt Spéder summarize the predicament faced by European elites in the following manner: "Low fertility can be viewed, from this quality of life perspective, as a consequence of freedom of choice and an aspect of daily behavior that is positively valued by European citizens. For this reason governments have been reluctant to define the practices that give rise to it as negative or to seek to change them in a heavy-handed way."[24] In other words, admiration of the root causes of European demographic decline make addressing it extremely difficult.

Gap Policy

The most obvious response to fertility decline would be an effort to raise fertility rates. Most of the nations of Europe believe fertility to be too low, believe they know why fertility is too low, and believe that they know how governments can influence domestic fertility rates.[25] According to a draft report of the European Parliament, fertility is "abnormally low and is not only the result of women's choice; . . . this alarming drop in fertility is also linked to the difficulty of reconciling work with family life, the anxiety-inducing social environment and a fear of the future."[26] Or, as the European Commission puts it, "The low fertility rate is the result of obstacles to private choices: late access to employment, job instability, expensive housing and lack of incentives (family benefits, parental leave, child care, equal pay)."[27]

In essence, governments across Europe have adopted various programs that seek to expand the European social model in order to reduce the "fear of the future" thought to be at the base of fertility decline. These programs include "job security, maternity and paternity leave, childcare, after-school programs, cash grants and allowances, priority housing, flexible work schedules and part-time employment."[28]

Why does Europe go down this path? It is easy and uncontroversial. European governments are unwilling to face the possibility that low fertility is not primarily caused by individual insecurities that could be mitigated by further expansion of the social welfare net, but instead that low fertility reflects profound cultural and normative changes concerning conceptions of individual human happiness and family life. Governments therefore adopt what can be called a "gap policy" as the only acceptable form of state-sponsored pronatalism. The gap refers to the difference between ideal fertility and actual fertility; the role of the government, in this conception, is to help to move society from the actual to the ideal number. According to the European Commission, "Europeans have a fertility rate which is insufficient to replace the population. Surveys have revealed the gap that exists between the number of children Europeans would like to have (2.3) and the number they actually have (1.3). This means that, if appropriate mechanisms existed to allow couples to have the number of children they want, the fertility rate could rise overall."[29]

This has proven to be a useful pursuit for three main reasons: first, if successful, it could return society to close-to-replacement rate of fertility (2.1 children per woman); second, it requires governments to make no value judgments concerning individual choices or to posit one set of choices as superior to another. As the European Commission admits, "Many governments are reluctant to formulate explicit pronatalist policies as there is widespread feeling that the government should not intervene and influence the private decisions of partners about their own fertility."[30] Here, governments need only assist individuals to achieve already existing preferences. As Wolfgang Lutz et al. put it, "This offers policymakers in Europe a seemingly convenient policy rationale to try to help couples to actually have the (higher) family size that they would like to have in any case."[31]

Third, and perhaps most important, the type of policies, such as generous maternity leave packages and flexible work scheduling, that have been implemented to fill in the gap can be consistent with feminism, constituting a kind of feminist pronatalism. The gap policy, it is thought, is still compatible with a society that encourages women to pursue careers outside of the home. In other words, this is a way to solve the population problem without challenging the current social values or mores that may be the root cause of the problem. For these multiple reasons, this policy has become an "almost universally acclaimed policy paradigm."[32]

But despite the expansion of the social welfare net in this direction, success—measured as a significant and enduring rise in fertility—has been elusive. According to the Population Division,

> The recent experience of low-fertility countries suggests that there is no reason to assume that their fertility will return anytime soon to the above-replacement level. Although governments in those countries have introduced, instead of explicit pronatalist policies, a variety of social welfare measures favorable for higher fertility, the long-term effectiveness of such measures is often called into question.[33]

Any increases in fertility that have occurred have also proven to be expensive, short-lived, and unsustainable, and fertility overall continues to fall.

Why hasn't the gap policy worked? There may be a simple, if troubling answer: for it to work, the gap theory is predicated upon a robust ideal family size. Once ideal fertility falls close to the real fertility rate, there is simply no important gap to close. Perhaps ideal family size is itself falling. Goldstein, Lutz, and Testa see evidence for this decline emerging throughout Europe:

> For younger cohorts ideal family size has fallen well below replacement in Austria and in both the former East and West Germany. . . . Younger cohorts generally preferred smaller family sizes than older ones. . . . We still see evidence of rapidly declining preferences in Germany and Austria, as well as Italy, Portugal, Spain, Ireland, and the Netherlands. . . . Family size ideals have fallen as part of societal shifts toward low-fertility norms. This shift occurs about one generation after below-replacement fertility ideals were reached, when new cohorts have been thoroughly submerged in a culture of small family sizes.[34]

Fahey and Spéder see similar trends, claiming that over the course of the last generation ideal family size in Europe has declined on average by one-third of a child.[35]

Why has ideal fertility declined? Rita Maria Testa and Leonardo Grilli have described what they call the Low Fertility Trap Hypothesis to explain the decline. Based upon their hypothesis, the lived experience of children in a low fertility setting changes their ideals; when these children grow to adulthood, the norm comes to match the real, as they experienced it in childhood.[36] So there really isn't a gap between real and ideal; rather there is a lag, a period of time for the ideal to catch up to the real. So what we are witnessing in Europe is a two-child ideal beginning to fall toward a one-child ideal.

One aspect of the Low Fertility Trap Hypothesis that warrants mention is that it would appear to illustrate how fertility could continue to fall in Europe, and to fall indefinitely. This is a "trap," a "downward spiral"; the fewer children now, the fewer children the next generation will want, leading to even fewer children born, leading to an even lower ideal after that. A second aspect of this problem is that it is, at least partly, a normative problem:

> It is assumed that through the processes of socialization and social learning, the social norms and in particular the family size ideals of the young generation are influenced by what they experience around them in term of families with young children. The fewer the children belonging to the environment that the young people experience, the lower the number of children that will be part of their normative system in terms of what is a desirable life.[37]

And this, in turn, means that there is no easy way out for the governments of Europe. If this hypothesis proves to be true, then the problem of demographic decline is not caused by some "fear of the future," as the European Parliament has surmised, a fear that can be assuaged by ever more generous social programs. Rather, the root cause is a different one: a *wish* for a future without children. "Then, unhappy governments will have to address the desire for children directly, rather than pointing at the politically convenient self-deception of only wanting to help couples to meet their desires."[38] Are the governments of Europe prepared to do this, to tell people they should want more children, since doing so seems to require interfering in areas related to personal autonomy and female empowerment?

There are two other considerations. First, it is at least conceivable that the gap policy may further decrease fertility, since in a zero-sum policy environment pursuing policies that encourage certain types of fertility—mainly, small-family fertility, or fertility that is most easily reconcilable with careers outside of the home—may discourage other types of fertility—mainly, large-family fertility. Also, these gap policies may further the microeconomic shift to the two-income family norm, making it potentially more difficult for single-income families (the prototypical arrangement for large-family fertility patterns) to live on one income. Second, it would be interesting to incorporate additional normative variables into the Low Fertility Trap Hypothesis. Such variables could include attitudes on family structure, marriage, religious observance, and state responsibilities. It is at least conceivable that norms for family size may be inter-related with other norms, that there may be alternate normative structures or worldviews, of which ideal family size is only one component. In other words, it is possible that the norms driving fertility downward may be more numerous and powerful—as they may be mutually reinforcing—than first thought. Ideal family size may be under siege.[39]

Immigration

Another obvious response to fertility decline is to increase, or at the very least continue, current levels of immigration. Belief in the efficacy of immigration is widespread. The European Parliament asserts that "the use of immigration is, and will continue to be, an element in the Union's demography and a positive contribution from an economic, social and cultural point of view."[40] *Eurostat* claims that "with relatively low birth rates in most Member States, migration is often the principal component of population change within the EU."[41]

But a UN Population Division report from 2001 on "replacement migration" cast doubts that immigration could replace the decades of "missing" native Europeans. The Population Division illustrates that merely maintaining overall population levels would be insufficient for upholding the current European social structures. The key is the "potential support ratio," the percentage of working-age citizens actually contributing through wealth creation and taxation to social welfare programs. To maintain the current support ratio, the number of immigrants needed would be both practically and politically impossible. According to the Population Division, "The annual number of immigrants needed to keep the potential support ratios constant at their 1995 levels is vastly larger, in every country, than any past experience . . . result[ing] in having between 59 per cent and 99 per cent of the population of all countries in 2050 composed of post-1995 migrants and their descendants. This scenario is clearly not realistic; therefore immigration cannot prevent ageing of the population."[42] Observers have noted the potentially destabilizing effects of current levels of European immigration. Joseph Chamie states,

> Many of today's immigrants to Europe come from Africa and Asia, raising concerns in host communities about cultural integrity and assimilation. . . . These conditions contribute to greater ethnic diversity and tensions within and among countries, raising concerns about cultural integrity, national identity, integration and national security.[43]

David Coleman makes this point even more emphatically, arguing that "if continued further to the end of the century and beyond, immigration combined with below-replacement fertility would lead to the eventual displacement of the original population from its majority position. The possible marginalization of European populations in Europe might be thought a rather momentous prospect, and a proper concern of policy, especially if it were an unintended consequence of policies entered into for other ends."[44] Thus, as with increased spending to encourage fertility, increased immigration may, in the longer term, only contribute to the destabilizing effects of the very demographic decline it is meant to mitigate.

Here ideology interferes again. Perhaps the most important unanswered question has to do with the fertility rate of Europe's immigrant population, especially its Muslim population. We do not know the answer to this question because most of the nations of Europe refuse to ask it, apparently as a bow to multicultural sensibilities. According to Mary Kent, "Because many European countries do not ask a person's religion on official forms or in censuses, it has been difficult to obtain accurate estimates of the number of childbearing rates of Muslims."[45] Thus, we do not know how low native European fertility actually happens to be or how severe the problem actually is. We do not know what percentage of France's relatively robust fertility rate is due to higher levels of immigrant fertility. Thus, a fertility rate that appears to point to demographic stability, and therefore greater societal cohesion, may in fact be masking the causes of greater internal civil strife. In fact, the Council on Foreign Relations estimates that the Muslim birthrate in France is three times higher than the non-Muslim birthrate.[46] If this conjecture is correct, and if it is generally accurate for most of the nations of Europe, then demographic decline may be more dire than the already dire picture appears.

Soft Power, Multilateralism, and the Obsolescence of Conventional War

The two mitigation strategies—raising fertility and increasing immigration—are perhaps obvious and commonsense responses to demographic decline. The adaptation strategy pursued by Europe, on the other hand, is audacious in the extreme: the governments of Europe hope to make conventional wars, fought with conventional armies, obsolete. Thus, it would no longer matter that Europe may not have the manpower or the money to field conventional armies that would be competitive with the armies of potential adversaries. How do these nations plan to achieve this? Tame the Hobbesian state of nature between nations with an international order, what Benita Ferrero-Waldner has called "a rule-based international order for the future."[47] So a chief strategy of the nations of Europe has been to reinforce the multilateral system coalescing around the United Nations. According to the *European Security Strategy*,

> The development of a stronger international order is our objective. We are committed to upholding and developing International Law. The fundamental framework for international relations is the United Nations Charter. . . . Strengthening the United Nations, equipping it to fulfill its responsibilities and to act effectively, is a European priority. We want international organizations, regimes and treaties to be effective in confronting threats to international peace and security, and must therefore be ready to act when their rules are broken.[48]

With this ever-strengthening international order, the governments of Europe believe they have overcome the threat of the type of conventional wars that marred the European history of the twentieth century. The *European Security Strategy* asserts that "large-scale aggression against any Member State is now improbable."[49] The European Defence Agency states that "all this has reduced the plausibility of scenarios, at least in the European context and for the foreseeable future, involving traditional state-on-state warfare, with conventional forces pitted against comparable opponents."[50]

It should be noted, however, that this shift to soft power and multilateralism is predicated upon an optimism that seemingly intractable problems have solutions that can be ascertained and implemented, and that goodwill can overcome long-standing animosities. In short, these nations assume that centuries-old problems can be addressed through reason and negotiation rather than force. In political philosophy shorthand, this would be the triumph of Kant over Hobbes.

Can this work? We do not know. On the one hand, the incredible success of the European project makes this idea seem plausible: it is widely considered inconceivable, for instance, that France and Germany would ever again resort to armed conflict against one another. On the other hand, the long experience of human history and the human condition would seem to temper this hope. At the very least, it would seem to entail that European governments must alter the long-standing perceptions of international relations as power relations with winners and losers. The European Defence Agency signals Europe's very departure from this type of thinking: "The objective is not 'victory' as traditionally understood, but moderation, balance of interests and peaceful resolution of conflicts—in short, stability."[51] But, even granting these points, their experiences in Afghanistan and Iraq seem to illustrate the continued importance of conventional armies, even in the process of creating stability rather than victory, a point admitted by the European Defence Agency: "The level of force required to achieve such outcomes may, in some scenarios, be substantial."[52]

It should also be noted that a major component in this quest to build an international order has been a drive by the developed world, including the nations of Europe, to depress the fertility of the developing world. This effort has been motivated by a neo-Malthusian belief that development requires fertility decline, as well as by the recognition of the *relative* demographic decline of Europe. Put simply, from a geopolitical perspective this demographic imbalance will mean that European nations will have difficulty staffing militaries, while their potential adversaries will not. According to John Van Oudenaren, "Small cohorts of draft-age males will mean that European countries, including Russia, will be militarily weaker relative to many non-European countries than the comparison of aggregate population figures alone would suggest."[53] What is more, some of the young men in non-European nations, as part of youth bulges, will potentially become radical and violent:

> Young men with few economic opportunities are easily recruited into radical causes. . . . In much of the volatile Middle East, exploding birthrates have created ultra-young societies. Saudi Arabia, Iraq and Pakistan all have median ages under 19, and are among the youngest and fastest-growing countries in the world. Unemployment, already a serious problem in these countries, is likely to get much worse in coming decades. A lack of economic prospects and fewer opportunities to emigrate, a byproduct of anti-terrorism, is quickly turning the region into a pressure cooker.[54]

Thus, over the past few decades, many in the West have considered the depressing of developing-world fertility rates to be within Western security interests. Richard Cincotta discusses the rise of a "more peaceful and secure world" if fertility continues to decline across the developing world:

> Both the results of our analyses and a robust literature on demographic change and security support the central—and hopeful—conclusion of this report: Progress through the demographic transition helps reduce the risk of civil conflict, and thus contributes to a more peaceful and secure world. . . . Most countries are moving toward what we call here a security demographic, a distinctive range of population structures and dynamics that make civil conflict less likely. Movement in this direction, however, is uneven and in peril. Continuing declines in birthrates and increases in life expectancy in the poorest and worst-governed countries will require much more international collaboration and assistance than are evident today.[55]

European nations have embraced this faith in shared fertility decline for many years, and have sought to provide the necessary "international collaboration and assistance." Although it is difficult to calculate total European investment in depressing developing world fertility, the commitment to the promotion of "reproductive health" and population programs is central to European foreign policy. According to Poul Nielson, the European Commissioner for Development and Humanitarian Aid, "Since the beginning of the 1990's, the EC has spent a total of about 650 million Euros on sexual and reproductive health in developing countries. Recent evaluations show that the EC provides approximately 5–10 percent of global support to the broader ICPD [International Conference on Population and Development] goals."[56]

What Europe apparently needs to do is buy time in order for potential adversaries to catch up to European fertility decline. As Gunnar Heinsohn emphasizes, "In another twenty years most of the Islamic youth bulges will have run their course—as they already have in Algeria, Iran, Lebanon, Morocco, Tunisia and Turkey. Therefore, defending against the aggression of the youth bulges that have hijacked Islam is not an insurmountable obstacle."[57] Thus, promoting worldwide fertility decline can be considered a kind of insurance policy, until the new multilateral order is more firmly established.

Pronatalism in a Post-Ideological Europe

So far, we have seen that Europe's mitigation strategies are hampered by ideological barriers, and that its adaptation strategy depends upon an unprecedented alteration of the international order. On this path, the geopolitical fate of the continent appears insecure. But what if ideology were not in play? What if Europe could address the real roots of fertility decline, free of modern presuppositions? A beginning of an answer can be found in Preference Theory, a sociological theory advanced by Catherine Hakim. According to Hakim, the second demographic transition has created an environment in which fertility outcomes are largely determined by the beliefs of individual women, especially in the way in which individual women decide to balance work and family. In modern societies, Hakim thinks there are three distinct normative choices, and therefore three distinct "types" of women, whom she labels "family-oriented," "career oriented," and "adaptive." To Hakim,

> Family-oriented women regard family life and children as the main priorities in life, and therefore decide not to work, unless economic needs force them to enter the labour market. . . . Being career-oriented, on the other hand, means giving value to a life devoted to work, either in paid employment or in the public arena. Career-oriented women strive for a high level of education and frequently remain unmarried and/or childless. Finally, adaptive women have no prevailing preference orientation. They usually

want to get the best of both worlds, combining work and family. Adaptive women are therefore fully engaged in the trade off between family and career.[58]

According to social survey data, adaptive women account for most of the women in European nations, while family oriented and career oriented women both account for between 10 to 30 percent of the population.

The essential point here is that there is a correlation between these belief structures (leading to the various designations) and actual fertility outcomes. In other words, family-oriented women should have more children than career-oriented women, and they do: "Indeed, Hakim provides evidence that her classification fits the British case and that it also fits actual fertility in Britain: family and work-centered women prove to be the most and the least fertile, respectively."[59] Agnese Vitali et al. agree, finding data to suggest that "the proportion of childless women in the work-oriented group was more than 10 per cent higher than that of women in the family-oriented group . . . while the proportion of women with 'large' families, i.e., three or more children, was higher among the family-centered than among the other two types: 16 vs... only 8 per cent among the careerists."[60]

If all of this proves to be true, family-oriented women may be the key to successfully addressing European demographic decline. In fact, demographically speaking, the value of each family-centered woman, each woman consciously choosing to establish a high fertility outcome as her goal, should be considered extremely high. In fact, this is exactly what Fahey and Spéder have discovered:

> Looking across countries at the present time, those countries with the lowest fertility rates were not necessarily those with a high level of childlessness; nor were they most likely to show a tendency among women to delay the start of childbearing years. Rather, fertility outcomes at the country level could be achieved by a wide range of combinations of these factors so that there is no model pattern of either high or low fertility within the range of fertility variation found in Europe today. However, one factor is strongly and consistently related to fertility outcomes at the country level, and this is the degree to which women go beyond the second child and have a third or fourth child.[61]

According to Fahey and Spéder, there is no statistically significant variable relating to fertility in Europe *except* for the desire for large families. Therefore, policies should be geared to large family creation. In terms of preference theory, this means policies geared to family-centered women.

But if this is an opportunity, it is also a challenge, for "family-oriented women are not responsive to employment policies and career-oriented women are not responsive to social family policies."[62] So, in a limited fiscal environment, pursuing one set of policies designed to assist one type of woman may make it more difficult to pursue another set designed to assist the other; policies may be mutually exclusive. And, on a more theoretical level, the very goal of encouraging one group may prove to discourage the other. Helping women to stay at home may make it more difficult for women who want to work to enter the workforce, and vice versa. To take a simple example: one-income households (the model for family-oriented women) become less practical as more career-oriented women successfully enter the workforce (making the two-income household the economic norm against which the family-oriented women must compete). So the question for the governments of Europe is not whether they should be pronatalist (the great majority of them seek, at least implicitly, to raise fertility), but rather whether they can be pronatalist in the correct way. Based upon the flaws of the existing gap policy, the implications of the Low Fertility Trap Hypothesis, and the insights emerging from Preference Theory and the scholarship of Fahey and Spéder, this will not prove easy. To shift the gap policy to target family-oriented women might entail that European governments recognize men and women are different, that some women do not want to pursue the same career paths as men, that some women want to be homemakers and mothers as their principal vocation, that single-income families must be able to afford three or more children, that marriage may be more conducive to large-family outcomes than cohabitation, that demographic data based upon religion and ethnicity must be available.

In sum, the nations of Europe must be willing to seek ways to advantage the family-oriented woman even at the potential expense of the career-oriented woman, as well as the native-born family-oriented woman at the expense of the immigrant family-oriented woman. Doing so, of course, would force Europe to abandon some of its most cherished tenets of feminism and multiculturalism, a step for which there is little evidence to suggest any European governments are prepared to take, despite the geopolitical consequences.

6

AMERICAN DEMOGRAPHIC EXCEPTIONALISM AND THE FUTURE OF U.S. MILITARY POWER

Susan Yoshihara

Introduction

American primacy defines world order. What was dubbed a "unipolar moment" in 1990 has lasted more than two decades.[1] But how long will it last? Even before the United States emerged from the Cold War as the sole superpower, scholars prophesied its imminent decline. Today, the rise of competitor economies, challenges from nontraditional military threats, and the financial burden of policing the world all seem too much to sustain in the long term.[2] In spite of this, some experts project continued U.S. dominance, citing unique American political and economic characteristics. Americans now seem to be exceptional in another way: their children. With the rest of the developed world facing plummeting fertility rates and the cost of aging societies, the United States sustains a near-replacement level birthrate along with robust immigration.[3]

The reasons for American demographic exceptionalism are not entirely known. Demographers have cited, in addition to economic and political factors, cultural and normative reasons: affinity for religious practice, attitudes of optimism, and a "frontier spirit" toward increasing population and urbanization.[4] The question this chapter seeks to answer is: can American demographic exceptionalism lead to continued American primacy, specifically military supremacy?

American power, from military might to normative influence, is founded upon its enormous economy. With an estimated fifteen trillion dollar gross domestic product, the United States produces more than a fifth of the world's

goods and services, and nearly 80 percent of its advanced and complex economy has transitioned to the services sector.[5] Though wars in Iraq and Afghanistan have garnered much public attention in the last several years, America's
most valuable military capability is its command and protection of the global
commons—air, space, cyberspace, and above all the seas, where its dominance
is unprecedented. Sea control allows the United States to command the flow of
the world's goods since 90 percent of the world's trade is seaborne.[6] Sea power
allows the United States to prevent the rise of a peer competitor in Asia and
Europe, and so it has underpinned American grand strategy for two centuries.

Yet several challenges loom. Policymakers target the military budget—particularly shipbuilding—to cut the deficit while military planners face skyrock-
eting costs for hardware and personnel. The United States already spends $50
billion a year on military medical care, which is taking up an increasing share of
the defense budget since it is sensitive to the costs of escalating American health
care. Active duty personnel cost twice what they did a decade ago with no increase in force size, and operational costs have risen some 87 percent in the
same period.[7] These costs have crowded out force modernization and research
and development, which hold the promise of more affordable and more capable
forces in the long run.[8] This stark reality led the U.S. secretary of defense Robert
Gates to announce in 2011 a drastic $78 billion budget, reducing the size of the
Army and Marine Corps in the midst of fighting the war in Afghanistan.[9]

There will be tremendous political pressure to cut even deeper. Aftershocks
from the 2008 economic crisis and 2010 health-care and economic stimulus
legislation have increased U.S. national debt and Washington's fiscal anxiety.
Adding to the angst is the retirement of the first wave of America's baby boomers, who turned sixty-five in 2011 and became eligible for Medicare and Social
Security benefits. The postwar generation will be drawing from these entitlements even longer than expected due to increased longevity. Funded by the
general revenue, much of the burgeoning expenses will crowd out discretionary
spending, of which defense is the largest portion.

Experts are deeply concerned that the wrong cuts today could hurt U.S.
strategic interests tomorrow. While the military budget is hefty at around $700
billion, it is less than 5 percent of the gross domestic product, a fraction of Cold
War and post–Cold War defense budgets.[10] Some worry that defense budgets
of recent history are inadequate to keep pace with U.S. strategic and military

requirements. Most important, there is concern that changes are not sufficiently tied to national strategy, resulting in a crisis of military force planning, programming, and budgeting. A prestigious expert commission headed by former national security advisor Stephen Hadley and former secretary of defense William J. Perry concluded that "the aging of the inventories and equipment used by the services, the decline in the size of the Navy, escalating personnel entitlements, overhead and procurement costs, and the growing stress on the force means that a train wreck is coming in the areas of personnel, acquisition, and force structure."[11]

Thus while long-term demographic exceptionalism would seem to support the optimists' projection of continued American primacy, political and economic realities could mitigate the advantage and vindicate the pessimists. This chapter will weigh the evidence on both sides and make some conclusions about whether, and under what circumstances, American demographic exceptionalism could tip the scales toward American power projection.

What Is Exceptional about American Demographic Trends?

In 2006, for the first time in thirty-five years, Americans produced enough children to replace themselves. Population experts heralded the achievement of replacement fertility of 2.1 children per woman as a sign of "demographic health."[12] The event put American demographic exceptionalism in the public eye, even if briefly, in 2007. Reaching a total population of 300 million in October 2006 also brought demographics to the fore.

The nation's total fertility rate (TFR)—a figure that represents the total number of children women bear—peaked at 3.8 in 1957, but fell precipitously during the 1960s and 1970s. In 1972, the rate seemed to fall below replacement, its nadir of 1.7 in 1976. It rose again in the late 1970s and 1980s, rising above 2.0 by the 1990s.[13] Demographers explained that the 1970s plunge in birthrates was because women were delaying childbirth due to career pursuits and later marriages, and not because they were deciding against having children. This made the TFR—a mere snapshot of a lifetime's childbearing—seem to dip and rise. In the future, the United Nations expects American fertility to fall only slightly to 1.9 between 2045 and 2050. If its highest estimates are borne out, the rate will be 2.35. The UN's 2010 forecast is even more optimistic, estimating U.S. fertility will remain near replacement levels through 2100.[14]

As a result of its healthy fertility rates, steady immigration, and declining mortality, the U.S. population has increased steadily over the last half century from 179.3 million to 308.7 million, according to the 2010 U.S. census.[15] It is expected to keep climbing, but at an increasingly slower rate, to 403.9 million by 2050 according to the UN's medium variant estimation.[16] The UN's low variant estimation projects population decline after 2045, from 358.2 to 357.1 million by 2050. A high variant assumption projects 455.6 million Americans, and if a constant fertility rate is assumed, there will be 425.2 million Americans in 2050.[17] Americans are younger than citizens of almost every other developed country, ranking fifty-first out of the 196 UN member nations with a median age of thirty-six and a half:[18] 17 percent of Americans are over the age of sixty, compared to the average of 21 percent for developed nations.

AGING OF THE DEPENDENCY RATIO

For every one hundred American workers in 2007, there were forty-nine children and old people, making this the lowest dependency ratio in decades. This dependency ratio is expected to rise again by 2050, when the same number of workers will support sixty-one dependents.[19] What is significant is that the rise will be due to an increase in the elderly population as baby boomers retire.[20] The child dependency ratio is not expected to change significantly, since the number of children born per woman is expected to remain stable.[21] While the dependency ratio was higher in 1960 than it is today, a larger number of those dependents in 1960 were children. By 2050, the dependent old will outnumber the dependent young. In other words, future American workers will not be investing in their own children so much as they will be paying to support the old and the very old, who require expensive medical care with social security, the most expensive medical costs occurring in the last few years of life. This matters because the growing share of federal funds devoted to health care will be the most significant threat to the U.S. military budget in the coming decades.[22]

NORMATIVE ASPECTS OF ROBUST FERTILITY AND IMMIGRATION

Experts have explained the exceptional U.S. fertility rate in various ways, highlighting immigration as an important part of the equation. Americans from Latin American origins have the highest fertility rate (2.9 children per woman), next are African Americans (2.1), Asians (1.9), and Whites (1.86). Yet Hispanics do not represent enough of the population to explain the trend entirely, and fertility has increased among Americans of all races and regions. Americans of European descent maintain higher fertility rates than their counterparts in the old world. Most of the difference in fertility rates between Europe and the United States is caused by the relatively high fertility among self-declared "Anglos" in the United States.[23]

Analysts have pointed to certain social, cultural, and religious attitudes to explain the difference between American and European fertility. Phil Longman notes that "in the USA . . . 47% of people who attend church weekly say their ideal family size is three or more children. By contrast, 27% of those who seldom attend church want that many kids."[24] Citizens of both the United States and Europe who say they attend church regularly, hold patriotic values, and value community, duty, and service ahead of individual self-fulfillment are far more likely to have children and to have more than one child. What is more, Longman says, "a segment of society in which single-child families are the norm will decline in population by at least 50% per generation and quite quickly disappear." Longman says this is because in the United States, "the 17.4% of baby boomer women who had one child account for a mere 9.2% of kids produced by their generation. But among children of the baby boom, nearly a quarter descend from the mere 10% of baby boomer women who had four or more kids."[25]

Optimism is another reason for higher total fertility. For example, German leaders credited positive attitudes among young people for a 30 percent increase in births in 2007, nine months after their country hosted a successful World Cup tournament and their national team took third.[26] Closer to home, Mayor Michael Bloomberg unveiled New York City's plan for accommodating a million more people into the aging city of 8 million, saying, "The predicament of our future is also our hope. The very same population growth that intensifies the challenges we face also offers us the resources for meeting them, and the means needed to help achieve sustainability."[27] The mayor's remarks also evinced an attitude of American expansionism and frontier spirit: "By 2030, our population will reach more than 9 million—the equivalent of adding the populations of Boston and Miami to the five boroughs. The result is a surge that is taking our population to new heights, and our city into uncharted waters. . . .

Our growing New York will always be the most diverse city on earth. It will remain a magnet for artists, entrepreneurs, and ambitious immigrants from every corner of the globe."[28]

Bloomberg's positive approach to population growth is characteristically American. John Quincy Adams reported in 1817 that Europeans feared "the gigantic growth of [American] population and power" would make it "a very dangerous member of the society of nations."[29] The Royal Institute of International Affairs (RIIA) predicted in 1945 that diverging attitudes would bring diverging population trends despite economic parity: "It may be asked whether the realization that the expansion—which is so central in American thought and feeling—is likely so soon to cease in its demographic aspect, will alter the attitude which has grown up with regard to immigration."[30]

The RIIA report predicted that the tight U.S. quota system and restriction of American immigration to European countries would eventually spark transatlantic competition as European armies felt the strain of dwindling pools of youth.[31] In fact, the Immigration and Nationality Act of 1965, adducing support from American attitudes about civil rights, overcame this potential rivalry and solved the supply problem.

Unlike Japan and Europe, the United States had exceptional flexibility in tailoring immigration to meet its economic needs. America's ability to generate an industrial working class in less than twenty years in the late nineteenth century and supplement its skilled technical class during the 1980s demonstrated this sort of demographic flexibility.[32] These are feats that, by some accounts, Europeans could not achieve without "massive social dislocation" and which Asia cannot accomplish on a broad scale.[33] The economic advantage in the coming decades could be significant, since by 2050 86 percent of U.S. population increase will be due to immigrants or their U.S.-born descendants.[34]

Military Recruiting Advantages from Demographic Exceptionalism

Three aspects of American population dynamics will bolster the future force. First, the U.S. military will draw from a much larger and more ethnically diverse pool of talent than any major power in the coming decades, due to both new immigration and the "echo boomer" effect—the relatively large generation born to the baby boomers. The working-age population will increase from 186 million in 2005 to 255 million in 2050. The share of population increase attributable to immigrants alone will increase from 15 percent to 23 percent between 2005 and 2050, while the White share will decrease from 68 percent to 45 percent of working-age adults. The growth in the next generation of workers, those seventeen and younger, is projected to be entirely due to immigration, rising from 73 million to 102 million between 2005 and 2050. In that period, more than one third of American children will be immigrants or their progeny, up from a quarter today. About four out of five immigrants are working-age adults, and so immigrants will make up almost a quarter of the recruitable population by 2050 (up from 15 percent in 2005).[35] Even while the rate of growth in the immigrant population today is not unprecedented, the overall percentage of immigrants is expected to reach 15 percent of the population between 2020 and 2025, slightly exceeding the record highs of the 1890s and 1910s.

Some of this advantage was mitigated by the fact that recruiting noncitizens was restricted after the events of September 11, 2001. Recruiters were no longer allowed to enlist prospective service members unless they have a green card in hand. Defense analysts from different political perspectives collaborated to address the restriction, and to push American policymakers to think even more broadly about recruiting noncitizens. Michael O'Hanlon and Max Boot proposed solving any recruiting shortfalls in the U.S. Army and Marine Corps by exchanging four-year enlistments for the prize of a green card.[36] They pointed out that this move is not unprecedented. American colonists used German and French soldiers during the Revolutionary War and locals in counterinsurgency operations in the Philippines.[37] In making a similar argument, army analyst George Quester has noted France's continued and extensive use of its Foreign Legion and Britain's Nepalese Gurkhas.[38]

Today, the U.S. military prides itself as one of the most racially egalitarian institutions in the country, and military force planners are open to immigrant-friendly recruitment policies. For example, at Congressional hearings regarding immigration legislation, Pentagon officials weighed in to move along legislation that would allow them to recruit the children of illegal immigrants who were born in the United States.[39] Additionally, they have already recruited foreigners as "heritage recruits," to lend linguistic and cultural expertise to the war on terrorism, and one heritage recruit has been awarded the prestigious Purple Heart. The waiting period for citizenship for military foreign nationals can be cut down from ten years to one year and fees can be eliminated. This provides an attractive recruitment tool, and recruiters report the need to make more immigrants aware of the opportunity.[40]

A second reason U.S. demographics uniquely benefit the military is the positive effects that large families have on military recruitment. Larger families are generally more likely to send a son or daughter to the military,[41] and in the United States larger families are more likely to be headed by parents holding conservative values.[42] These parents, in turn, are more likely to put values such as national service ahead of more individualistic concerns, which can have positive effects for recruiting.[43] The U.S. Army undertook a $1.35 billion media campaign directed at parents for this reason.[44] A third reason U.S. demographics benefit military recruiting is that regional demographics and military enlistments have mutually reinforcing effects. Recruitment for, and representation in, the armed forces is highest in the South and West.[45] These are the same regions the 2010 Census shows to have the highest growth rates and which are projected to have the highest growth through 2025.[46] Conversely, the recruit-to-population ratio is lowest in New England and other states projected to show relatively static growths in population in the coming decades.[47]

THE VALUE OF THE ALL-VOLUNTEER FORCE

Some of the same attitudes that explain U.S. demographic exceptionalism also account for U.S. military superiority. Even more than technological advancement, leadership experts credit such characteristics as driving leadership to the lowest levels as a key advantage of the all-volunteer military and the reason it prevailed in the Cold War.[48] This analysis assumes that the United States will maintain the nearly forty-year-old All-Volunteer Force (AVF) in the decades ahead. Americans resorted to a draft only four times in their history: the Civil War, two World Wars, and during the Cold War (the longest period in which the draft was in place). While some politicians raised the possibility of its reinstatement during the Iraq War,[49] defense leadership eschews the idea, warning of a significant decrease in quality and diversity of servicemen under the draft, with insufficient fiscal benefits.[50] The quality of the All-Volunteer Force has been vindicated by its performance in recent wars. U.S. military recruiters and military commanders have translated American demographic exceptionalism into unprecedented levels of service quality and operational capability, with relatively few combat casualties in comparison to previous wars.

The AVF is younger than the broader American population, more educated, and more racially diverse.[51] More than half the enlisted force is younger than twenty-five, while the same age group in the general population is 14 percent.[52] High school graduates among those twenty-five years or older account for 98.6 percent of enlisted personnel, compared to 86.6 percent in the population.[53] Among active duty personnel, 64 percent are White, 17 percent are Black, 11 percent are Hispanic, and 3.4 percent are Asian, whereas in the general population 80 percent of the general population is non-Hispanic White.[54] In general, 15 percent of the forces are women, with the highest percentage (19 percent) in the Air Force and the lowest (6 percent) in the Marine Corps.[55]

Part of the reason the AVF was able to boost retention despite wartime operational tempos is the camaraderie of shared combat. Since 2008, another reason is the souring economy, which makes staying in military service more attractive. Before then, the Afghanistan and Iraq wars created the double pressure of increasing troops while facing the toughest recruiting landscape since the Vietnam War. The "propensity package"—a combination of factors the Navy uses to indicate whether a youth will enlist—reached its lowest point since the All-Volunteer Force was established in 1973.[56] The package includes the disposition of parents, whose resistance to allowing their sons and daughters to join the military is seen as a major hurdle for recruiters.

While the Navy and Air Force had little trouble with retention as they reduced their total force numbers, the U.S. Army and Marine Corps faced more daunting challenges of family separation and personal hardship as troops returned from third and fourth deployments to war zones. Even though some recruiting restrictions had to be loosened during the wars in Iraq and Afghanistan, including the preclusion of criminal records, they were quickly reinstated. In fact, restrictions are so tight that only 25 percent of the available population can be recruited.[57]

The case of the National Guard in New England shows that the expense of recruiting and retaining the AVF pays dividends in readiness. Monetary and career incentives allowed the United States to continue to fight two wars and provide homeland security forces, despite an adverse recruiting and retention climate. The recruiting landscape in these states is arguably the most unfavorable in the country, yet recruiters reached their goal recruitment figures due to five incentives they could offer young people: student loans, bonuses, dental benefits, health care, and affordable life insurance.[58] Support for education includes federal and state tuition assistance and the post–September 11, 2001, Montgomery G.I. Bill, which can offer full tuition plus housing and book stipends, all of which is transferable to the serviceman's spouse and children. Recruiters say that more young people are looking to stay in the military for a career and do not see the service merely as a stepping-stone to education and other jobs. Recruits report that this is due to the private sector's increasing retirement age and rise in part-time jobs without benefits.

Many young people leave the New England states after high school or college to look for jobs. In some states, lack of familiarity with the military and even some anti-military attitudes diminish the recruiting pool.[59] To overcome these obstacles, recruiters use competitive tactics to increase market share, such as social media outreach and celebrity sponsorship, like with famed snowboarder Hannah Teter, who promotes the Guard in her native Vermont. While many recruiters remain optimistic that women provide an underrepresented pool of talent, they point out that if their state has a command with few or no career tracks open to women, such as armor, they will not be able to increase the number of women they recruit. In the active duty forces, the Navy has employed a pilot program allowing women a three-year sabbatical via "on and off ramps" to raise children and come back to military service.[60] Because of the trend toward dual-income households in the economy, the armed forces are also allowing more "homesteading," in what is called a "geo-stability package," to accommodate working spouses. Barring a draft scenario, there is little evidence that women would compensate for a dwindling recruiting pool in the case of a significant decline in American fertility.

Recruitment and retention incentives come at a cost to sustainability. The Hadley-Perry commission concluded that while the AVF has been an "unqualified success," its recent and dramatic growth in cost makes it unsustainable in the long term.[61] The commission said, "A failure to address the increasing costs of the All-Volunteer Force will likely result in a reduction in the force structure, a reduction in benefits, or a compromised All-Volunteer Force," and it recommended changes in retention, promotion, compensation, and professional military education policies—the very things recruiters attribute to successful manpower levels.[62] Some proposed changes are politically sensitive. For example, another study critiquing the bonus system found that while some ethnic groups respond well to monetary incentives, servicemen from some groups leave the force despite bonuses. An official policy remunerating on the basis of race is unlikely, no matter the fiscal benefits.

Defense Secretary Robert Gates proposed various ways to "grow the force small" and cut costs through the personnel system. These included slashing the number of flag and general officer billets, filling senior officer billets with lower-ranking officers, cutting senior enlisted billets, and increasing medical care copays of retirees. Some military human resources experts say this does not go far enough. They propose changing the "up or out" career progression that has been in place since the Second World War.[63] This would entail adjusting the twenty-year retirement eligibility based upon career specialty, such that a combat pilot could still retire at twenty years, but an administrative specialist would have to wait until thirty or even forty years.

The defense secretary maintained that "the future of our maritime services will ultimately depend less on the quality of their hardware than on the quality of their leaders."[64] That quality depends on the overall quality of the American workforce from which the nation will draw its future military leadership. The current leveling off in the number of U.S. high school graduates indicates that the competition for educated young workers will increase in the years ahead.

Perhaps an even more serious concern is the rise of obesity among Americans. A 2010 study found that between 1959 and 2008, the percentage of military-age men and women who satisfy enlistment standards for weight-to-height ratio and percent body fat has fallen considerably.[65] This is because the percentage of the overweight and overfat has doubled for men and more than tripled for women in that timeframe.[66] While the absolute number of those fit to serve continues to increase due to a relatively robust fertility rate, the percentage of recruitable youths is dwindling. Since the military will not waive the physical fitness requirement, the competition for healthy young workers will increase in the decades ahead. If the United States reinstated the draft, the effects of obesity would be even more severe. And if the fertility rate declines significantly in the years ahead, it is possible that this added restriction would mean there will not be enough young people to fill essential military billets. Thus, America's demographic exceptionalism, together with the AVF, have so far been the military's antidote to a growing health crisis among American youth.

Why "Declinists" Could be Right: Force Planning Threats to the AVF

The All-Volunteer Force is sustained by the ability to recruit and retain educated, physically fit, and dedicated young people from diverse backgrounds and equip them with the best technology and training. The question is, are American civilian and military leaders capitalizing on American demographic exceptionalism, or has it made them complacent? Are current plans to cut major systems and recruiting and retention benefits being made strategically, or as a reaction to political pressure in the midst of a severe economic crisis? The Obama administration's strategic planning documents do not instill confidence that defense cuts are based upon coordinated strategy, nor that demographic trends are sufficiently accounted for.

Military analysts often express exasperation with the lack of sincere efforts to link planning, programming, and budgeting to strategy. Long-range force planning looks only five years into the future; beyond that, the single best statement of future force needs is the *Quadrennial Defense Review* (QDR).[67] The QDR and the *National Security Strategy* (NSS), which the White House released later even though it is meant to guide defense decisions, do not reflect a tight synchronization so much as a justification of current plans.

American grand strategy—the coordination of national foreign and military strategies—is missing from the texts. In particular, the role of sea power and alliances in preventing the rise of peer competitors in Asia and Europe, a core tenet of American grand strategy, is obscured by emergent but less existential threats and capabilities such as terrorism and counterinsurgency.[68] The QDR calls for a "cooperative" international approach and "tailored" defense posture, both signaling retreat from American leadership on the world stage. Instead of threat-based planning, the Obama administration's QDR uses the less precise scenario-based planning. Capabilities-based planning was rejected as too platform-centric and too costly. The drawback with the QDR's planning construct is that without knowing what military forces should be capable of doing in the years ahead, it is difficult to discern whether the right budget choices are being made today. The plan seeks to hedge against such uncertainty by suggesting a "balancing" of long-term and near-term risks as well as a host of other risks, such as operational, force management, and future operations risks.

The Hadley-Perry commission charged with assessing the QDR called its lack of a clear force-planning construct a "missed opportunity."[69] The commission found that the QDR force structure does not provide sufficient capability to respond simultaneously to a domestic catastrophe during ongoing contingency operations abroad. The experts feared that under the plan, America's number-one interest—protection of the homeland—cannot be met because National Guard components were neither dedicated to nor funded for homeland defense. They expressed concern about the need to modernize and recapitalize equipment that was worn out ahead of schedule due to heavy use in combat operations. The long-term cost of not recapitalizing would be even greater than the short-term costs, no matter the temptation to skirt recapitalization in the rush to achieve cost savings in acquisition and overhead. Additionally, the force size must be increased to meet other top threats, including anti-access, cyber threats, and post-conflict stabilization. They highlighted a "significant and growing gap between the force structure of the military—its size and its inventory of equipment—and the missions it will be called on to perform in the future." [70] At the very heart of the force-planning problem, the experts said, is "a failure of our political leadership to explicitly recognize and clearly define these essential strategic interests." [71]

For its part, the NSS is imprecise about the long-term security environment. It cites three concerns: violent extremism, rogue states possessing WMD, and the rise of military power challenger states. Notably, these are all concentrated in Asia and Eurasia, leading experts to emphasize the need for U.S. maritime presence in the western Pacific to ensure economic and security interests. More than presence, what is needed is the ability to transit freely, "protect American lives and territory, ensure the free flow of commerce, maintain stability, and defend our allies in the region." [72] Only a robust force structure, "rooted in maritime strategy," can secure these vital national interests, the commission concluded. [73] Yet this is the very quality most threatened by current plans to cut defense deeply in order to pay for America's swollen national debt and burgeoning entitlements obligations.

FISCAL THREATS TO THE AVF: THE ENTITLEMENTS "SQUEEZE"

Down-to-the wire congressional budget battles in the summer of 2011 showed that, along with strategic drift, America's military power is threatened by broader economic woes. With days to go before the lack of a budget deal would have allegedly threatened default on American debt repayments, both political parties agreed to massive and arbitrary defense spending cuts as a way to achieve agreement while avoiding tough decisions about entitlement reform.

Even without such dramatic showdowns, the increasing share of the budget dedicated to mandatory funding for expenses such as health care and social security, means that discretionary funds like the military budget will inevitably be constrained.

In the general budget, unfunded liabilities alone are estimated at some $100 trillion. These include mandatory spending for which there is no dedicated revenue source, such as taxes or health-care premiums. Medicare is estimated at $88 trillion, and Social Security is estimated at $17.5 trillion. Meanwhile, the net worth of Americans is estimated at half that much. On top of these commitments is an enormous public debt, estimated at $13.7 trillion. The latest health-care reform legislation and stimulus legislation is reported to have added an additional trillion dollars to this figure. These liabilities, which comprise mandatory spending, will no doubt crowd out discretionary spending such as defense in the coming decades.

Pushing mandatory spending higher will be the rising cost of medical care. Over the past thirty years, American spending on health care has more than doubled as a share of gross domestic product (GDP) and costs continue to account for a steadily growing share of GDP. That share will double again by 2035 to 30 percent of GDP, according to Congressional Budget Office (CBO) estimates published before the U.S. Congress passed its 2010 health-care reform legislation.[74] Health-care costs are expected to reach more than 40 percent of GDP by 2060 and almost 50 percent by 2082.[75] Since the enactment of the 2010 health-care legislation, the CBO has estimated that at the current spending levels, the U.S. federal debt will surpass the historical high of 110 percent GDP by 2025. The CBO warns that this is an "unsupportable" level and will constrain America's ability respond to domestic and international problems and which will make the country vulnerable to a fiscal crisis in the near term.[76]

While aging is often seen as a primary reason for increases in Medicare and Medicaid spending, an older population is only part of the reason for cost growth, according to the CBO. The main cause is the degree to which health-care spending cost growth exceeds economic growth.[77] Federal spending on

Medicare and Medicaid, which accounted for 4 percent of the GDP in 2010, is projected to rise to 9 percent by 2035, and to 19 percent by 2082.[78] Experts are still arguing what impact health-care reform legislation will have. Estimates project that it will add more than $500 billion to the deficit over the next ten years and $1.5 trillion in the following decade.[79]

What is certain is that parts of Medicare—including medical visits and prescription drugs—do not have dedicated funding streams and will therefore compete with national defense for a portion of the general revenue. On the state level, funding for guard and reserve forces will compete with rising costs of the mandatory expansion of Medicaid coverage included in the 2010 health re-form legislation. States will also have to pay for people formerly uninsured and those who shift from private insurers.[80]

An equally serious challenge for the U.S. economy in the next thirty years is the unfunded liabilities associated with Social Security. According to a recent study, the official estimates regarding the imbalance between what is owed to retiring workers and what the nation can afford is woefully underestimated.[81] What is more, official estimates do not take into account important demo-graphic factors that will affect worker productivity in the years ahead.

Assessments of demography and power often oversimplify a nation's pros-pects of worker productivity by looking merely at the projected number of workers. However, worker quality matters. And while assessments of quality often focus on education, social and demographic factors matter too. American worker quality will increase in the coming years due to more capital and bet-ter technology per worker, but it will face challenges, such as leveling-off high school graduation rates and fewer integrated families.[82] Immigrant groups with higher fertility also tend to have lower education acquisition propensity, lower employment, and longer average periods of unemployment according to Jag-deesh Gokhale. He says this will hurt U.S. worker productivity, balancing out the positive aspects of future worker quality.[83]

Integrated families—in which the elderly, adult children, and grandchil-dren live together—promote higher worker productivity. These families pass on to the younger generation noncognitive learning of important attitudes and skills such as persistence, focus, and willingness to learn. High divorce rates, people remaining single, and single-headed households indicate a decrease in integrated families and the prospect of lower worker quality in the future.[84]

According to the Population Reference Bureau (PRB), American children are more likely to see their parents' marriage break up than any other children in the developed world.[85] PRB reports: "Eight percent of children living with their mothers encounter three or more maternal partnerships by the time the children are 15 years old." That percentage is three times as many as in Sweden, the country in second place, where 2.6 percent of children go through the same experience. "This high frequency of turnovers and transitions is a distinctive aspect of American families," the report says.[86] This, too, threatens to undermine American worker productivity.

INTRA-DEFENSE THREATS TO THE AVF: THE NEED FOR COST CONTROL

Along with broader American fiscal challenges, defense budget battles could also threaten the future force. Cost growth for "research and development, test and evaluation" rose an astonishing 40 percent in the first eight years of this century. At the same time, military acquisition costs rose an equally remarkable 26 percent.[87] What is more, the problem is metastasizing. Anthony Cordesman has shown how the portion of military programs with more than 25 percent cost escalation rose from 37 percent to 44 percent. At the same time, the delay in delivering these programs rose on average from sixteen months to twenty-one months.[88]

Cost escalation is not only a military planning challenge, it is also a political problem. The Pentagon is perceived by Congress to underestimate costs, and this has created a lower level of trust between the services and Capitol Hill, leading to pressure to cut some of the costliest programs. Indeed, after the full weight of the budget crisis came to bear in 2010, the Secretary of Defense told Navy supporters, "At the end of the day, we have to ask whether the nation can really afford a Navy that relies on 3- to 6-billion-dollar destroyers, billion-dollar submarines, and 11-billion-dollar carriers."[89] In 2010 Secretary Gates announced the services would cancel major programs and curtail others. This included ending plans for a third engine for the Joint Strike Fighter, and cancellation of the C-17 Globemaster strategic lift aircraft. The 2010 QDR announced more cuts in major weapons systems whose costs had escalated out of control: the F-22A Raptor stealth fighter whose costs escalated 177 percent, while the quantity to be procured decreased by 71 percent; the DDG1000 Zumwalt Class destroyer, for which the Navy showed a $200 million per ship increase over the service's 2008 estimate for the first five ships;[90] and the littoral combat ship, which had risen from $220 million to more than $600 million.[91]

These cuts come at a time when the pace of Navy shipbuilding is already so slow that some experts say it severely threatens future U.S. security interests. A RAND study concluded that over the past four decades, the rate of growth of Navy shipbuilding costs has exceeded the rate of inflation, "outstripping the Navy's ability to pay for them." [92] The study found that since the Navy's budget is unlikely to rise due to fiscal constraints, it must find a way to build more on the same budget or face the fact that its fleet will inevitably shrink. Indeed, a CBO report on Navy shipbuilding for 2011 confirmed that the U.S. Navy's construction plan is not sufficient to achieve the goal of a 322- or 323-ship fleet.[93] The CBO's estimates of the Navy's plan are 18 percent higher than Navy projections and 37 percent higher in the final ten years of the twenty-year plan. Hans Ulrich Kaeser and Anthony Cordesman conclude that "the costs [of shipbuilding] already are high enough to make the U.S. Navy the greatest single peacetime threat to the U.S. Navy."[94]

What is worse, building fewer ships may be more costly to the U.S. taxpayer than building more, due to the increasing maintenance costs of older ships. Kaeser and Cordesman concluded that "the industrial shipbuilding base is designed to support a larger fleet than can be afforded today. Maintaining or closing excess supply capacities will incur large costs on the industrial base that are not figured into the Navy budgets."[95] On the other hand, closing public shipyards has already cost the nation dearly in terms of future security interests. Since the complex skills required in shipbuilding must be learned over the course of many years, the United States can no longer reconstitute its public shipbuilding and repair capability in time to meet an emerging naval threat like the one it faced in the Second World War.[96]

The defense secretary justified the situation this way: "It is important to remember that, as much as the U.S. battle fleet has shrunk since the end of the Cold War, the rest of the world's navies have shrunk even more. So, in relative terms, the U.S. Navy is as strong as it has ever been."[97] Critics argue that this is specious, since the real question is which navies the United States will face in the future, such as China's, which is growing at an unprecedented rate. In fact, the defense secretary admitted that the "virtual monopoly the U.S. has enjoyed with precision guided weapons is eroding—especially with long-range, accurate anti-ship cruise and ballistic missiles that can potentially strike from over the horizon."[98] At the same time, the secretary submitted a budget cutting R&D spending by more than 4 percent.

Contrary to what these actions would suggest, the defense budget does not put a significant strain on the overall U.S. budget. In fact, defense spending as a percentage of GDP is as low as it has been since World War II (when it was nearly 40 percent). The 2010 defense budget appropriation, at around $726 billion for fiscal year 2011, was just 4.8 percent of GDP. The base 2010 defense budget was $550 billion, including $158 billion for the cost of overseas contingency operations, primarily in Iraq and Afghanistan.[99] In comparison to the enormous and rapidly rising costs of Medicare, Social Security, and health-care costs, the defense budget is economical.[100] While ending the Iraq War will decrease national security costs to the GDP, it will do so only by about $100 billion a year. Meanwhile, shifting focus and resources to Afghanistan will likely offset these savings.[101]

Thus, what will continue to drive the increasing burden on federal spending in the coming years will be the rising cost of civil, not military, programs.[102] The burden of health-care reform and stimulus legislation is likely to grow if more large financial institutions get into trouble.[103] While the American economy has been able to attract investments from abroad for now, it cannot continue to do so unless and until it credibly reduces entitlements.[104]

Accomplishing major shifts from national defense spending to pay for civil programs will inevitably require major and lasting reductions in American strategic commitments abroad. But this is not inevitable. Discretionary spending, especially military budgets, are caught between rising costs of mandatory spending and entitlements. Tough choices that contain costs must be made sooner not later.

Conclusion

In his 1987 opus *The Rise and Fall of the Great Powers*, acclaimed historian Paul Kennedy predicted the decline of America's relative power among great nations due to overreaching in its security commitments. Thus began an intensive debate among scholars about the denouement of American influence. While it was dampened somewhat by the end of the Cold War and unpredicted rapid demise of the Soviet Union, pessimism persisted; in 1997, Kennedy again surmised the United States was in the throes of "imperial overstretch."[105] The events of September 11, 2001, prolonged campaigns in Iraq and Afghanistan, and the economic slowdown have created a second wave of intellectual pessimism.[106] Mark Haas argues that "to pay for the massive fiscal costs associated with its aging population, the United States will in all likelihood have to scale back the scope of its international policies," and that "the economic effects of an aging population will likely deny even the United States the fiscal room necessary to maintain the extent of its current global position, let alone adopt major new international initiatives."[107]

It was during the first wave of pessimism that Samuel Huntington called America's critics "declinists" and argued they paid too much attention to material factors such as relative changes in military and economic indicators and not enough accounting of the internal factors that would determine the future of American power.[108] American demographic exceptionalism and the adaptability and technical advances of its workforce and its military equivalent, the All-Volunteer Force, mean the United States has significant manpower advantages over the rest of the world that many scholars miss in their analyses. American leaders should seize upon the population advantage. While lower-level planning guidance addresses the operational consequences of shifting demographics, national strategic documents need to be better informed.[109]

Ironically, it may be due to their nation's demographic health that leaders have become complacent, putting off difficult decisions regarding civilian spending and not anchoring current military force planning decisions to strategy. An abundance of youth and the financial ability to recruit and retain them during two ground wars has also led to a strategic drift away from the traditional American grand strategy that emphasizes sea power and balancing against a the rise of a peer competitor. Without swift attention to its shipbuilding and strategic alliances, America's role as a Pacific power could be eclipsed in China's rise, whether peaceful or turbulent.

The problem then seems to be less about "imperial overstretch," as declinists would argue, and more about strategic indecision and a lack of cost control. The rising cost of platforms must be contained, but not at the expense of American maritime superiority, which ensures economic and security interests, especially in the Asia-Pacific region. The rising cost of the All-Volunteer Force has to be controlled, but in a way that is attuned to changing demographics regionally and generationally. When the Obama administration announced it would cut retention incentives, critics rightly warned that it might have negative effects on force quality. National Guard commands, which are vital to homeland security, are affected by regional demographic disparities that may be exacerbated by a "one size fits all" cut in recruiting and retention incentives. Competition for American high school graduates will increase due to a leveling off in the number of those with a high school diploma. The rise in child obesity means that even though the number of recruitable youths is increasing due to relatively high fertility rates, the portion of youth who are eligible for military service will decrease, especially among women, who are harder to recruit and retain in the first place. The decline of the traditional American family and extended family has been linked to a decrease in worker quality in the recruitable population. While the cost of the All-Volunteer Force is rightly scrutinized, these health and education problems would be even more of a problem if the United States faces a great power war and must return to the draft.

Fortunately, American demographic prospects offer policymakers a way forward: there is evidence that America's demographic exceptionalism will continue. While fertility declined during the Great Depression, it rose during the smaller recessions since the 1930s, when Americans responded by having more, not fewer, children. The economic stimulus of World War II and a burgeoning workforce from the postwar baby boom followed. Since the 2008 recession, it appears that Americans are not appreciably reducing their family sizes, according to preliminary reports.[110] This means that the United States is nowhere near the straits European policymakers find themselves in, a situation that has led to an unprecedented partnership between Britain and France, which includes sharing aircraft carriers and nuclear weapons technology. The European situation is a harbinger of impending retreat among America's NATO allies from what will be unrelenting security threats calling for a military response. America's share of the burden to keep the peace and secure the economic sea-lanes will only increase.

To meet the challenge, or at least to avoid the "train wreck" some security analysts are predicting, tough choices about health-care costs and entitlements have to be made today. The temptation to solve short-term deficit problems by cutting costly defense systems without regard to national strategy must be resisted. Force planning decisions must be tied to a well-defined strategy and a long-term budget. America's demographic health, in the form of an aging population projected to draw from entitlements longer than any previous generation, will only increase the temptation to make short-sighted defense cuts in the coming decades. American demographic exceptionalism—in particular its robust fertility rate that gives it a strong and growing workforce—has ironically allowed Washington to defer these tough choices too long. Policymakers should seize the demographic advantage to chart the way ahead.

PART III.
TURBULENCE IN ASIA'S RISE

7

THE SETTING SUN?
STRATEGIC IMPLICATIONS OF JAPAN'S
DEMOGRAPHIC TRANSITION

Toshi Yoshihara

That Japan is undergoing an unprecedented demographic transformation is well known. For years scholars and policymakers have held up Japan as a classic case study of a rapidly aging society. As a frontrunner in global aging, Japan has become an unfolding experiment for those examining the future of the postmodern, developed world. Most studies have focused on the economic and social impact of Japan's demographic dilemma.[1] This is understandable. As a leading economy in the world, Japan's weakening capacity to convert human capital into a source of growth could have global consequences. Yet, observers have consistently overlooked the implications of Japan's demographic decline from a national security and defense perspective.

The security dimension of Japan's population predicament is critical, not least because manpower is essential for the physical defense of the homeland and for discharging the nation's international responsibilities. Demography's impact on Japan's national security boils down to two questions. First, will Japan become less able to defend itself as its population ages and shrinks? Second, will Tokyo be less able to help maintain the peace and security of the international system with the expected demographic shift?

To answer these two questions, this study aims to (1) highlight the demographic challenge to Japan's basic defense requirements; (2) posit two scenarios on how population decline could impact Tokyo's strategic position; and (3) explore the broader strategic implications of demography for Japan, the United States, and regional/global security. A key finding of this chapter is that wrenching decisions await Japanese policymakers and defense planners as depopulation pressures begin to limit Tokyo's strategic options in the decades to come.

Japan's Demographic Future

Projections of Japan's population are uniformly troubling. In statistics compiled by the United Nations, Japan tops the global list of categories on aging, fertility decline, and population decline. Japan is the front-runner in the graying process by which the proportion of older people increases relative to those of younger people. The speed of population aging is expected to accelerate in the coming years. As Richard Jackson and Neil Howe explain, "Japan's massive age wave is the result of a perfect demographic storm: plunging fertility, soaring life expectancy, and negligible net immigration."[2] Japan experienced a steep fertility decline in the postwar period. In the 1950s, the fertility rate averaged 2.58. In the 1960s and 1970s, the birthrate fell slightly below the so-called "replacement rate" of 2.1 to 2 and 1.98, respectively. The downward trend continued, bottoming out at 1.28 over the past decade.[3] The birthrate has fallen to a level that the United Nations describes as "unprecedented in human history."[4] Consequently, Japan's median age was 44.4 in 2009, while the percentage of the elderly population aged sixty and older stood at 29.7 percent in 2009.[5] The United Nations foresees a jump in the median age to 52.3 and a rise in the proportion of the aged to 41.5 percent by 2050.[6] In absolute terms, the elderly cohort will grow from 38.6 million out of 126.5 million in 2010 to 45 million out of 108.5 million in 2050.[7]

Beyond the aging problem, the declining birthrate has set the stage for a sustained depopulation process. The United Nations Population Division forecasts three pathways for Japan's demographic future. The more generous calculation predicts a drop to 114 million in 2050 from the peak of 127 million in 2005. The more pessimistic assessment anticipates a dramatic dive to 90 million four decades hence, representing an astounding 30 percent decrease in Japan's population.[8] Official Japanese figures corroborate these estimates. In 2002 Japan's National Institute of Population and Social Security Research projected that slightly over 100 million of its citizens will inhabit the nation in 2050 and that 35.7 percent of the population will be aged.[9] Four years later, the Institute published a revised estimate, finding that Japan's population will fall faster than initially predicted to 95 million, of which 39.6 percent will be sixty-five or older by 2050.[10] A private Japanese research institute estimates that Japan's population will drop to 94 million people during the same period.[11]

The looming demographic trends have not gone unnoticed in Japan's defense community. The Council on Security and Defense Capabilities (CSDC) issued a report in 2004 that for the first time outlined a comprehensive national security strategy for Japan. The report foresaw a significant expansion of Japan's regional and global responsibilities. At the same time, it bluntly noted that Tokyo faces "constraining factors" that could inhibit efforts at improving Japan's defense. Notably, it ranked the "dwindling birthrate" as the primary constraint.[12] The report supplied a vehicle to set the tone and direction of Tokyo's 2004 National Defense Program Guideline (NDPG), which sets forth broad contours for Japanese security policy, defense priorities, and anticipated force levels, both in qualitative and quantitative terms.[13] Reflecting the demographic concerns expressed by the council, the NDPG noted, "In developing Japan's defense forces, we have to take into account the fact that while the roles that our defense forces have to play are multiplying, the number of young people in Japan is declining as a result of the low birth rate, and fiscal conditions continue to deteriorate."[14] The NDPG thus pledged to "recruit, cultivate, train and educate high quality personnel to meet the challenge of the diversification and internationalization of Self-Defense Forces [SDF] missions."[15]

Owing to the rapidly changing security environment, the Japanese government reconvened the council to consider the nation's future strategic direction. The 2010 report urged Tokyo "to grow from an inward-looking pacifist nation to an outward-looking 'Peace-Creating Japan' that imaginatively and skillfully plays a greater and more active role in the sphere of international security."[16] But it, too, conceded that Japan's "rapidly aging society and declining birthrate will make it difficult to allocate resources to defense capabilities," tempering any expectations that the defense budget would grow in the future.[17] The 2010 NDPG also acknowledged the need to "appropriately adapt to the declining birth rate ... and the diversification of SDF missions."[18]

Similarly, annual defense white papers produced by Japan's Ministry of Defense have explicitly noted that population trends will harm recruitment and will likely exert downward pressures on the end strength of SDF personnel. For instance, the 2005 report observed that the male population eligible to join the Self-Defense Forces (aged eighteen to twenty-six) peaked at 9 million in

1994.[19] In other words, the pool of recruits has been shrinking for well over a decade. In 2006 those between the ages of eighteen and twenty-six stood at 6.68 million, representing a 25 percent decline over twelve years.[20] UN statistics bear out these trends. According to the UN's *World Population Prospects*, the number of Japanese males aged fifteen to twenty-four declined from 9.5 million in 1995 to 7.2 million in 2005.[21] The Ministry of Defense predicts that eligible male recruits will fall somewhere between 5.5 and 6 million by 2018.[22] By way of comparison, a similar pool of potential military recruits aged eighteen to twenty-four years in the United States will increase by 16 percent over roughly the same period (1995–2020).[23] By 2030 this age group in Japan could fall as low as 4.8 million.[24] These figures suggest that the youth available to join the ranks of the armed services could shrink to unsustainable levels.

These projections and statistics clearly place Japan at the forefront of low-growth developed states. Japan will be smaller twenty years from now, and one of the demographic ranges that will be hardest hit could harm the SDF's ability to meet its personnel needs. To compound the expected recruitment difficulties, security threats—ranging from homeland defense to peacekeeping operations—that place a premium on manpower may remain unchanged or could very well increase in the coming years. What impact such an expected chasm between manpower and basic defense requirements portends for Japan's security remains to be seen. But it is nevertheless useful to postulate alternative futures that explicitly link demographics to national security because such scenarios help forecast the more likely challenges that Japan will face in the coming years.

Scenarios for Low-Growth Developed States

Developed states suffering from low growth rates face two distinct types of scenarios that threaten national security. The first scenario is premised on (admittedly crude) balance-of-power calculations and interstate competition. Specifically, demographics contribute directly to conflict between states with inverse growth rates. The second scenario rests on a more nuanced cost-benefit analysis of a state's growing inability to defend itself against threats or to intervene in crises. In this case, manpower shortages gradually reduce the strategic options of states that have a stake in maintaining the current regional and world orders. In contrast to the first scenario, which predicts the potential for war between states, the second one foresees a steady withdrawal of states from international security commitments as the means to project power overseas diminish.

For Japan, the first scenario is not relevant at the moment because Tokyo's strategic position immunizes it from security threats that large population imbalances produce. The second scenario, on the other hand, will more likely assume a prominent place in Tokyo's strategic calculus as Japan expands its security responsibilities in Asia and beyond. More importantly, the two scenarios are not mutually exclusive. If Japan fails to meet the challenges of the second scenario effectively, then the first, less probable, scenario is more likely to rear its ugly head in the future.

SCENARIO 1: IMBALANCE OF POWER

Akin to realist explanations of international relations, the imbalance-of-power scenario posits that large population differentials can produce a major disequilibrium in the conventional military balance between two states. Such an imbalance could in theory stimulate geostrategic calculations on both sides that are more conducive to war. A much larger or faster-growing state may be more inclined toward aggression because it can tap into a huge reservoir of manpower to overwhelm a smaller neighbor. A state with a slower growth rate, or a significantly smaller population, may be tempted to strike preemptively against a larger power in order to preclude the expected intolerable shift in the balance of power.[25]

But there are four intervening variables that would serve as brakes to such a simplistic, offensively oriented construct. First, geography matters. If the two states are separated by a nautical border, either side may be blunted by "the stopping power of water."[26] For example, despite the tremendous disparity in populations between mainland China and Taiwan, the ninety miles of water separating the two states have prevented either side from invading the other for decades.[27]

Second, even if two states share a land border, specific geographic features may favor the defense sufficiently to blunt predatory or preemptive temptations. Difficult terrain, such as mountains, jungles, and rivers, could prove to be a sufficient physical buffer. If a state boasts a large territory or enjoys sanctuaries, its potential ability to maximize strategic depth and wage a war of protraction and attrition could serve to deter aggressors. During the 1979 Sino-Vietnamese

War, the far larger Chinese side suffered tremendous human losses with no tangible gains due in large part to the difficult operating environment along the invasion routes.

Third, the presence of nuclear weapons on both sides is likely to deter direct aggression between two states with significant population differentials. The destructive power of nuclear weapons may make even a modest attack on a populous state unacceptably painful. Although several crises over the past decade brought India and Pakistan to the brink, the ongoing standoff over Kashmir has not spiraled into conflict since both sides tested nuclear devices in 1998. Islamabad has overtly adopted a first-strike posture to deter the much larger Indian army from entering into a conventional war that Pakistan cannot hope to win.[28]

Finally, the larger state must be able to translate its human potential into credible offensive power. In light of the ongoing advances in military technologies, quality has increasingly trumped quantity. Smaller states armed with first-class, high-tech militaries may be able to generate enough combat power to more than compensate for their numerical inferiority. The small state of Israel has repeatedly defeated its demographically larger Arab neighbors due to its emphasis on operational excellence and technological superiority in weaponry.[29] Arab states, on the other hand, have been unable to convert their far larger populations into effective fighting forces.

How do these variables and considerations apply to Japan? The only potential competitor in Northeast Asia that possesses a large enough population to threaten Japan is China. Despite a looming demographic crisis of its own, China boasts a population ten times larger than that of Japan. Historical animosities, territorial disputes, and a budding rivalry for leadership in Asia have frequently produced turbulence in bilateral ties. One might be tempted to conclude that conflict is inevitable.

The four constraining factors noted above, however, are all present to dampen the demographic sources of confrontation. Most obviously, Japan and China are separated by the East China Sea and the Yellow Sea. The distance from Shanghai to Naha, Okinawa, for example, is 511 miles. If China cannot cross the 90-mile-wide body of water separating it from Taiwan today, then the Japanese home islands will be safe from a Chinese amphibious assault for many decades to come. Japan's mountainous terrain and the few pockets of densely populated urban areas make for an operational nightmare, even if China could successfully reach the home islands. Beijing's small nuclear arsenal, which has long targeted major U.S. bases in Japan, is counterbalanced by the extension of America's nuclear umbrella to Tokyo.[30] Finally, despite China's impressive military modernization efforts over the past two decades, Japan's SDF boasts a small but world-class navy and air force that are sufficiently lethal to deter Chinese aggression. A demographically driven conflict between Beijing and Tokyo, then, is improbable for the foreseeable future.

SCENARIO 2: RESOURCE MISMATCH

This scenario envisions a low-growth state undergoing an enervating transition propelled by four trends. First, population decline inevitably leads to a gradual decrease in eligible manpower that can be recruited and fielded for combat. Second, higher demand for social services from a growing retiree population crowds out resources for defense expenditures, including finances for recruiting, training, and retaining military personnel. Third, as competition over the productive members of society intensifies, the better-paying private sector attracts and lures away the best and the brightest that the military needs to command and operate a modern force. Fourth, risk aversion begins to characterize decision-making in government, particularly in aging democracies. An older electorate may be temperamentally inclined towards conciliatory policies while smaller families may become reluctant to place their children in harm's way.[31]

As a consequence of such developments, low-growth nations may increasingly acquire a taste for technological solutions to make up for labor shortages. In particular, states may exhibit strategic preferences for standoff precision-strike weaponry, unmanned platforms, and other high-tech gadgetry to reduce casualty concerns while still maintaining the capacity to respond robustly to threats. However, the proclivity to rely on technology to compensate for declining manpower creates its own pathology. With fewer and more highly skilled people operating very expensive high-tech platforms, casualty and risk aversion could increase for a state unwilling to lose its high-value resources. Moreover, the military campaigns in Afghanistan and in Iraq over the past decade vividly demonstrate the limits of technology. The "transformation" that former secretary of defense Donald Rumsfeld touted certainly produced spectacular operational successes at the conventional level of war. But the inability of the U.S. military to quell the subsequent insurgency underscored the reality that manpower is still required for a range of military operations other than war. As such, as long as the specter of failed or failing states that threaten to provide safe havens for terrorists remain, the pressure to muster resources for manpower-intensive stability operations in "ungoverned spaces" will mount for developed nations.[32]

Over the longer term, an even more troubling outcome looms. Even if the political will existed among developed states to maintain regional and global order, declining populations and the diminishing returns from technology investments will likely reach a kind of crossover point. If manpower and technology combined can no longer meet the demands of stability operations, for example, then strategic paralysis might very well ensue. Aptly illustrating the stark choices for developed nations, Peter Peterson argues that

> even if military capital is successfully substituted for military labor, the deployment option may be dangerously limited. Developed nations facing a threat may feel they have only two extreme (but relatively inexpensive) choices: a low-level response (antiterrorist strikes and cruise-missile diplomacy) or a high-level response (an all-out attack with strategic weapons).[33]

In other words, developed countries may find themselves unable to issue threats or take military actions that correspond proportionately to the varying levels of threats. Put in even more dramatic terms, developed nations may become trapped between a policy of appeasement resembling that of British diplomacy during the inter-war period and a strategy of massive nuclear retaliation adopted by the Eisenhower administration during the early years of the Cold War. Confronted with either inaction or over-reaction as policy choices, regional and global powers may be unable or unwilling to fulfill multiple security responsibilities.

A Looming Strategy-Resource Mismatch?

The second scenario perhaps best describes Japan's future predicament. As noted, Tokyo clearly recognizes the coming demographic crisis in security terms. Yet, at the same time, Japan has in recent years promised to engage in a range of international operations that it had previously shunned. The 2010 CSDC report, for example, deemed improving the international security environment as important to Japanese national security as the physical defense of the nation. As the commissioners sweepingly asserted, "Preventing conflicts in all corners of the world, or managing the risks of emerging conflicts is an important factor for Japan's security."[34] Indeed, the report designated SDF involvement in stabilizing the global security environment as a "primary role."[35] To achieve the twin goals of national defense and international stability, declared the council, Tokyo needed to (a) depend on its own efforts, (b) act in concert with Japan's main ally, the United States, and (c) engage in "multilayered security cooperation" with South Korea, Australia, NATO, India, China, Russia, and the United Nations.[36]

The commissioners further argued that "Japan should aim at acquiring the capability for adequate response to 'complex contingencies' in which various events may break out simultaneously or continuously rather than separately."[37] More concretely, the report proposed entrusting an array of missions to the Self-Defense Forces. Among the missions it contemplated were ballistic- and cruise-missile defense; counterterrorism; defense of remote islands, territorial waters, and airspace; and exclusive economic zones, non-combatant evacuation operations, and disaster response. The council reiterated the possibility that these threats could arise concurrently, severely challenging the responsiveness and effectiveness of the SDF.

The 2010 NDPG reaffirmed the commission's assertion that national security and international stability are indivisible, pledging to "participate more actively in . . . United Nations peace-keeping activities and activities to deal with nontraditional security issues, such as humanitarian assistance, disaster relief, and counterpiracy initiatives."[38] For operations closer to home, the document mandated the capacity to defend against ballistic-missile attacks, cope with cyber attacks, respond to incursions by enemy special-operations forces, defeat an invasion of Japan's offshore islands, patrol and prevent intrusion into Japan's surrounding seas and airspace, and manage the effects of WMD attacks. In addition, the SDF must conduct "continuous" intelligence-gathering, surveillance, and reconnaissance operations while engaging in joint training and exercises with other militaries and in "international peace cooperation activities."[39] Japanese defense planners clearly plan to keep the SDF very busy on a more or less permanent basis.

Policy documents issued under the rubric of the U.S.-Japanese alliance in recent years strongly endorsed this decidedly forward-leaning posture on global security affairs. In February 2005 the Security Consultative Committee (SCC), the highest-level official working group bringing together the Japanese ministers of foreign affairs and defense with their American counterparts, issued a joint statement boldly setting forth "global common strategic objectives." The alliance specifically identified "international peace cooperation activities" and "the stability of the global energy supply" as areas demanding closer collaboration between the two partners. [40] That October the SCC reiterated the common strategic objectives set forth in February, called on both countries to develop "flexible capabilities," and opened the door for third-party participation in allied endeavors. [41]

The 2007 SCC joint statement specifically identified "the redefinition of the SDF's primary mission to include international peace keeping operations, international disaster relief operations, and responses to situations in areas surrounding Japan" as an area of major breakthrough. [42] In June 2011, the SCC identified twenty-four common strategic objectives that included maintaining regional security, assuring access to the global commons, promoting stability in the Middle East, and strengthening international cooperation. [43] The joint statement explicitly endorsed the goals that the SCC set forth in 2005 and 2007, underscoring the enduring nature of the alliance's global outlook. In short, as Japan assumes greater global responsibilities, the demands and accompanying stresses on the SDF promise to multiply.

At the same time, Japan will be confronting a range of interrelated constraints that would stand in the way of the new national security objectives Tokyo aspires to. The expected decreases in manpower availability previously noted will certainly be one factor. In the post–Cold War period, Japan has consistently maintained an active-duty force of 240,000 members, representing roughly 0.18 percent of the overall population. [44] By comparison, 0.5 percent of the U.S. population is in active-duty service. If Japan were to maintain force levels in absolute or relative terms, then demographic pressures appear manageable over the next decade. Assuming that Japan decreases to 123 million people by 2020, the total number of SDF personnel would slide to 231,000 if Tokyo fixed the ratio of active duty to population at 0.18 percent. Keeping troop levels at 240,000 in 2020 would require slightly less than 0.2 percent of the population.

If Tokyo moves forward to integrate international operations into its defense portfolio, then present force levels are not likely to be enough. Medium-size European powers that engage actively in international operations and boast power projection capabilities provide a useful benchmark. Both the United Kingdom and France field active-duty forces that constitute roughly 0.3 percent of their respective populations. If Japan were to replicate equivalent force sizes, the SDF would need to recruit, train, and deploy 140,000 additional active-duty personnel. Given the narrowing band of eligible recruits, such expansion will be difficult at best.

It should be noted, however, that force size alone is only one crude measure of Japan's ability to fulfill its international responsibilities. The age distribution of personnel in the officer and noncommissioned ranks is another useful qualitative indicator. Ideally, the nation's youth—from the late teens to the early twenties—fill the most junior ranks of a healthy, vigorous military. Japan's personnel system, by contrast, encourages the exact opposite phenomenon. The retirement age of the three lowest officer ranks is fifty-four.[45] Consequently, 60 percent of fifty-two-year-old officers serve as captains and lieutenants in the Ground Self-Defense Force (GSDF). This demographic group is twenty years older than their U.S. counterparts occupying similar ranks. Overall, the GSDF's average age is forty-one, roughly seven years older than the U.S. Army's.[46] The 2010 CSDC report admitted that the average age of junior officers in charge of front-line units is higher than those serving in the United States and the United Kingdom. It bluntly conceded that "the SDF is, in fact, getting older across the board."[47] From an operational perspective, the U.S. military would consider the majority of Japan's tactical leaders too old to serve in the field. In other words, increases in personnel may be a necessary but insufficient condition for the SDF's combat effectiveness to keep up with new demands.

Moreover, this age structure partially masks the looming shortages in recruits. The luxury to retain junior officers for two to three decades substantially reduces the strain to refill the billets of lower ranks, depressing recruitment needs. By way of (an admittedly extreme) comparison, the U.S. military operates under a pressurized promotion system in which service members must be promoted within a certain time frame to stay in the military or, failing that, face mandatory retirement. This "up or out" approach ensures a steady supply of young officers to lead frontline units. If the SDF were to pursue a more demographically balanced force, then recruitment targets would almost certainly surge above current levels. Whether the SDF could meet higher benchmarks in light of the coming squeeze on eligible male recruits remains to be seen.

Perhaps more troubling, there are already some telling signs that the SDF is beginning to strain under the weight of current operations. Some senior leaders of the Ground Self-Defense Force have voiced concerns about manpower shortages. The former commandant of Japan's officer candidate school, General Joji Higuchi, claims that post–Cold War reductions in personnel and equipment have already "compressed and skeletonized" the current force structure.[48] He concludes ominously that amid the rush to field new weaponry such as ballistic missile defense systems, "the minimal defense capabilities that Japan should retain as an independent nation have already been forfeited." Some frontline units are under-strength by 20 percent, severely undermining readiness. As a result, a former GSDF field officer laments, "It is doubtful that the SDF with the current strength level will be able to carry out PKO [peacekeeping operations], countermeasures to deal with pirates, or the raid and search mission."[49]

The Maritime Self-Defense Force (MSDF) faces similar challenges. Following Tokyo's dispatch of a naval task force to the Indian Ocean in support of U.S.-led antiterrorism activities, the Japanese media began to question whether the deployment was creating a gap for homeland defense. Among the four escort fleets available, two (and up to three) are either in training or under repair at any given time. As a result, the Indian Ocean mission left only one major flotilla at homeport to provide for the nation's defense.[50] It was later revealed that the former chief of staff of the MSDF, Admiral Koichi Furusho, worried that Japan lacked the maritime capacity to monitor missile launches from North Korea following Pyongyang's admission that it possessed an illicit nuclear program in late 2002.[51] After North Korea launched a series of ballistic missiles in July 2006, similar concerns were raised about the availability of MSDF destroyers to protect Japan.[52]

Such apparent overcommitment has led Admiral Furusho to openly express fears that the naval service may soon reach a breaking point. As new missions have proliferated, even while manpower has remained fixed over the past two decades, the MSDF has turned to stopgap measures, siphoning off servicemen from frontline destroyers, training, and support units to fulfill the additional obligations. As a result, some ships are shorthanded by 30 percent. If the personnel needs are unmet, Admiral Furusho warns, then "a collapse involving insufficient manpower resources for recruitment, education and training (schools), and rear-area support" could result. He asserts, "It can be predicted that the combat capabilities of the MSDF as a whole will be weakened."[53] The Ministry of Defense's plans to transfer sailors from four destroyers decommissioned ahead of schedule to replenish undermanned ships in the fleet reflect the persistence of this human resource scarcity.[54]

Over the longer term, whether Japan can harness the wherewithal to build more ships and to generate the crews to operate them remains uncertain. The escalating costs of advanced surface combatants suggest that Tokyo will encounter difficulties in substantially expanding its force structure and personnel. For instance, the *Aegis* destroyers armed with state-of-the-art antiballistic missile systems are prohibitively expensive.[55] Moreover, they provide a relatively narrow range of capabilities in the context of manpower-intensive international peacekeeping operations. Even if modern ships equipped with automated systems require fewer crew members, the MSDF would have to grow by several orders of magnitude in order to be able to conduct sea-lane defense, interdict WMD, intercept ballistic missiles, provide relief in the aftermath of major disasters, participate in international operations, and prepare for conventional at-sea engagements. Such an expansion seems highly unlikely. Revealingly, the 2010 CSDC report more or less decreed that the MSDF would have to do more with less as aging ships and aircraft are decommissioned without the prospects of replacement. In response to the downward pressures on the naval force structure, the council urged the maritime service to extend the service life of front-line units as an interim measure.[56]

Financially, the SDF has labored under an informal cap on the defense budget at 1 percent of GDP for decades. In absolute terms, Japan's defense budget has remained stagnant over the past decade even as personnel expenditures, including ever-growing pensions, occupy a larger share of the spending. It remains to be seen whether the massive reconstruction efforts following the March 2011 tsunami and earthquake will add more pressure on defense expenditures. Competition over young and skilled workers will intensify to cutthroat levels as business demand for workers to fill vacancies left behind by retired baby boomers is met by a dwindling supply of potential employees. The 2006 edition of *Defense of Japan*, for example, anticipated a recruitment crunch as private firms hire more employees to offset the anticipated wave of baby-boomer retirements.[57]

To rival the private sector, the SDF will have to pay far more to recruit and retain its soldiers than ever before.

Moreover, as Japan focuses on increasing the quality of troops via better training and education for existing and new missions, personnel expenses are likely to grow at an even faster pace. And if Japan assumes more overseas missions, the demand for larger personnel increases will likely follow, adding even more pressure on a tightly circumscribed budget. These factors together would crowd out funds for military modernization programs that are critical for Tokyo to project power effectively to distant shores.

To compound an already stressful situation, a fiscal crisis looms, and this crisis will only worsen as depopulation shrinks the tax revenue base in the coming years. An advisory panel on the future of Japan's fiscal policy projected severe spending cuts that would be needed to restore the government's financial health by 2015. The commission speculated that if the Japanese government were to rely exclusively on spending reductions, expenditures would have to be scaled back by 32 percent at the 2006 fiscal level. The panel warned that such cuts would slash the defense budget by 70 percent, threatening the SDF's ability to provide disaster relief to Japanese citizens at home.[58] While it would be too politically painful for Tokyo to undertake such drastic measures, the bleak outlook illustrated by the commissioners demonstrate that the Defense Ministry's pleas for more manpower will more likely fall on deaf ears in the future.

Misplaced Faith in Technology?

What, then, explains Japan's bold (and perhaps ill-founded) decision to broaden its security responsibilities even in the face of daunting resource scarcity both in terms of manpower and finances? In a word, technology. Japan's defense community has apparently come to believe that technological advances premised on the so-called Revolution in Military Affairs (RMA), a concept that has been in vogue since the first Gulf War, would overcome quantitative inferiority. Such expectations are somewhat understandable from a nation as technologically oriented as Japan. But faith in technology may be misplaced, particularly in the unforgiving environment of war and conflict prevention.

In 2000, the Japanese government released a report entitled *Info-RMA: Study on Info-RMA and the Future of the Self-Defense Forces*, which sparked a lively debate within the defense community. It argued that pursuing Japan's own brand of RMA would produce "a defense posture that could perform most efficiently with a minimum of reaction time, and could respond flexibly in accordance with rapidly changing situations."[59] Notably, the term "efficiency," connoting a more effective use of scarce resources such as human capital, stands out as an expected operational outcome of the RMA

As Tokyo wrestled with the RMA concept, the terms and language associated with it began to surface in official documents, including the annual defense white papers.[60] Indeed, the 2007 issue seems to have internalized the concept completely, and its authors enthusiastically endorsed the RMA in glowing terms. The report exclaimed, "Technological advancements led by the information and communications technology have not simply sparked spectacular improvements in combat capabilities, but brought about fundamental transformation of military powers."[61]

This confidence in the promise of technology has also found expression in the keystone documents cited earlier in this chapter. The 2004 CSDC report, for example, voiced hope that the armed forces could offset manpower and other resource challenges by squeezing new efficiencies out of government contractors, using information technology as a force multiplier, streamlining the chain of command, and improving education and training in the ranks. The SDF, in short, must "perform many functions without enlarging the size of the force."[62] The 2004 NDPG similarly declared that Japan would build a "multi-functional, flexible, and effective defense force . . . without expanding its size." It pledged that "the Government of Japan will rationalize and streamline personnel, equipment, and operations so as to attain greater results with limited resources that are available."[63] In other words, technology would enable the SDF to do more with the same or, perhaps, with less.

Japanese defense planners are already examining a range of technological solutions designed to substitute capital for labor.[64] One promising area is the development of unmanned systems. In December 2009 the SDF successfully flight tested a prototype of Japan's first high-speed unmanned aerial vehicle (UAV).[65] According to the 2010 defense budget, the medium-range UAV would be designed to perform peacetime reconnaissance missions.[66] More ambitious, Nisohachi Hyodo argues that the Self-Defense Forces must aggressively develop robotics technologies that can take over dangerous and tedious human duties ranging from border and sea-lane patrols to disaster relief.[67] Tokyo has also exhibited an interest in standoff precision-strike weaponry as another technological alternative. Before being ousted from power, the Liberal Democratic Party issued an electoral manifesto on defense policy that boldly articulated plans to marry Japan's proven space-based technologies with missiles. It proposes the combined use of satellites and long-range cruise or ballistic missiles for conducting strike missions against enemy missile bases.[68] Presumably, offensive missiles would take the place of manned airpower, thus reducing the risk of casualties in high-threat environments.

Japan's debate over policy, strategy, and resources for its Self-Defense Forces recalls former secretary of defense Donald Rumsfeld's obsession with "transforming" the U.S. armed forces. Rumsfeld sought to jettison heavy formations and capabilities, particularly in the manpower-intensive ground services, on the logic that "networked" forces relying on high technology could achieve more with less. Technology, he argued, can compensate for numbers. As a corollary, the assumption seems to be that forces optimized for high-intensity warfare can perform all lesser missions—"lesser includeds," in the awkward phraseology used by the Pentagon—with few if any additional assets. Japan's high-end military force designed for major combat operations, then, should be able to discharge stability operations using existing assets.

But can it? Three enduring strategic risks stand in the way of a technological silver bullet. First, military transformation or even a partial RMA is not cheap. The U.S. experience in the 1990s suggests that acquisition costs will likely skyrocket for states seeking to transform their armed forces for high-tech, information-based warfare.[69] Looming fiscal constraints would place severe limits on the innovative potential of Japan's scientific and engineering communities. Second, a less technologically sophisticated adversary could employ numerical superiority to swamp a smaller, high-tech force. As the *Info-RMA* report observed, "If the pre-RMA force massively overwhelmed the post-RMA force, even the post-RMA force would have difficulty [turning] the tables, since the precision-engagement capability of the post-RMA force would become saturated."[70] China, for example, could impose costs by throwing the weight of its large, obsolescent units against its enemies, even while reserving its more modern forces for other purposes.

Third, nontraditional security threats ranging from humanitarian crises to failed states may be impervious to high-technology options, demanding the staying power of troops on the ground. As the internal think tank of the Ministry of Defense observes, wars often "require large-scale military activity during the follow-up processes of restoring order and reconstruction." Thus, it counsels defense planners to consider "sustainability to handle prolonged activities based on the understanding that many situations in today's security environment call for continuous defense operations of an intermediate nature between peacetime and emergency activities."[71] The authors have clearly taken to heart the lessons of postwar Iraq. The March 2011 tsunami disaster, too, was a stark reminder that manpower still matters. In the largest deployment of troops in Japan's postwar history, Tokyo called up over 100,000 SDF personnel to engage in disaster relief operations. Technology, then, clearly has its limits for missions ranging from traditional homeland defense to increasingly prevalent stability operations. The lesson may be that Japan will need to scale back its ambitions related to international peace operations. In the future, Tokyo may have to confine itself to low-impact, rear-area support missions that require no substantial commitment of manpower.

Strategic Implications for Japan

Unless the policy statements issued by Japan are empty rhetoric, it is safe to assume that Tokyo genuinely intends to expand its security responsibilities. Otherwise it would not have engaged in an unprecedented internal reassessment process, nor would it have so publicly declared its intentions before the world. As Tokyo gazes into a future in which a smaller Japan will inhabit the international system, there are critical considerations and decisions that demand attention now.

First, there is clearly a policy-strategy-resource mismatch. Given the expected manpower shortages, it is exceedingly doubtful whether the SDF could cope with multiple, simultaneous, or near-simultaneous contingencies, prosecuting some combination of conventional and stability operations. If Tokyo hopes to attain its wide-ranging set of political objectives, Japanese leaders must set clearer priorities—in effect establishing a hierarchy among traditional warfighting tasks and the nontraditional tasks Tokyo anticipates. They must also consider the strategic, operational, and force-structure implications of any priorities they choose to set. Do, say, humanitarian missions outweigh counterpiracy operations along the approaches to the Strait of Malacca?

Second, Japanese decision makers should challenge the largely unexamined assumptions underlying the nation's new strategic direction. They should define much more concretely "international peace cooperation activities," a vague umbrella term which obscures more than it conveys. Military operations other than war span a wide spectrum of tasks that impose many different operational demands. While Tokyo could easily provide token forces for certain low-tempo peacekeeping operations, Japan will likely be hard pressed to contribute to manpower-intensive stability operations. Thus, analytical rigor is at a premium for Tokyo as it debates how to respond to its immediate surroundings and beyond, both of which are in flux. Japanese leaders must disabuse themselves of the notions that technology trumps manpower, that more can be done with less, and that a one-size-fits-all force structure can achieve their nation's goals. That Japan wants to be a good international citizen while minding its own security interests is praiseworthy. Whether it can do everything it wants to do is another question.

Third, Tokyo's pledges to do more on the international stage and the potential inability to fulfill those promises could have dire consequences for the U.S.-Japan alliance. As previously noted, the fanfare surrounding Japan's display of greater self-confidence was largely celebrated in the context of the alliance. Washington will clearly expect (and demand) more from Tokyo. Indeed, former secretary of defense Robert Gates publicly endorsed the Japanese government's plans to pass a permanent legislation that would enable the SDF to deploy more readily as circumstances warrant.[72] (At present, Japan's Diet must pass laws approving the dispatch of the SDF on a case-by-case basis.) The risk is that Japan's potential failure to meet higher expectations from the United States, even for symbolic purposes, could harm the health of the relationship. For example, as depopulation pressures increase, the likelihood that Japan is forced to bow out of U.S.-led international initiatives could grow. Despite Washington's insistent calls for Tokyo to "show the flag" or "put boots on the ground," Brad Glosserman and Tomoko Tsunoda bluntly assert that "there will be no feet to put in those boots, nor hands to hold the flag."[73] The consequences of Tokyo's unwillingness or inability to participate in "coalitions of the willing" operations remain to be seen.

Fourth, over the longer term it is conceivable that Japan will become even more dependent on the United States for its defense. This dependence prom-

ises to be a double-edged sword. On the one hand, Tokyo may feel compelled
to integrate its forces with their U.S. counterparts. Enhanced interoperability
would not only bind the two nations closer strategically, but such "jointness"
would also serve as force multipliers that generate greater combat power for the
SDF, which will not grow significantly in size. Such an outcome clearly dove-
tails with the Defense Ministry's philosophy on the IT-RMA. Ongoing efforts
to permit the SDF to operate more seamlessly with U.S. forces are clearly intended to improve the efficiency of Japanese forces.[74] On the other hand, allied
integration at the operational level could erode Japan's strategic independence
by heightening the risk of Japanese entanglement in crises and conflicts that
Tokyo would otherwise seek to avoid. Consider, for instance, the SDF finding
itself inadvertently embroiled in a U.S.-China confrontation over Taiwan due to
its tight operational linkages to U.S. forces deployed in Asia. Dependence could
also lead to *over*dependence on the United States, tempting Japanese decision
makers to hitch a "free ride" on U.S. security commitments. Japan may hand
off defense responsibilities to the United States to such an extent that the SDF
becomes a hollow, unusable force. Neither scenario bodes well for the integrity
of the alliance.

Fifth, strategic options, including a nuclear breakout, that were once inconceivable could become thinkable for Japan. In a forecast of the international
system in 2025, the National Intelligence Council identifies "emerging unfavorable demographic trends" and "more intensive military competitions" as potential sources of insecurity for Japan.[75] Leading Japanese politicians already
fret about long-term national decline and the prospective inability to compete
militarily with China, attributing their fears directly to low fertility and aging.[76]
Such anxieties could become particularly acute if the Japanese polity perceives
a weakened U.S. resolve to fulfill its security commitment to Tokyo. A Japan
that felt under siege and alone could very well pursue the ultimate weapon as a
desperate measure. A congressional report on Japan's nuclear future amplifies
this point:

> Another wild card is the likelihood that Japan will face a major demo-
> graphic challenge because of its rapidly ageing population: such a shock
> could either drive Japan closer to the United States because of heightened

insecurity, or could spur nationalism that may lean toward developing more autonomy.[77]

The latter, worst-case scenario may be farfetched at the moment. But it is worth considering how Tokyo would arrive at such an outcome. If the negative trends in the U.S.-Japanese alliance illustrated above unfold, then either party or both sides could lose confidence in the credibility of the security partnership. Washington may withdraw its security guarantees or Tokyo may question America's extended deterrence. In the absence of a U.S. nuclear umbrella, it is possible that Japan would seriously consider developing its own nuclear arsenal in order to shore up its independent defensive capabilities. Indeed, Japanese observers have already begun to explore nuclear options that were once considered taboo. As one Japanese analyst forcefully declares, "A 'nuclear umbrella' to be provided by someone else cannot protect Japan from the Chinese military's nuclear missiles, the capability of which has been improving steadily every year. *Japan needs to have its own autonomous nuclear deterrence capability.*"[78] This nuclear scenario clearly portends dangers for regional and global stability.

Finally, in light of the gloomy prognosis in the foregoing paragraphs, an analytical caveat is warranted. This study assumes that key strategic parameters, such as the informal cap on the defense budget and the authorized end strength of active-duty personnel, will remain fixed indefinitely. But radical policy changes are possible under extraordinary circumstances. Wild cards and systemic shocks could shake deeply felt beliefs or undermine longstanding principles, producing sharp turns in strategic orientation. Japan is certainly no stranger to such about-faces. The decision to abandon isolationism during the Meiji era and another one to embrace an American-led international order in the postwar period are decisive turning points in Japanese history. A dramatic departure from the status quo of similar magnitude should not be discounted out of hand. Violent or peaceful unification of the Korean states hostile to Tokyo or a naval war with China over disputed maritime claims could trigger a fundamental reassessment of Japan's options. Perceptions of American inaction or ineptitude over a cross-strait conflict that leads to the forcible Chinese unification of Taiwan would be another game changer. The bottom line is that there is nothing inevitable about Japan's self-imposed constraints. It would be prudent for defense planners to keep an open mind about the role of contingency in international politics.

Concluding Thoughts

In an article provocatively entitled "A Geriatric Peace? The Future of U.S. Power in a World of Aging Populations," Mark Haas argues that global aging will inaugurate a long period of peaceful ties among the great powers. He contends that Washington's healthier demographic profile will enable the United States to widen its lead over major European and Asian states across key indexes of national power. This power gap, he asserts, will cement and prolong American hegemony and "therefore decreases the probability that either hot or cold wars will develop between the United States and the other great powers."[79] While this conclusion is imminently plausible and reasonable, it vastly oversimplifies the complexities of international politics by focusing exclusively on what depopulation might mean for the United States. For example, no one could seriously argue today that conflict between Japan and United States is conceivable even in the absence of the demographic crisis gripping Tokyo. This study demonstrates that while global aging could dampen the potential for conflicts between the United States and other great powers, depopulation could also make other forms of great power interactions more destabilizing. The case of Japan shows that demographics could add tremendous volatility to alliance politics and trigger competitive great power dynamics at the regional level that could nevertheless have global reverberations.

As such, the security dilemmas arising from Japan's population decline can no longer be ignored. Indeed, Tokyo, Washington, and other capitals overlook this demographic dimension of international security at their peril. The population crisis for Japan is undoubtedly approaching, and this crunch will be accompanied by unprecedented strategic pressures. The anguishing decisions and choices to mitigate the security-related consequences of aging are already evident today and will only become more difficult to make as the strategy-resource mismatches worsen in the coming years. It thus behooves policymakers to devote their attention to this looming problem sooner rather than later and, more importantly, before it becomes unmanageable.

8

THE GEOPOLITICAL CONSEQUENCES OF CHINA'S DEMOGRAPHIC TURMOIL

Gordon G. Chang

The author gratefully acknowledges the invaluable assistance of Lydia Chang and Zhang Yifei. Certain material in this chapter has been reprinted with the permission of Forbes Media LLC © 2010.

"More people means more power. This is the truth."

—Fang Feng (online alias)

Why does China loom so large in the popular imagination? There are many reasons, but the most important of them is that it is the world's most populous nation, with perhaps as many as 1.5 billion people living within its borders.[1] The image of a fifth of humanity awes foreigners—and instills great pride in China's own people. "What is the real fulcrum of China's strength?" asked a popular Chinese website in 2009. "Population!"[2]

If "the true power of China's rise is a powerful reproductive force," as many of its citizens evidently believe, the country is in for a reversal of fortune.[3] Mao Zedong, the founder of the People's Republic, generally believed there should be as many Chinese in the world as possible. This pro-growth attitude meant that at one point, in the beginning of the 1970s, there were 5.9 births per female. The rate, of course, was unsustainable, and Beijing's technocrats adopted the mostly voluntary *wan, xi, shao*—"late, long, few"—program to limit population growth. They included population targets in a five-year plan for the first time when the fourth plan was introduced in 1970.

Beijing's efforts were effective, with the birthrate falling by half in less than a decade. Mao's successor, Deng Xiaoping, was not satisfied, however. He instituted the one-child policy in 1979 as one of his first initiatives after assuming power. During the existence of the coercive program, "probably the largest social experiment in human history,"[4] China's birthrate declined from 2.9 births per female to an estimated 1.54 in 2011,[5] a figure well below the replacement rate of 2.1.

Chinese leaders these days congratulate themselves for the success of this much-criticized policy, which they credit for preventing 400 million births.[6] Yet the program, which remains in effect, has inevitably created demographic abnormalities that cannot be remedied for decades. As Nicholas Eberstadt of the American Enterprise Institute writes, "These problems will compromise economic development, strain social harmony and place the traditional Chinese family structure under severe pressure; in fact, they could shake Chinese civilization to its very foundations."[7]

These foundation-shaking problems include the almost complete disappearance of aunts, uncles, and cousins. Moreover, in a society that places great importance on producing male heirs, parents have killed newborn girls to ensure that their only child is a boy, and prospective mothers and fathers have used sonograms and sex-selective abortions to weed out female fetuses. As a result of this "gendercide," China in the one-child era has produced the world's most abnormal sex ratios.[8]

The country's 2010 census showed that the sex ratio at birth, expressed as the number of boys per 100 girls, was 118[9]—whereas the global average was somewhere between 103 to 106. Some provinces have recently reported ratios exceeding 130. The ratio for second children is about 146. Spot checks in some areas reveal ratios as high as 156.[10]

The abnormal ratios are inevitably leading to strange demographic phenomena. There are 51.3 million more males than females.[11] This imbalance means many males cannot find wives, and the lack of women has resulted in, among other maladies, increased prostitution, elevated HIV-infection rates, and renewed trafficking in females. Gangs are abducting females in Russia, Mongolia, North Korea, Burma, and Vietnam and transporting them to China, where they are sold and resold to husbands in the "bachelor villages."

Can Beijing alleviate these problems by relaxing its population policy? After all, Chinese officials created strange demographic patterns, so they should also be able to remedy them. Moreover, a new direction would seem, at first glance, likely because the one-child policy is hated at home and condemned abroad.

Almost every Chinese demographer will say—at least in private—that the program does not make sense at this stage of the country's development.[12] It is not even being enforced in all locations. Not surprisingly, there have been efforts to ameliorate the worst aspects of the program and even experiments aimed to liberalize it. Beijing, for instance, sensibly eased the policy for families who had lost their only child in the Sichuan earthquake of May 2008.[13] Some even suggest a two-child policy is coming.[14]

Chinese officials believe the gender imbalance could take fifteen years to correct,[15] but that won't happen unless Beijing scraps its one-child policy. Unfortunately, the program looks like it is here to stay. First, the policy is administered by a large bureaucracy that has been tenaciously fighting to keep the status quo. Second, the population-planning apparatus is one of the Communist Party's most effective means of controlling people both in the countryside and the city. At a time when China has been plagued by increasing incidences of protest and other signs of social discontent, an increasingly repressive leadership is unlikely to surrender the power the policy provides.

Third, a reversal in long-held population programs, which have been strenuously defended, would inevitably call into question the Party's judgment—and therefore its legitimacy. No wonder penalties have grown tougher for violations of the one-child policy,[16] and officials have consistently reaffirmed their support for the population control measures.[17] Because Chinese officials are obviously determined to keep the one-child policy,[18] we need to think about its effects and long-term implications, especially the skewed sex ratio. As Eberstadt notes, "The country's gender balance has headed off in an eerie and utterly unfamiliar direction."[19] The absence of historical parallels has naturally given rise to interesting theories regarding China's future.

If we peer far enough ahead, the scenarios look mostly reassuring. A scarcity of women of childbearing age must, in the absence of unprecedented immigration, lead to rapid demographic decline. As China's population quickly shrinks—which it undoubtedly will by the fourth decade of this century—the nation's foreign policy should become less aggressive. After all, a quickly aging society usually tends to be a pacific one.[20]

Countries dominated by the elderly would not be inclined to pick fights and, even if they did, probably would not have the resources to engage in prolonged combat. If we want to see how falling population affects geopolitical ambition, perhaps Japan, with its narrowing horizons, is the best nation in Asia to watch. So far, the decline in population there seems to be shaking its confidence. As a result, a resurgence of Japanese aggression, which scarred Asia in the last century, is unlikely anytime soon.

China's population, however, will not start falling for at least another ten years, perhaps fifteen.[21] So how will the country's skewed gender ratios affect events in the interim? Security demographics may be a new field, but there is no lack of dire predictions.

Consequences of Abnormal Sex Ratios

One set of dire predictions comes from Valerie Hudson and Andrea den Boer in their much-discussed book, *Bare Branches: Security Implications of Asia's Surplus Male Population*. Hudson and den Boer suggest a link between the existence of large numbers of unmarriageable males—the so-called bare branches—and the adoption of risk-taking foreign policies. "The security logic of high-sex-ratio cultures predisposes nations to see some utility in interstate conflict," Hudson and den Boer argue.[22]

Why? As Christian Mesquida and Neil Wiener note, "controlling elites" sponsor military campaigns abroad so that the aggression of single males is directed at foreigners and not at themselves.[23]

Chinese demographers seem to agree with Hudson and den Boer. Bare branches, write Jiang Zhenghua and Mi Hong in *Population Security*, are a "huge humanitarian disaster."[24] Li Jianxin, writing in *The Structure of Chinese Population*, describes excess males as part of a set of "time-bomb factors."[25]

There is also evidence suggesting Beijing's current leaders in fact accept the bare-branches thesis.[26] In any event, they are keen students of Chinese history. As such, they surely know that one bare branch, Zhu Yuanzhang, founded the Ming dynasty and that the Ming house was eventually destroyed by another, Li Zicheng. The next emperors, the Qing rulers, were in part ruined by the consequences of sex-ratio imbalances. "China, it seems, is re-creating the vast army of bare branches that plagued it during the nineteenth century," write Hudson and den Boer.[27]

Hudson and den Boer also make the interesting argument that the existence of bare branches in a society impedes democratization: "High-sex-ratio societies are governable only by authoritarian regimes capable of suppressing violence at home."[28] Accordingly, they think the prospect for "full democracy" in China is "poor."[29] If one accepts the notion that free societies do not go to war with one another—the so-called democratic peace theory—then the deferral of the liberalization of the Chinese political system could ultimately have important geopolitical consequences.

Should we blame China's ills on its unmarriageable men? There actually may be some validity to the Hudson and den Boer thesis on democratization. Li Jianxin states that behind the mass-violence incidents of recent years are "shadows of surplus males," who will magnify the challenges of maintaining social stability in the future.[30]

The Chinese government, as it sought to quell this civil turmoil especially evident since the first decade of this century, has noticeably become more repressive. Consequently, in responding to increasing social disorder—most of it caused by males—Beijing has increased law enforcement efforts and repression, its typical reaction to disobedience of any kind. As a result, liberalization has been postponed yet again.

The part of the Hudson–den Boer thesis regarding the link between excess males and aggressive foreign policies is harder to establish. Single males may indeed be "testosterone-powered violence machines"[31]—a crude sexual stereotype that nonetheless appears accurate—but that does not necessarily mean a country with too many of them will embark on misadventure abroad. For one thing, bare branches can cause so much trouble at home that a country's leadership would become preoccupied maintaining internal stability. Civil turmoil, instead of external conflict, would appear to be the more likely consequence of extreme gender imbalance as tens of millions of bare branches travel the countryside and mill in the slums of great cities.

On the other hand, we know that at the same time that China has endured bare-branch violence, its foreign policies have become assertive and even hostile. Perhaps the most important cause of this new approach is the rise of the People's Liberation Army (PLA). In the last three decades of the twentieth century, the PLA had been losing power as fewer and fewer generals and admirals held posts in top Communist Party organs. This trend was reversed in the last decade. The current civilian leadership team, led by General Secretary Hu Jintao, appears to have been unnerved by the rising tide of unrest evident throughout China—unrest partly caused by the infamous bare branches. Due to bare-branch aggression and other factors, the Party's leaders, more than at any time since the Tiananmen massacre of 1989, rely on the troops of the PLA and the People's Armed Police to maintain order and keep themselves in power.

As a result, flag officers have recently gained influence, and they have not passed up the opportunity to exercise their strength. Unfortunately, they have been pushing the country's foreign policies in more aggressive directions, getting the leadership to finally abandon the long-honored "bide time and keep a low profile" philosophy of Deng Xiaoping. So there is something to the Hudson–den Boer thesis, even if the link between abnormal sex ratios and the country's external relations is attenuated.

Just because unusual sex ratios look like they are leading to more assertive foreign policies today does not necessarily mean they will do so tomorrow. Tomorrow, these sex ratios might even push Chinese foreign policy in the other direction. One consequence of the one-child policy may be attitudinal changes in Chinese society that make the use of force less—not more—likely.

What prevents great nations from going to war in these modern times? The most important factor is the increasing intolerance of casualties.[32] In preindustrial societies, the sorrow over the loss of a son in battle was tempered by the knowledge that a family usually had many more of them.

In a one-child nation, however, a son's death in combat means the extinction of the family line. That, for many parents in a society attaching great importance to continuing bloodlines, would be completely unacceptable. China's "little emperors" may or may not be selfish, spoiled, and self-indulgent—and therefore not likely to sacrifice themselves for the nation[33]—but Chinese parents are surely more protective of the lives of their only sons than their counterparts in the Maoist era.

But would autocratic Chinese leaders care what parents thought of military adventures abroad? Even nominally top-down political systems like China's must be responsive to public opinion—and China's may be more sensitive to popular attitudes than most democracies due to the extreme insecurity of Beijing's leaders. Consequently, mass-casualty wars started by China could easily become a thing of the past. The country is unlikely to become as "debellicized" as Western Europe in the next, say, two decades, but in China's demographic profile we can, even today, see the beginnings of the trend toward "warlessness."[34]

Of course, we can only speculate as to the psyches of Chinese leaders. Yet we can say the relentlessly enforced one-child policy has created some of the most unusual demographic patterns ever recorded in the absence of war and pestilence, and so the policy has the potential for affecting the country's external policies in dramatic ways. This means, at a minimum, Hudson and den Boer are right to suggest that bare branches can sway the governments of mighty nations. At this point, however, we do not know exactly how.

Population Pressure on Borders

Of course, gender imbalance is not the only demographic factor that can affect Beijing's external relations. For fifteen or so years, China's population will continue to grow. Its billion-and-a-half people will crowd into a land increasingly unable to support them. The fear in Asia, as one former Japanese prime minister said recently, is that Beijing is seeking *Lebensraum*.[35]

Whether or not that is true, China needs all the land it can acquire. It may be the fourth biggest nation in terms of geographical size,[36] yet the continent-like country lacks fields suitable for crops. It possesses about 20 percent of the planet's population, but only seven percent of its arable land. Yet that is not the end of the story. China is losing thousands of square miles of arable land annually to pollution, desertification, and breakneck development.

In short, China's good earth cannot support its still-expanding population. This shortfall would not create a geopolitical problem if Beijing were content to rely on international markets to buy food. Yet it is not. And because of official insistence that the country be self-sufficient in foodstuffs, central government technocrats are now developing plans sure to increase tensions with other states.

Chinese authorities, for instance, are encouraging state enterprises to buy or lease agricultural land. So far, Beijing has largely focused its acquisition efforts on Africa, but for various reasons agriculture on that continent is uneconomic for China. Beijing is also establishing farms in Southeast Asia, where the flood of Chinese workers and migrants—especially in Laos, Cambodia, Burma, and Vietnam—is creating friction. Friction is also evident along China's western boundaries, particularly in Kazakhstan.

In December 2009 Kazakhstan's president Nursultan Nazarbayev announced that Beijing had expressed an interest in leasing one million hectares in his country for farming soy and rapeseed. The proposed deal triggered a rare protest there because people, in the words of the country's first ambassador to Beijing, were worried about the "Chinese colonization of Kazakhstan."[37]

China inflames passions because its citizens have already poured into Kazakhstan in large numbers. There could be as many as half a million legal and illegal Chinese immigrants in the country, and the flow of undocumented workers from China is considered by some Kazakhs to be "the biggest threat" to their homeland.[38] Surprisingly, many Chinese have ended up near Kazakhstan's boundary with Russia. This curious phenomenon is the result of Astana's policy to make sure the Chinese remain far away from the China border.[39] Kazakh officials fear Beijing might one day try to annex border areas with Chinese populations, and the concern is shared by leaders of the other post-Soviet states. Chinese residents are forming fast-expanding Chinatowns across the region, creating potential conflict with local populations. Kyrgyzstan is already scarred by anti-China sentiments, friction, and violence.[40] Because Beijing is now more willing—and certainly more able—to defend its citizens wherever they may live, none of the Central Asian republics wants to give China's army a pretext to march west.

To its credit, Beijing has worked with authorities in the region to persuade Chinese migrants to settle away from areas boarding China. Beijing has no grand territorial ambitions in Central Asia, and its playbook there appears to be similar to the one it uses for the islands in the Pacific Ocean: gain influence through the presence of Chinese citizens. Although China has been trying to maintain friendly relations, the sheer size of its outbound migration causes concern. Its plan to lease or buy agricultural land is bound, therefore, to cause troubles in the post-Soviet states.

At the moment, troubles are most evident in the most important post-Soviet state. Beijing is already leasing land for farming in the Russian Federation, the largest of the fourteen nations sharing a land border with China. Russia's Far East, a continent-size area from Lake Baikal to the Pacific Ocean, is home to about 6.3 million people, and it is depopulating faster than other parts of the rapidly shrinking nation. Projections show that the number of people there will fall to 4.5 million by 2015.

Meanwhile, on the portion of the China-Russia border east of Mongolia, there are three Chinese provinces—Heilongjiang, Jilin, and Inner Mongolia. Together, they are home to about 90.5 million souls. Some of them, the ambitious and the restless, have left overcrowded villages and headed to Russia, especially since 1991, when Moscow began to welcome tourism from China and when the Russian government's influence in the region weakened. Now nobody knows how many Chinese citizens live in the Russian Far East because many of them have overstayed their visas, but there could be as many as five hundred thousand.[41]

So far, the problem is manageable from Moscow's point of view. The Chinese, legal or otherwise, make the economy in the Far East hum. They trade goods in open-air markets, farm the soil, try to stay out of trouble, marry Russian women, and work hard. And, despite deep-seated xenophobia—Russians refer to the "yellow peril" when they forget to use the more polite "Sinification"— there is no evidence that Beijing has a master plan to settle the Russian Far East with Chinese settlers in preparation of annexation.

But Beijing does not need a plan to do that. All it needs to do is to let ongoing migration take its course now, watch assimilation fail, and stoke nationalism later.[42] And Moscow can see this coming. One Russian military officer expressed the Kremlin's fears: "We see the overpopulation of the neighboring nation. They will come here, give birth to multitudes of slit-eyed people and then claim political autonomy."[43]

Would Chinese migrants in the Russian Far East seek Beijing's protection? Some of them in fact see themselves as settlers laying the groundwork for China's eventual claims.[44] In any event, the Chinese migrants are clannish, as most recent immigrants tend to be, and Moscow has done nothing to integrate them into Russian society. It would not be hard to imagine Beijing coming to their aid—whether they wanted it or not—in the aftermath of a racially charged event. A diplomatic incident over the treatment of Chinese citizens living in the Russian Far East is not just probable—it is virtually inevitable, given the potential for friction there.

Moreover, it does not help that the irredentist leaders of the People's Republic have often grumbled about "lost territory," which includes land now under the Kremlin's control. Portions of what the Russians call their Far East, including the port of Vladivostok, were in fact once ruled by Qing emperors. The then-tottering Qing dynasty ceded the area to Russia in two "unequal treaties"—the Chinese term for the agreements—in 1858 and 1860. Since then, Beijing and Moscow have exchanged harsh words, and sometimes even gunfire, over their common border, the fifth longest in the world at almost 2,700 miles. Yet in a series of recent agreements, the last signed in July 2008, the two sides have finally delineated the line separating their territories.

The Russians and the Chinese know from their common experience, however, that no border is ever really final, especially one between peoples who were adversaries in the past and competitors today. Illegal Chinese migration, propelled by demographic pressure, is changing the facts on the ground fast. If there is one reason for the two giants to quarrel in the future, it is this continuous flow of Chinese citizens into Russia's territory.

Moscow's response to Chinese immigration has to been to fortify its military in the region and urge ethnic Russians to resettle in the Far East. Moreover, it has begun to offer financial incentives for births across the country. None of these measures looks like it will have much of an effect. The Russians have what the Chinese need—land and a market for inexpensive items—so the economic imperative will ensure migration continues indefinitely. And as it does, the Russians are bound to become even more insecure in their own homeland.

The Russians are by no means the only ones wary of the presence of Chinese immigrants. The Mongolians, for instance, have an even greater fear of them. There are about ninety thousand Chinese citizens in Mongolia—including ten thousand illegals—constituting perhaps as much as 9 percent of the country's total workforce.[45] Whatever the number, the Mongolians are worried about their presence.

Mongolians are worried about China because their landlocked nation, nestled between the giant Russian and Chinese states, is sparsely populated, just 5.2 people for each square mile. China, on the other hand, has a population density 70 times greater—and a population 428 times larger.

Moscow no longer defends Mongolia, as it did during most of the twentieth century, and in many ways the Mongolian state exists at the mercy of Beijing. As one American consultant living in the capital of Ulan Bator remarked, "China could overrun this country in two days."[46]

In a sense, the Chinese already have. They dominate the sectors open to foreign businesses, for instance. They would account for an even bigger slice where it not for Mongolian restrictions on foreign investment, which were put in place largely to prevent China's money taking over the country.[47] The Chinese are, in a word, feared. Beijing does little to disguise its desire to absorb Mongolia, which in China is often called Outer Mongolia. That term is in contrast with Inner Mongolia, one of the thirty-three provinces and provincial-level areas making up the People's Republic. Beijing calls the area an Autonomous Region, but that term is an Orwellian misnomer. Mongolians can see that the Han, China's dominant ethnic group, are bent on assimilating the Mongolians in Inner Mongolia, and worry about Beijing's designs on their independent—for the moment—nation.

Mongolia declared independence from China when the Qing dynasty fell at the end of 1911. The Chinese reclaimed the country in 1919, but the Mongolians eventually prevailed, forming their present state in 1921. Beijing today recognizes Mongolia as a separate nation, but Deng Xiaoping mentioned taking it back after recovering Taiwan and Hong Kong. The Han today claim that Genghis Khan, Mongolia's national hero, was really "Chinese." That expansive belief—the proposition that anyone who ever conquered China was "Chinese"—is the historical justification for the re-annexation of Mongolia. To China's inhabitants, the grand project of uniting with (absorbing) Mongolia makes sense because, in addition to other reasons, they need Mongolia's land.

Demographic pressure, therefore, looks like the motor for China's problems with nations on its northern and western borders and could cause friction in the south. But what about the east? Beijing wants Taiwan, the island that China claims as its thirty-fourth province but which more resembles an independent state. Beijing has tried a range of tactics to absorb the island into the People's Republic, but it has recently settled on simultaneously threatening force and offering economic blandishments.

With regard to the blandishments, Beijing is trying to foster integration by employing population tactics, encouraging people from Taiwan to live in China and Chinese to live on the island. At present, there may be as many as a million Taiwan citizens working on "the Mainland" but only 270,000 Chinese citizens—virtually all of them brides—in Taiwan.[48]

Taipei's restrictive immigration laws mean that Beijing cannot flood the Republic of China (as the island formally calls itself) with Han settlers as it has done in other areas it considers its own, especially restive Tibet and Xinjiang. Therefore, it is no surprise that Beijing pushed hard for the inclusion in the Economic Cooperation Framework Agreement, a bilateral trade and investment deal inked in June 2010, of provisions authorizing Taiwan visas for its investors. Many Taiwanese contend these new visa rules, one of which potentially allows unlimited immigration from China,[49] will result in their island becoming just another Chinese colony. Beijing's tactics are subtle and may backfire, but Chinese officials evidently believe the country's population is a weapon to be used against smaller societies.

Future Geopolitical Consequences of Population Trends

Just about everyone at the moment says we are living in "China's century." If that country does not yet own this epoch, most assume it will do so soon. The periods of European and American ascendancy, we are told, look like nothing more than minor interruptions in the natural state of Chinese domination of world affairs. Even today, Eliot Cohen of Johns Hopkins calls China "the most important power in the world."[50]

Whether or not that assessment is correct, the Chinese evidently believe they are century-owners and that now is the time for them to get what they want. Among other things, the Chinese want territory now under the control of others[51] and exclusion of foreigners from neighboring seas.[52] They are seeking "to change the rules of the game," according to a recent comment by a Chinese foreign policy specialist,[53] and "to become world number one, the top power," as one senior colonel wrote in late 2009.[54]

Yes, the country has grand ambitions, but its demographic problems ultimately undermine them. Is demography destiny? It surely does not determine everything, but population trends define the realm of the possible and are generally unforgiving.[55] Policy mistakes, once they scar a country's demographic profile, can take generations to correct. That is a problem for China because its government has, through unusual population programs, become committed to a course with few good outcomes.

Outcomes look unfavorable in part because the People's Republic has relentlessly pursued two contradictory policies. Mao's speedup and Deng's slowdown of births in the past mean Chinese population swings today are both large and occurring rapidly. Their effects, consequently, could be wrenching.

For one thing, these diametrically opposed policies have created a bulge of older Chinese, who either have left or are now leaving the workforce. The country, in short, is about to be hit by an "age wave." In 2009 the number of "aged"—those sixty and older—soared by 7.25 million to 167.14 million. The group's share of total population that year jumped a half percentage point to 12.5 percent, the biggest annual increase in history.[56] This age cohort will more than double by 2030.[57] The aging of China will happen much faster than demographers expected just a few years ago.

As the Chinese age, China's workforce shrinks. The country has been short of labor since 2004,[58] and the number of people in the workforce will level off soon. Demographer Wang Guangzhou thinks that will happen in 2013, and Cai Fang believes China will reach its peak in 2015.[59] The National Population and Family Planning Commission estimates the date to be 2016, when the workforce—defined as those fifteen to sixty-four[60]—will number 1.01 billion people.[61]

In any event, this group will shrink rapidly. The working-age population will fall from about 995.8 million people in 2015 to 789.0 million in 2050 according to UN statistics. The proportion of working-age Chinese has already peaked at 72 percent in 2010 and is in seemingly irreversible decline.[62]

The start of that decline marks the end of China's "demographic dividend," a bulge in the percentage of the population in the workforce. The country's dependency ratio—the ratio of children and the elderly to the working-age population—started moving in the wrong direction in 2010, a reversal of a positive trend beginning in 1968.[63] The demographic dividend has now become the "demographic tax." Cai thinks the ending of the dividend is the greatest threat to China's economic growth,[64] and the prominent demographer may be right. The dividend, for one thing, helps explain how China's share of the global economy could grow so rapidly while its percentage of global population shrank.[65]

Changes in the country's workforce are already shaking the economy. For instance, a tight labor supply in the crucial export sector led to a rash of strikes that began at a Honda plant in Guangdong Province in May 2010. Unrest then raced up the coast to the Yangtze River delta and Tianjin and to inland Chongqing, as well as other locations. The work stoppages were eventually settled with large wage increases, and those increases led manufacturers to begin shifting production to lower-cost countries.

China's shedding of low-value manufacturing could be a positive development, but the problem is that the country could lose bottom-rung jobs faster than it can replace them with better-paying ones. Moreover, its export manufacturing sector could shrivel long before it develops consumer-based growth. In any event, we are witnessing a tumultuous transformation of the Chinese economy triggered in large part by demographic factors. When American futurologist George Gilder told us "the single greatest untapped resource in the world economy is the Chinese people," he was absolutely right.[66] But he wrote those words in 1989, and today that statement is no longer true.

Today, China has to think about the cost of providing for its elderly, many of whom are not covered by pensions. The expense must rise as the ranks of the old increase and as the responsibility for their care shifts from families to the government. While these trends continue and as both the number of workers and their percentage in the population decrease, the burden on the rest of society gets heavier.

Demographers these days talk of China's "inverted pyramid." Due to the one-child policy, one worker may end up supporting two parents and four grandparents. Other nations face similar problems, but many of them, such as Japan, are well off. Japan is the world's most aged society, but in a generation China will be older than Japan.[67] In 2009 China's per capita gross domestic product was only a fifth of Japan's.[68] The Chinese call it the "aging before affluence" phenomenon.

There will, of course, be factors other than demography that will ultimately determine China's economic performance, but now the economy will have to overcome population factors instead of being aided by them. In general, a shrinking workforce and shrinking population will, in all probability, mean shrinking economic output, which in turn will mean fewer resources. And fewer resources will lead, inevitably, to smaller budgets for the People's Liberation Army and other instruments of state power. "One of the most stunning demographic transformations in its history"[69] will eventually result in the diminution of Beijing's ability to influence events abroad.

Demography, once China's best friend, will soon become a foe. Of course, there is no straight-line relationship between changes in a nation's population and changes in its power. If, for instance, the United States can attain the status of sole superpower with less than 5 percent of the planet's people, China should be able to do so with a population five times larger. But if "babies win wars,"[70] as the Chinese evidently believe, then the paucity of newborns creates strategic concerns for policymakers in Beijing. In a one-child society, who will fill the ranks of China's soldiers, sailors, and pilots? The pool of potential recruits will, over the course of decades, fall fast.

There are, however, several mitigating factors in the interim. First, the People's Liberation Army has begun to attract university graduates because there are so few opportunities available for them in other fields. These days, the highly educated in China are accepting positions as, among other things, domestic servants, nannies, and collectors of "night soil"—at one point in 2010, more than eleven hundred university graduates applied for eight jobs gathering excrement in prosperous Wenzhou, in Zhejiang Province.[71]

In these circumstances, who would not want to serve as a second lieutenant? In 2009, 130,000 college graduates joined the PLA. That was more than three times the number in the preceding year and sixty-five times more than in 2001. Increases in educational levels should help China's armed forces eventually deliver a more destructive punch, even if their numbers are smaller.

Second, fertility rates in Asia are also low for strategic competitors like Russia and Japan, which have their own "depopulation bombs" to worry about. Moreover, many of the countries more fertile than China are small. Vietnam, Laos, Burma, Bhutan, and Nepal all have higher fertility than China, but all are too far behind to ever catch up to the Chinese, no matter how fast they grow.

That's not true of India, however. Because the Chinese are obviously obsessed by population and believe the Americans are in terminal decline, they see the Indians as their long-term competitors. Whether or not they are right about the United States, they have good reason to be concerned about India. In perhaps as few as ten years[72] the Indians—not the Chinese—will be living in the world's most populous nation. Not only will China lose the population crown, which it has held for centuries, but it will also have to hand it over to the rival it fears most. UN demographers believe India's population will peak about thirty-five years after China's does, at which time there will be over 500 million more Indians than Chinese.[73] The economic impact of India's population increase will undoubtedly be enormous: some Chinese demographic analysts believe that in about two decades, that country will have twice the number of workers as China.[74] "What are the factors that can propel India past China?" asks Xue Yong, a Chinese academic. "Number one is demography."[75]

China's relegation to second place will be traumatic for a people who think the inevitability of their hegemony is due to the heft of their numbers. Because Beijing is full of population determinists,[76] China's unenviable demographic trends are creating a mood of long-term pessimism. Li Jianxin, for one, believes that, for demographic reasons, China will be overtaken by "our biggest competitor, India,"[77] which might end up dominating the middle of this century.[78]

Beijing, not surprisingly, has been connecting the dots between China's impending demographic decline and India's continuing population rise. And because the Chinese are over-the-horizon strategic thinkers, some in Beijing evidently feel that they have only a limited window to prevail over New Delhi. "When you see a country's population decline, the country will definitely degrade into a second-rate one," notes Yao Yang, vice director of Peking University's China Center for Economic Research.[79]

It cannot be a coincidence that, as the Chinese started to focus on unfavorable demographic trends in the last few years, Beijing's strategists began to talk about India as a threat and urged China's military to teach New Delhi a "lesson" that would last a half century.[80] Will China strike while it still has the population advantage?

The signs do not look good. At the moment, Chinese and Indian troops are skirmishing high in the Himalayas. Neither side, however, will admit what is happening across their disputed border in Arunachal Pradesh, Aksai Chin, and Ladakh. New Delhi and Beijing hold round after round of border talks, but the two sides are no closer to settling disputes that led them to war in 1962.

The number of incursions by China's troops into Indian-controlled territory appears to be on the rise. The Chinese are thinking of military solutions because, among other reasons, they are worried that the Indians will use their superior numbers to bolster their claims. Beijing, for instance, is complaining that New Delhi is flooding disputed territory in Arunachal Pradesh with migrants to strengthen its hold on the area.[81] Apparently, unfavorable demographic trends weigh heavily on the minds of Chinese leaders.

Indians still refer to former prime minister Nehru's "*Hindi-Chini bhai-bhai*" slogan, promoting the notion that the two Asian nations are brothers. Beijing, if it sees itself as a sibling, has been more like Cain than Abel. The Chinese, for instance, are now supporting Islamabad's campaign of terror against the Indian nation.[82] In August 2009 Zhan Lue, a Chinese strategist connected to the Ministry of National Defense, even suggested that Beijing try to break up India into as many as thirty states. The article, widely circulated in Chinese policy circles, appears to represent increasingly hard-line views in that country.

Some Indians are noticing China's hostility. Bharat Verma, the editor of India's leading defense journal, predicted that China will attack India before 2012.[83] Whether or not the Chinese decide to teach the Indians "the final lesson," as Verma puts it, the People's Liberation Army is reinforcing its border garrisons and building infrastructure so that it can maintain sustained operations against India.

Moreover, Beijing looks like it is rehearsing for war. Just three days after the thirteenth round of border talks with New Delhi ended in failure in August 2009, the Chinese started Stride-2009, their "largest-ever tactical military exercise."[84] Designed to improve the country's long-range force projection, the two-month massive war game involved sending troops to bordering Tibet. In 1962 China had surprised India with its ability to fight in hostile terrain far from its bases. Now, the Chinese are quickly improving their ability to do so. In short, Beijing is ramping up the pressure on India at a time when the Indians would prefer to work out an accommodation. If anything, recent Chinese tactics betray a sense that there is a limited time in which to act. Unfortunately, Beijing apparently sees India through the lens of demography.

Perhaps that is the correct assessment for a China that will surely be surpassed by its most feared strategic rival. After all, Chinese leaders, recognizing reality, have decided not to compete with India on population size. They may run an authoritarian state, but they know they cannot command their people to out-procreate a society at an earlier stage of development.[85] As Peking University's Yao Yang, fearing India's growing strength notes, "Demography is one thing you cannot change."[86]

Is This China's Century?

The onset of adverse demographic trends is occurring at one of the worst possible moments for a China set on realizing centuries-old ambitions. As its geopolitical horizons expand, its population is peaking. Worse, favorable population trends are not only reversing—they are reversing fast. China may not be the next Japan, but it is apparent that the Chinese are traveling down the same road. That's a serious concern for the leaders of the People's Republic, who have always believed population and power go hand-in-hand.

So what effect will the country's fast-moving demographic changes have on strategic thinking in Beijing? The current crop of senior Chinese leaders have not publicly linked population trends to their foreign policies, but their focus on "comprehensive national power" indicates that they consider adverse demography to be a critical factor.

As technocrats, they know their position in the international system ultimately rests on the strength of their economy. Their economy, they know, has been largely propelled by the dividends of extraordinary population growth. And as they peer into the years ahead, they realize they must overcome the effects of accelerating demographic decline. If that arc does not create a sense of urgency, then at least it suggests to officials that they may have a short window of time in which to achieve their goals, as the uptick in Chinese hostility to India seems to reveal. And, as China's officials see it, there is much for them to do before they must accept the limits imposed by a smaller, graying society.

There are also limits imposed by a more peaceful populace. Even authoritarians—and maybe they in particular—must be sensitive to public attitudes. Eventually China will become benign as its population ages. But before the country enters an era of Japanese-like tranquillity, other nations must endure the current period of turbulence.

Although we cannot draw straight-line links between the now-famous "bare branches" and unusually assertive foreign policies, almost every analyst notes that Beijing's policymakers are constrained by the inflamed opinions held by young Chinese—most of them males—especially on matters relating to the United States and Japan. Demography, of course, does not dictate policy, but it influences it nonetheless.

From day to day, population trends may not have a discernible effect on China's external relations. In a land of a billion people and a "million truths," perhaps no one factor can stand out as determinative of any particular decision or event. Yet demography, one way or another, sets the course for an especially troubled society.

Beijing's supremos at this moment know they are playing a bad hand. Population trends are, after all, a "relentless maker and breaker of civilizations."[87] As Li Jianxin, the demographer, writes, "Population is the most basic driving force of a country, of a society, of a people, and of a civilization."[88] Because that is correct, this century will not be kind to the Chinese.

9

INDIA'S DEMOGRAPHIC TRENDS AND IMPLICATIONS FOR THE ASIAN STRATEGIC LANDSCAPE

Lisa Curtis

The author would like to extend special thanks to Nicholas Hamise-vicz, formerly research associate in the Asian Studies Center at the Heritage Foundation, for his assistance in conducting research for this article. Mr. Hamisevicz is currently the Director of Research and Academic Affairs at the Korea Economic Institute.

For most of the country's history, Indians viewed their burgeoning population as a disadvantage for future development prospects and in maintaining social and political stability. Several years of strong economic growth, a robust military modernization campaign, and growing recognition of India's emerging global status is changing perceptions about current demographic trends. With a population of around 1.2 billion, India is now the second most populous nation in the world, and poised to surpass China to take the number-one spot sometime around 2025. With half its population under the age of twenty-five, India will add about 11 million workers each year to its workforce over the next decade.

India is potentially facing what Harvard demographer David Bloom called a "demographic dividend"—when a country's working-age population grows and the number of dependents lessens, resulting in increased savings and capital creation. Indeed, a recent study from Goldman Sachs says India could potentially add four percentage points per year to its GDP growth rate, so long as it overturns outdated labor laws, brings more women into the workforce, and invests more in training and education.[1] However, these are major hurdles for India, and would require the government and private sector to begin planning now for the surge in workforce numbers. Fortunately, there are signs India is beginning to grasp the challenges that lie ahead in dealing with its youth bulge and to recognize that swelling numbers of working-age men and women do not automatically translate into economic success.

This chapter seeks to address the impact of India's demographic trends on its desire and ability to project power beyond its immediate borders. Will India's youth bulge mean the government is more consumed with managing internal challenges, like increasing urbanization and growing Naxalism in the rural areas?[2] Or will a more robust working-age population enable India to grow its GDP at increasingly higher levels, thus providing the means for military modernization programs and the confidence to project power abroad? As Nandan Nilekani, author of *Imagining India*, describes it:

> A billion people may offer us a deep base of human capital, but it also signals a potentially massive, detrimental burden on our environment, food production and resources, as millions of people join the middle class, ramp up their consumption, and per capita energy intake grows.[3]

This chapter argues that while India's demographic trends will bring new internal challenges, they will also create economic and manpower benefits that will facilitate India's rise as both a regional and global power. India will be forced to spend increasing amounts of energy and resources on dealing with internal issues, such as the Naxalite-Maoist problem and increasing urbanization. Yet these challenges are unlikely to sap its ability to continue its military modernization programs and enhance its strategic role in the world. Overall, India's youthful population will likely serve as an asset in fulfilling its geopolitical ambitions and contribute to its ability to project power beyond the Indian periphery and into the broader Asia-Pacific region.

Brief History of Indian Population Policies

India's first prime minister, Jawaharlal Nehru, emphasized that family planning was essential to the social economy, family happiness, and national planning.[4] Each of India's early five-year plans emphasized population policy, and a population policy committee was constituted in April 1952 inside the Planning Commission. This committee focused on advocating family planning policies and instituting public health programs. The third five-year plan, announced in 1961, stated that "the objective of stabilizing population . . . must be at the center of planned development."[5] Despite these efforts, population growth rose substantially in the 1950s and grew at an average annual rate of about 2.5 percent during the 1960s, frustrating Indian planners.

In the mid-1970s, Prime Minister Indira Gandhi favored taking drastic steps to reduce population growth rates and instituted forced sterilization campaigns that caused widespread anger.[6] During the period of Emergency Rule from 1975 to 1977, sterilizations reportedly rose from 1.35 million to 8.06 million. By contrast, in 1978, after the elections that overturned Gandhi's rule and brought the Janata Party to power, sterilizations dropped to under 1 million.[7] The new government announced a revised population policy that replaced the phrase family "planning" with family "welfare." Family planning was now viewed as a completely voluntary concept and part of a comprehensive policy focused on education as well as child and maternal health.

Population policies in the 1980s and 1990s focused on reducing child mortality and improving maternal health, but it was not until 2000 that a National Population Policy (NPP) was approved by the Cabinet. The NPP acknowledged that "the overriding objective of economic and social development is to improve the quality of lives that people lead . . . and to provide them with opportunities and choices to become productive assets of society." It asserted that stabilization of the population was essential for promoting sustainable development and set the goal of achieving replacement-level fertility of 2.1 children per woman nationally by the year 2010.[8]

The government's focus on improving female social and economic welfare, along with rising living standards and increased literacy, has led to falling population growth rates. Indian population growth has slowed from nearly 2.5 percent in the 1970s to about 1.6 percent today. The rate has reportedly fallen even further—to between 1–1.5 percent—in some southern and western parts of India. India's 2011 census data revealed significant decreases in the population growth rates of the six most populous states in India, although differences in the growth rates between poorer northern states and more economically advanced southern and western states persist. Most striking are differences in the age structure among the various states, due in part to the varied timing of the onset of demographic transition.[9]

India has followed the typical demographic transition profile of most developing nations by initially experiencing high birthrates and death rates, then moving to a period of high birthrates and low death rates—leading to high rates of population growth—and finally to experiencing both low birth and death rates. The fertility rate in India has come down from more than 6 children per woman in the 1960s to 2.7 today, but is still well above the 2.1 goal set in the National Population Policy.

Challenges of the Youth Wave

To achieve the "demographic dividend" of higher savings, investment, and GDP growth rates from the surge in numbers of the working-age population, India must cope with a number of socioeconomic challenges that are being exacerbated by the same demographic indicators. These challenges may require Indian policymakers to make difficult resource-allocation decisions between maintaining internal security and projecting power beyond India's periphery. The more attention Indian officials pay now to coming up with solutions that address these socioeconomic challenges, the better poised India will be in the future to ensure its growing working-age population will translate into more leverage and influence on the international stage and within the Asian power balance.

EDUCATION

An improved education system in India is crucial both to controlling population and to ensuring that the tens of millions of young Indians approaching working age will be productively employed. If these waves of Indian youth are educated adequately, they can be trained for productive employment. If, on the other hand, they are unprepared to enter the workforce, they are likely to contribute to social tensions and become a drag on the economy, rather than part of the expected economic "dividend."[10] Although India produces the second largest number of engineers in the world every year, a quarter of the population is still illiterate.

Regional divisions and diverse languages made the idea of a single, common education system impossible for India in its early years. Education was designated a state subject and the central government was given only a very limited role in setting standards and regulations.[11] Throughout the 1960s and 1970s the government's focus with regard to education was primarily on building up infrastructure for schools, not on teacher training and performance measurement. Although some states in the south—such as Tamil Nadu and Kerala—emphasized schooling for the poor, many other states—like Bihar, Rajasthan, and Uttar Pradesh—failed to move in this direction, primarily because of feudal politics.

In 2009 India passed legislation that mandated free public education for all citizens. While this was a step in the right direction, the government will have to follow it up with concrete moves to incentivize education, particularly for the rural poor. The education bill includes provisions for free and compulsory education for all children ages six through fourteen; construction of schools in all communities within three years; outlawing discrimination against the disadvantaged; private schools to reserve 25 percent of their slots for the disadvantaged; and a standardized national curriculum.[12]

Many in India believe the best policy the government can pursue to encourage basic education is to simply get out of the way and allow the private sector to meet increased demand. Already about 50 percent of primary students are educated at private institutions. Since the public education system has failed to meet the demands of the poor, they have increasingly turned to cheap private schools. Some of the poorest families in India are setting aside as much as one-fourth of their income for their children's education.[13] The idea of school vouchers—government funding students rather than schools—also is gaining steam. Many argue that when a student determines where public funding goes, it brings more competition and thus better education.[14]

Another innovative and promising project is the Indian corporate sector's work with the government to help create a skilled workforce by setting up a public-private initiative, the National Skills Development Corporation. The objective of this program is to catalyze the creation of more for-profit vocational training institutes.[15]

AGRICULTURE SECTOR AND LABOR FLEXIBILITY

What transpires in India's agriculture sector and the degree to which labor can easily move from agriculture to other more productive sectors of the economy will largely determine whether Indian demographic trends will be a boost or a drag on India's ability to project power in the region. Whereas 60 percent of India's current workforce is in the agriculture sector, this sector only produces about 17 percent of the GDP. The services sector, on the other hand, makes up one-third of the workforce but accounts for more than half of India's GDP. The vast majority of Indian farmers are small landowners who own between one and five acres of land. They have no skills or education that can be used in the urban marketplace and often end up in city slums or as migrant laborers when they are forced off their land.[16] There are already an estimated 60 million redundant agriculture workers.

Thus there is a strong need for more labor flexibility that will lead to greater employment in manufacturing. India's manufacturing sector grew by 7 percent annually for sixteen years but then slowed to 2.4 percent in 2008–2009, in part because of the global economic downturn. But as Jayant Davar, president of Automotive Component Manufacturers Association of India, recently put it, "We can't be a capitalist country that has socialist labor laws." Indian manufacturers currently must adhere to the Industrial Disputes Act of 1947, which requires companies with more than one hundred employees to gain government permission before dismissing workers, and the Contract Labour Act of 1970, which prohibits employers from using temporary workers for long-term jobs.[17] Relaxing labor laws would create efficiencies that will ultimately allow companies to hire more workers and attract more manufacturers to India, thus raising wages.

The debate over labor reform in India is fierce. There are those who argue for reforms to reflect new economic realities, and those who are unwilling to let go of protections that they believe cushioned them from the worst economic downturns in the 1960s and 1970s.[18] Labor unions are extremely powerful in India and an entrenched part of the political landscape. India's labor laws were formed around periods of economic slowdown, and may have helped provide an important social cushion, but they are now outdated and constitute one of the biggest drags on Indian economic growth prospects.

URBANIZATION

Three out of ten of the world's largest cities are in India. India has seven cities with populations over 4 million, and thirty-five cities with populations over 1 million. By 2050, 55 percent of India is expected to be urbanized, compared to 30 percent today. Mumbai is projected to be the most populous city in the world by 2020, with a forecasted population of 28.5 million.

Managing the influx of urban residents will be one of India's greatest challenges over the coming decade. Sprawling, impoverished cities are more vulnerable to gang activity and crime and provide recruits for internationally connected terrorist organizations. Seventy-five percent of India's urban population earns under $2 per day.

To cope with the challenges of increased urbanization and rapidly growing cities, India must prioritize municipal planning and strong local governance to unburden city planners from state-level bureaucracy. Historically, India has recognized mainly the governing authority of the center and the state (the central government collects income and excise tax while the state governments collect sales tax, stamp duty, and excise tax on alcohol), without devolving much power to municipal authorities. City-level decision-making is subject to state-level bureaucracy, and municipal expenditures are only a small fraction of the state's GDP.[19]

According to a recent McKinsey Global Institute study, if India handles urban expansion effectively, it could add as much as 1.5 percent to GDP growth. But if India fails to invest in managing the challenges of urbanization, investors will be deterred and growth will lag, risking high unemployment. As cities expand, demand for services is set to increase seven-fold by 2025. Yet Indian cities could also face a severe gap in affordable housing and tremendous deficiencies in infrastructure, including in sanitation management and sewage facilities.[20] The majority of India's urban population is already living in substandard sanitary conditions, and slums account for a quarter of all urban housing. In Mumbai alone, more than half the people live in slums. According to the McKinsey report, India has grossly underinvested in its cities. While India spends $17 per capita on capital investments in urban infrastructure annually, China spends $116, or almost seven times as much. To fund urban infrastructure, many argue that Indian city planners should develop ways of generating money internally that are in turn backed by the central government.

NAXALITE-MAOIST PROBLEM

Demographic trends in India could exacerbate the Naxalite-Maoist problem, which would force India to expend an increasing amount of security resources to contain the insurgency, and possibly even deploy regular army units to the insurgency-affected areas. India has fought insurgency in the state of Jammu and Kashmir for several years and still has around 400,000 army and paramilitary forces stationed in the region. More recently, however, Indian government officials have acknowledged that the primary internal security threat for India is rising Naxalism, particularly in the eastern and central states of West Bengal, Bihar, Jharkhand, Chhattisgarh, Madhya Pradesh, and Orissa—the so-called Red Corridor.

The main factors in the original outbreak of the Naxalite insurgency in the late 1960s were unemployment and lack of access to land. Continuing their claim of fighting on behalf of the landless poor, Naxalites have increased their activity over the last decade, thriving in areas where economic growth has lagged and good governance is lacking. In 2006, for the first time, attacks from Naxalites outstripped those by Kashmiri militants.[21] Naxalites launched their deadliest attack yet in April 2010 in the state of Chhattisgarh, killing seventy-six members of the Central Reserve Police Force.[22] In July 2010 Union Home Minister Palaniappan Chidambaram revealed that in the first six months of 2010 over two hundred Indian security personnel had died from Maoist attacks. The South Asia Terrorism Portal (SATP) recently reported that Maoist violence led to over 1,100 Indian civilian and security forces deaths in 2010, the highest annual figure for Maoist-related fatalities to date.

Prime Minister Manmohan Singh acknowledged in May 2010 that Naxalism was India's biggest internal security challenge and that the problem must be controlled to ensure the country's continued economic growth.[23] As India's population and economy grows, it increasingly looks to the eastern areas of the country, which contain vital natural resources like 85 percent of India's coal reserves.[24] Growing Naxalism poses a threat not only to resource security and development; it also tears at the social fabric of the nation.[25]

The Indian government is seeking to deal with Naxalism through a two-pronged strategy of stepping up police action and increasing economic development projects. In late 2009 India launched Operation Green Hunt, a counteroffensive involving the deployment of fifty thousand paramilitary soldiers to the most affected regions. Maoist attacks declined dramatically in the state of Andhra Pradesh over the last few years after state authorities massively increased the size and budget of the police forces.[26]

SEX SELECTION

Despite economic development and social change in India, the preference for sons remains high and could pose another internal security challenge for India. Sex selective abortions have led to a sex ratio of 914 girls born for every 1,000 boys born in India. The 2011 Indian census revealed an increase in the sex ratio in favor of males since the last census in 2001, particularly in the states of Punjab and Gujarat. It appears that a combination of fertility decline, the increased availability of technologies such as ultrasound and amniocentesis, and traditional discriminatory attitudes toward women continue to lead to the abortion of more female fetuses. The Indian government enacted a law in 1994 banning the use of prenatal testing for sex selection, but it has been difficult to enforce.

If the number of Indian women continues to decrease relative to the number of Indian men, this could become a significant source of social instability. When marriage rates decline, unmarried men have trouble finding jobs: observers note that societies with large numbers of single young men are more likely to suffer higher crime rates and more internal unrest and violence than societies in which most men marry and have children.[27] A landmark study by Valerie Hudson and Andrea den Boer on the "bare branches" phenomenon in Asia notes that by 2020 there will be 28 million young adult "bare branches" in India.[28] This issue was first highlighted by Nobel Peace Prize winner Dr. Amartya Sen, who blasted the sex selection phenomenon both on ethical and national security grounds, arguing that skewing the sex ratio in favor of men would impede economic and democratic development and jeopardize internal stability in India.[29] When sex selection trends combine with the various ethnic and communal-based conflicts in India, the challenges to maintaining social cohesion are compounded.

The sex selection problem is also linked to human trafficking inside India. Indian government leaders have identified human trafficking as a major social problem, with estimates of possibly 100 million people involved. Indian states with fewer women, such as Punjab and Haryana, can become destinations for women and girls trafficked from poorer states such as Assam, Jharkhand, and West Bengal.[30] Poor Indian women and girls are either sold by their families or lured by the promise of employment into bonded labor, forced marriage, or even forced prostitution. There are also reports of increased incidents of polyandry—individual women married simultaneously to brothers and uncles in one family, essentially making them sex slaves.[31]

HINDU-MUSLIM TENSIONS

Although India's population is 80 percent Hindu, it has a sizable Muslim population of about 160 million, which makes it the state with the third largest Muslim population in the world. There are fairly wide differences between the growth rates of the Hindu and Muslim populations in India, which have been exploited to provoke communal tensions. The Muslim community in India grew by around 30 percent between 1991 and 2001, while the number of Hindus rose 20 percent, according to data from India's 2001 census. India has a history of communal violence and rioting, and there were well-founded fears that the data released in the 2001 census would be used by those seeking to stoke communal tensions.

Indeed, some Hindu chauvinist leaders have called on Hindu families to produce more children to counter the current demographic trends. The former leader of the grassroots Hindu organization Rashtriya Swayamsevak Sangh (RSS), K. S. Sudarshan, for instance, has appealed to Hindu families to "have a dozen sons."[32] Another grassroots Hindu chauvinist organization, the Vishwa Hindu Parishad, announced several years ago plans to launch an action program to educate the community on the dangers of the "falling" Hindu population.[33] Studies published by the RSS going back to the early 1990s emphasize the growth in the Muslim population and the threat it poses to the Hindu majority.[34]

The demographic trends of the Muslim community in India are most likely attributable to broader trends in their socio-economic status, which is generally much lower than the national average. Although Muslims make up 13.4 percent of the population, they hold fewer than 5 percent of government positions and make up only 4 percent of the undergraduate student body in India.[35] There is a growing perception among Muslims in India that they have been excluded from economic, political, and educational opportunities through systemic discrimination.[36]

The Congress-led government has taken initial steps to seek to deal with the marginalization of the Indian Muslim community. To explore the level of disaffection among Muslims in India and seek ways to address the issue, Prime Minister Singh established a high-level committee in 2005 to prepare a report on the social, economic, and educational status of Muslims in India. The *Sachar Committee Report*, named after the chairman of the committee, Justice Rajindar Sachar, was released in November 2006. It found that India's Muslims lag behind the rest of the Indian population in literacy, employment rates, and income, and that there has been a general decline in the socioeconomic conditions of Muslims in India. The report offered recommendations to ensure equity and equality of opportunity for Muslims, especially in employment and education. There have been numerous complaints that the government is moving too slowly in following up on the report's proposals, however.[37]

The Threat of Muslim Radicalization

If the Indian government fails to address Muslim grievances adequately, there is a danger that global terrorist groups will exploit these grievances and convince increasing numbers of India's large Muslim minority to engage in terrorist acts. The Gujarat riots of 2002, when more than a thousand Muslims were killed at the hands of Hindu zealots, have contributed to a sense of alienation of India's Muslim community. Another major episode of communal violence in India could lead Indian Muslims to radicalize on a broader scale.

There already is concern in India about the threat posed by homegrown Islamist extremists who are linking domestic grievances to pan-Islamic agendas. From May 2008 until the November 2008 attacks in Mumbai, India suffered at least eight major attacks inside the country, with a death toll of more than four hundred. While a domestic group identifying itself as the Indian Mujahideen (IM) claimed responsibility for some of those attacks, it has been firmly established that the Pakistan-based Lashkar-e-Taiba carried out the Mumbai rampage.

The Indian domestic terrorist organization, the Students Islamic Movement of India (SIMI), was formed in April 1977 at the Aligarh Muslim University in Uttar Pradesh with a mission to revive Islam in India and transform the country into an Islamic state. One year after the destruction of the Babri Mosque by Hindu zealots in December 1992, SIMI-linked operatives carried out terrorist strikes across India. In a 1996 statement, a SIMI leader declared that since democracy and secularism had failed to protect Muslims in India, the sole option was to struggle for the Caliphate. After 9/11, SIMI members held demonstrations in support of Osama bin Laden, prompting the Indian government to ban the organization. Analysts believe that SIMI may have about four hundred full-time activists and twenty thousand regular members.[38] Some experts believe the IM is an offshoot of SIMI.[39]

Indian terrorism experts and government officials increasingly acknowledge that alienation among Indian Muslim communities is contributing to the problem of homegrown terrorism. They have further noted that increased prosperity in the country has not necessarily led to increased integration among various religious communities. Perpetrators of some of the 2008 terrorist attacks were apparently motivated by speeches that focused on perceived wrongs against the Muslim community in India, such as the demolition of the Babri Mosque by Hindu zealots in 1992 and the communal riots in Gujarat in 2002.

The rate of growth of the Indian Muslim population relative to other religions in the country, in and of itself, will not determine whether Indian Muslims pose an increasing security threat to India and globally. Whether or not the Indian Muslim community becomes more radicalized in coming years will likely be determined by a complex set of factors involving socioeconomic conditions; societal and political trends regarding Hindu nationalism; Pakistani interference; and the influence of global terrorist movements through the media and Internet.

India-China: Demographic Trends Feed Strategic Competition

India's population will surpass that of China's in about fifteen years. While not the decisive factor in determining the overall power balance between the two Asian giants, this demographic trend will play a role in regional security dynamics. The most striking difference in the Indian and Chinese demographic pictures over the coming decades is the onset of India's youth bulge at the same time that China finds its population graying. U.S. Census Bureau analysts estimate that new entrants into China's labor force may be near its upper limits of 124 million, as the population of Chinese aged twenty to twenty-four peaks this year. India's population of twenty- to twenty-four-year-olds, on the other hand, is not expected to peak until 2024, when it hits 116 million. While India's workforce will increase by 110 million over the next decade, China's will increase by less than 20 million, according to a Goldman Sachs study.[40]

India's demographic dividend could fuel India's economy in ways that make it a peer competitor to China, in particular pushing Indian growth rates ahead of China's.[41] At present the Chinese economy is vastly larger than India's. China's GDP, at over \$4.7 trillion, is four times that of India's; its GDP per capita, at about \$3,565, is three times that of India's; and China produces about 12 percent of the world's GDP, while India produces about 5 percent.[42] The Chinese also hold socioeconomic advantages over India that could play in Beijing's favor. Adult literacy in China stands at about 91 percent, compared to about 74 percent in India.

A brief look at knowledge production in each country, as measured by the number of patents granted by the United States, also reflects some differences. The number of patents the United States granted to China from 2004 to 2008 (3,464) is about one-third higher than the number granted to India during the same time period (2,408).[43] India may be a world leader in IT, but it clearly lags behind other IT leaders when it comes to patents.[44] While no Indian information technology companies featured in the top 200 list of filers with the International Patent Office in 2008, six Indian domestic pharmaceutical and biotech companies appeared in the top one hundred list of filers.[45] The higher figures for U.S. patents granted to Chinese companies may reflect that China is doing more broad-based research, while India is focused on specific areas like pharmaceuticals.

At the same time, the density of India's population (measured in people per square kilometer) is expected to increase from 369 to 476 between now and 2040. During this same period, China's population density is expected to increase from 141 to 152. Thus India must manage a faster-growing population in a smaller mass of land than China. This means greater pressure on natural resources and public goods.[46] Although 17 percent of the world's population lives in India, it only has 4 percent of the world's freshwater, and water tables have dropped as much as 70 percent in recent years in some parts of the country.[47] China's resource stresses are also considerable, but not as daunting as India's.

Still, the demographic trends are largely in India's favor, and China is watching India's emergence with wariness. China is particularly apprehensive of U.S. efforts to strengthen ties with India, including the civil nuclear deal and closer U.S.-India defense cooperation, since China claims such collaboration is aimed at containing its own power in the region.

Indeed the United States and India share concerns about China's military modernization and seek greater transparency from China on its strategic plans and intentions. Both countries also view signs of Chinese military presence in and around the Indian Ocean with concern, and are carefully considering what it means for energy and sea-lane security. China's attempt to scuttle the civil nuclear agreement at the September 2008 Nuclear Suppliers Group (NSG) meeting was evidence for many Indians that China does not willingly accept India's rise on the world stage, nor the prospect of closer U.S.-India ties.[48]

The future direction of relations between China and India, two booming economies that together account for more than one-third of the world's population, will be a major factor in determining broader political and economic trends in Asia, which directly affect U.S. interests. While trade and economic ties between India and China are improving (bilateral trade has increased from around $5 billion in 2002 to over $60 billion in 2010), both sides continue to harbor deep suspicions of the other's strategic intentions.

Signs of India's and China's deep-seated disagreements have begun to surface over the last five years, and it is likely that such friction will continue, given their unsettled borders, China's interest in consolidating its hold on Tibet, and India's expanding influence in Asia. In recent years, China has increasingly pressured India over their disputed borders by questioning Indian sovereignty over Arunachal Pradesh, stepping up probing operations along different parts of their shared frontier, and building up its military infrastructure, as well as expanding its network of road, rail, and air links in the border areas.

Former Indian ambassador to the U.S. Lalit Mansingh recently commented that "China is intruding into our security space in a big way."[49] Indian leaders are not interpreting China's newfound assertiveness as Beijing necessarily preparing for conflict, and they continue to calculate the overall probability of another Sino-Indian war to be low. However, they believe China may be trying to enhance its bargaining position in their ongoing border negotiations.[50] India accuses China of illegally occupying more than fourteen thousand square miles of its territory on its northern border in Kashmir, while China lays claim to more than thirty-four thousand square miles of India's northeastern state of Arunachal Pradesh. India is a long-term host to the Dalai Lama and about 100,000 Tibetan refugees, although the Indian government forbids them from participating in any political activity.

The history of events leading up to the Sino-Indian border war of 1962, and the severe Indian disillusionment with the Chinese in the aftermath of that conflict, provides a useful context for assessing current developments in Chinese-Indian relations. When China simultaneously invaded the eastern and western sectors of their shared borders in 1962, India was taken off guard and felt betrayed by a country it had supported in the international arena. The Indian parliament accused Prime Minister Jawaharlal Nehru of turning a blind eye to Chinese construction of a road a few years earlier through what was then Indian territory in the Aksai Chin. Indian strategic analysts now warn officials not to make the mistakes of the past by downplaying provocative Chinese actions in the border areas.

India has somewhat belatedly sought to match the Chinese moves and to reinforce its own claims in their disputed border areas by augmenting forces and constructing roads in the border areas. These measures include the deployment of two squadrons of Su-30MKI fighter jets in Tezpur and Chhabua in Assam and the raising of two mountain divisions for deployment in Arunachal Pradesh.[51] India also redeployed elements of its Twenty-seventh Mountain Division from Jammu and Kashmir to the patch of land that intersects India, Tibet, and Bhutan, and that links India with the rest of its northeastern states.

China is also strengthening ties to its traditional ally Pakistan and slowly gaining influence with other South Asian states. Beijing is developing strategic port facilities in Sittwe, Burma; Hambantota, Sri Lanka; and Gwadar, Pakistan, in order to protect sea-lanes and ensure uninterrupted energy supplies. China also uses military and other assistance to court these nations, especially when India and other Western states attempt to use their assistance programs to encourage respect for human rights and democracy.

China maintains a robust defense relationship with Pakistan, and views a strong partnership with Pakistan as a useful way to contain Indian power in the region and divert Indian military force and strategic attention away from China. The China-Pakistan partnership serves both Chinese and Pakistani interests by presenting India with a potential two-front theater in the event of war with either country. Chinese officials also view a certain degree of India-Pakistan tension as advancing their own strategic interests as such friction bogs India down in South Asia and interferes with New Delhi's ability to assert its global ambitions and compete with China at the international level. China transferred equipment and technology and provided scientific expertise to Pakistan's nuclear weapons and ballistic missile programs throughout the 1980s and 1990s, enhancing Pakistan's strength in the South Asian strategic balance.[52] China helped Pakistan build two nuclear reactors at the Chasma site in the Punjab Province under agreements made before it joined the NSG in 2004.[53] More recently, China has proposed selling two new nuclear reactors to Pakistan (Chasma III and Chasma IV); however, the United States has indicated Beijing must first seek an exemption from the NSG for the nuclear transfers. Since some NSG members could vote against such an exemption because of Pakistan's poor non-proliferation record, China may have to decide whether to move ahead with the deal without the NSG exemption.

Beijing has demonstrated in recent years that it favors bilateral Indo-Pakistani negotiations to resolve their differences and has played a helpful role in preventing the outbreak of full-scale war between the two countries, especially during the 1999 Indo-Pakistani border conflict in the heights of Kargil.[54]

For its part, India is seeking to build political and economic ties with the states of Southeast Asia, which generally welcome India's involvement to balance growing Chinese influence. India became a full dialogue partner of the Association of Southeast Asian Nations (ASEAN) in 1995, joined the ASEAN Regional Forum in 1996, and became a member of the East Asia Summit in December 2005. India signed a free trade deal with the ASEAN countries in December 2008 after four years of talks and has also enhanced its naval profile in Southeast Asia, holding periodic joint exercises.

Also with an eye on China, India has prioritized strengthening relations with Japan through increasing military contacts, maritime cooperation, and trade and investment ties. Tokyo has pledged $4.5 billion in soft loans for the Delhi-Mumbai railway freight corridor, and the two sides are preparing to sign a Comprehensive Economic Partnership Agreement to enhance bilateral trade, which currently stands at a paltry $10.4 billion.[55] In a significant turnaround from its past tough stance toward India's nuclear program, Tokyo is currently negotiating a civil nuclear deal with New Delhi.[56]

India-China strategic competition increasingly revolves around naval issues. As Robert Kaplan described in a recent article in *Foreign Affairs*, "China's worldwide scouring for resources brings it into conflict with . . . countries such as India and Russia, against whose own spheres of influence China is bumping up."[57] China's economy increasingly depends on ensuring access to open sea-lanes. Its dependence on energy imports makes the Malacca Straits, which straddle its oil supply routes, a key choke point. No doubt India's rising defense budgets and growing navy concern Beijing, as China's energy lifeline that passes through the Malacca Straits will increasingly be at the mercy of India.[58] India has the world's fifth largest navy. It has one aircraft carrier and is striving to put into place three carriers by 2020 as part of its naval expansion and desire to project power throughout the Indo-Pacific.[59]

Demographics and Indian Military Modernization

In 2020 there will be 1 billion fighting-age men (ages fifteen to twenty-nine) in the world.[60] India alone will account for over 183 million of that total and Europe 65 million.[61] The size of India's military currently stands at 1.3 million, a little less than half of China's 2.8 million–strong force. India clearly has the potential to vastly increase the size of its military in the coming decade, if it so chooses.

But India will need to balance the possibility of increasing the size of its military with its desire to pursue an ambitious military modernization campaign. In the simplest terms, this means India must consider whether it wants to spend its military budget on personnel (salaries, pensions, etc.) versus sophisticated weapons systems. India already spends about 15 percent of its defense budget on pensions, compared to Russia, which spends 12 percent.[62] India's annual defense budget was announced at $36 billion in 2011, representing an 11 percent increase from previous year's budget. About 40 percent of the defense budget will be spent on capital expenditures.[63]

Indian strategic planners need to pay attention to the quality, not merely the quantity, of their future forces. Indian planners must consider issues such as costs of training a larger army, since training larger numbers of soldiers could detract from their ability to use advanced systems. Indeed, China and Russia have each made decisions in the past to forego expanding their armies in order to save money for technologically advanced systems.[64] Sheer military size is not what allows a country to maintain conventional superiority.[65] Moreover, in the context of nuclear weapons capabilities, which both China and Pakistan possess, a large standing army becomes less important in strategic terms.

India's robust military modernization effort is one of the most striking features of the changing strategic landscape in Asia today. India plans to spend up to $30 billion modernizing its military over the next few years and has imported about $28 billion worth of military equipment over the last ten years, mostly from Russia, but also increasingly from countries like Israel, France, and the United States. Indian strategic affairs analyst Raja Mohan has argued that China's neighbors are eager to expand defense ties with India, which is partly driving its military modernization.[66] Over the next decade, India is expected to purchase one thousand aircraft worth $100 billion. Its request for 126 Multi-Role Combat Aircraft worth over $10 billion is one of the largest deals of its kind. Indian strategic planners see air power as one of the most important areas for military investment and expenditure, given the need to meet exigencies arising on their borders and potentially for expeditionary purposes.[67]

The civil nuclear deal with the United States was expected to raise the confidence of the Indian defense establishment in the United States as a reliable supplier and thus set the stage for a much broader and deeper defense relationship between the two countries over the next several years. U.S. Under Secretary of Defense Michèle Flournoy, while commenting on the importance of U.S.-India maritime cooperation during a trip to India last year, said, "We also have to respond to maritime security and freedom of navigation and against those contesting the accepted rules of the world. We will have to work to prevent that. We have to be prepared in terms of capability."[68] Following are some major milestones in the U.S.-India defense relationship:

- In the last three years, the United States and India have signed deals worth nearly $8 billion to provide India with six C130-J Hercules military transport aircraft, eight P-81 maritime reconnaissance aircraft, and ten C-17 Globemaster III aircraft.
- The two sides have held regular joint exercises across all services at increasing levels of complexity, and including multilateral exercises like the Malabar naval exercise in 2009 that included Japanese participation.
- In 2006 the U.S. Congress authorized the transfer of the USS *Trenton* amphibious transport dock to India.
- In 2005 India and the United States signed a ten-year defense framework agreement that calls for expanded joint military exercises, increased defense-related trade, and the establishment of a defense and procurement production group.

Indian Power Projection in the Asia-Pacific

Demographics alone do not determine a country's power potential. Military capabilities and the ability to leverage economic and diplomatic clout also determine a country's ability to project power. Indian leaders certainly view India's future demographic trends and its human resource base as its two greatest assets.[69] But studies exploring the dynamics of power emphasize that it is important to examine a variety of factors in addition to human resources, including technology, enterprise/entrepreneurship, financial/capital resources, and physical resources.[70]

According to South Asia expert George Perkovich, India deserves credit for "making steady progress under democratic governance and without trampling on its neighbors," and achieves greatness by "improving the quality of life of its free citizens."[71] Other South Asia scholars, like Dan Twining of the German Marshall Fund, argue that integral to India's ability to achieve great power status is whether or not it can lead in the transformation of South Asia into an "economically thriving democratic region." Otherwise, Twining argues, India's rise will be undermined by ongoing problems in the region.

If India is to reap the economic benefits of its demographic boom, it must invest now in policies that address long-festering problems, like lack of labor flexibility and an inadequate education system. The key to expanding education may lie in the private sector, but the government can facilitate the process by setting standards for curriculum and following through with implementation of the universal education bill passed last year. The government has placed too much emphasis on the benefits of its youthful population without addressing the challenges of ensuring productive employment for the coming waves of job-seeking youth. Not only has this led to a policy void, with no current preparations to meet the challenge, it also has likely raised false expectations that could add to frustration when jobs are not available.

Despite the internal challenges India faces in managing its demographic transition, it will continue to play an increasingly influential role on the global stage, particularly in the Asia-Pacific region. Growing Indian trade, currently at $500 billion, and increased Indian reliance on foreign resources (India's energy needs alone are expected to increase 3.5 times by 2025) dictate that India will continue to invest in maritime security in order to protect the free flow of this trade.[72] It is likely that India will seek to project military power throughout the Asia-Pacific even as it copes with its internal demographic transformation. The U.S. Defense Department's Quadrennial Defense Review released last year acknowledged the potential for Indian power projection when it stated that "as its military capabilities grow, India will contribute to Asia as a net provider of security in the Indian Ocean and beyond."[73]

India will have to manage a balancing act, though, as it seeks to expand economic opportunity for all its citizens, while projecting strength outside its borders and managing border tensions with Pakistan on one side and China on the other. There are several developments that could tip this balance further in either direction. A major upsurge in the Maoist insurgency, for example, could force India to deploy regular army troops to insurgent-affected areas, thus detracting from its ability to maintain forces in other traditional hot spots, like Kashmir along the Pakistan border, or in Arunachal Pradesh along its border with China. Moreover, the potential for military conflict with Pakistan, precipitated by a high-profile terrorist attack conducted by Pakistan-based terrorists along the lines of the Mumbai 2008 tragedy, remains relatively high. Any potential conflict between India and Pakistan would likely be short-lived, but it would form an important basis for continued robust investment in India's defense sector.

Even if defense spending trends remain high, they will not likely have a major economic impact on India until the population begins to gray, in about twenty-five years. India's "demographic dividend" will peak around 2035, and by 2050 there will be 236 million Indians over the age of sixty-five. So while India does not face the immediate trade-off between funding defense and elderly care, it must begin to factor rising pensions into strategic plans, and to put programs in place now to cope with becoming one of the oldest countries in the world.

Separating India's demographics from its strategic destiny is nearly impossible. For the next two decades, India will be forced to address the challenges of its demographic boom. Yet with China's rapid global rise and its more assertive stance on India-China border issues, India must also increasingly project power, both hard and soft, beyond its borders to compete with—but not necessarily confront—the Chinese. Given U.S. concerns about lack of transparency in Chinese defense modernization, and China's newfound assertiveness in the seas off its eastern coast, Washington should welcome India's enhanced role in the Asia-Pacific region and develop policies that support India in coping with its demographic challenges.

Buttressed by a strong U.S.-India partnership, India's demographic and strategic destiny will ultimately impact the Asian strategic balance in ways that promote healthy competition among regional powers and push the region toward greater economic and political stability.

CONCLUSION

POPULATION, POWER, AND PURPOSE

Susan Yoshihara

The world is entering uncharted and turbulent waters. Unprecedented population decline and global aging will bring profound shifts in national power and international politics. No course correction can avoid the changes or reverse the fertility decline of the preceding decades. Leaders can, however, navigate the worst effects on global stability.

For some four decades, scholarship on population and security has maintained that fewer people would make the world more secure. The conventional wisdom helped build an international economic and development architecture advancing fertility control and population decline. Only in the last few years have demographers and social scientists who challenge the "less is better" thesis been given a more prominent place in the debate about demographics and international security. Recently, landmark studies have uncovered the coming crisis within the great powers and its geopolitical ramifications. This book has built upon that work, and fills a void in the scholarship by focusing specifically on military and strategic effects of global aging. The authors of this volume have examined the lessons manifest in yesterday's superpowers, Japan and Russia; today's leaders, Europe and the Unites States; and contenders for tomorrow, China and India—giving due consideration to crosscutting normative, technological, social, and political drivers that will remake the global order.

What emerges can be summarized according to several ongoing debates about population, power, and security: Will global aging lead to a "geriatric peace" among the great powers? Will technology compensate for population decline as a military force multiplier? Do normative changes attendant to aging and diverging fertility patterns bode well or ill for national power? Will aging powers become less innovative and uncompetitive, or can they manage an "elegant decline"? Finally, will the United States have to "go it alone" as its allies retreat from the world stage?

This study has uncovered several surprising conclusions that challenge the conventional wisdom. The "less is better" hypothesis is wrong for several reasons. The authors of this volume find that the world is headed for a period of instability among the great powers on account of population decline.

"Geriatric Peace" or Clash of the Titans?

Jim Holmes's analysis of the Peloponnesian War testifies to the negative strategic effects of dwindling manpower. In the case of Athens and Sparta, regime type was one of many intervening variables in the relationship between population and security. The Spartan leadership believed it could no longer afford to risk major army contingents when an earthquake killed a significant number of fighting-age men. On the other hand, population shock resulting from a prolonged plague enhanced military adventurism on the part of the Athenians, just as it had amplified risk aversion on the part of the Spartans. More recent history brings into question the conventional wisdom that older societies are inherently more conservative. Some aging societies—such as Germany in the 1930s and Serbia in the 1990s—have been prone to aggression.[1]

Today, some argue that the aging of the powers will bring about a "geriatric peace" whereby elderly, fiscally constrained societies will inevitably become more tranquil. Our analysis finds that aging could instead add tremendous volatility to alliance politics and trigger competitive great power dynamics at the regional level that could have global reverberations.

Part of the "geriatric peace" thesis is that America's demographic exceptionalism will so widen its advantage over the other powers that the ensuing American hegemony will decrease the probability of hot or cold wars developing between the United States and the other great powers.[2] The cases examined in this study demonstrate that while global aging could dampen the potential for conflicts between the United States and other great powers, depopulation could also make other forms of great power interactions more destabilizing.

Toshi Yoshihara identifies two scenarios for nations with a low-growth rate that may threaten their national security. The first scenario, based on balance of power calculations and interstate competition, predicts the potential for war between states. In the second scenario, "manpower shortages gradually reduce the strategic options of states with a stake in maintaining the current regional and world orders." The result is "a steady withdrawal of states from international security commitments as the means to project power overseas diminish." While the first scenario, war between states, is less likely in the short term, Yoshihara points out that if Japan and other developed nations do not rise to the challenges of reconciling demographic realities with security policy, then the second scenario, defaulting on security commitments, is more likely in the future.

Another destabilizing effect demographics may have is what Gordon Chang calls the "closing windows" aging nations face on their main foreign policy goals. As the contraction of China's working population restricts military manpower, China will have to consider dealing with manpower-intensive operations such as taking over Taiwan, Mongolia, and other disputed areas sooner rather than later. Chang demonstrates that China is already skirmishing with its neighbors, Russia and India, and that tensions are on the rise. Beijing encourages the continuous flow of immigrants into Russia, even though it makes Moscow uneasy. Seeing a window closing, China is using its temporarily growing population to virtually incorporate key contested areas by assimilation. For its part, Russia has chosen to ignore the incursions rather than allow them to interfere with tightening economic ties with China, but how long Moscow will look the other way is uncertain.

Closing windows on Russia's foreign policy objectives also threaten to make Eurasia more unstable in the coming decades. Murray Feshbach alerts us to a public health crisis in Russia that has led to a dramatic drop in population and population density—to three times below the world average. In the short term, this threatens to undermine Russia's force modernization plans. In the longer term, it will lead to Moscow's diminishing military and political influence regionally and globally. In particular, Russia will be less able to police its "near abroad" where ethnic divisions and unresolved border disputes persist.

Lisa Curtis finds that diverging fertility trends within nations can bring about internal destabilization that may translate into less global stability. In the case of India, higher fertility rates among the less educated northern population and declining fertility in the south will make converting to a high-technology service economy more of a challenge, and, more worrying, will threaten to exacerbate religious and ethnic tensions between Muslims and Hindus.

In addition to the inattention to coming turbulence within alliance politics, the notion that aging nations are inevitably more peaceful misses major policy-strategy mismatches in most of the powers' strategic plans. To what extent do Western nations recognize the coming security challenges caused by population decline? Feshbach has identified a clear mismatch between Russia's force modernization plans and its dwindling pool of eligible youth. On the other hand, Tokyo has explicitly accounted for the inevitable consequences of aging. Japan's recent strategic plan bluntly noted that the "dwindling birthrate" was the primary constraint on improving Japan's defense. That strategy, set out by the Araki Commission, in turn set the tone for Tokyo's subsequent defense guidelines, which warned, "In developing Japan's defense forces, we have to take into account the fact that while the roles that our defense forces have to play are multiplying, the number of young people in Japan is declining as a result of the low birth rate, and fiscal conditions continue to deteriorate."[3] Japanese defense white papers also note explicitly that recruitment will be undermined by the birth dearth and that this will hamper the end strength of Self-Defense Forces personnel.

Even though Europe is not far behind Japan in its demographic demise, Europe's strategic planning documents ignore the problem. The 2003 European Security Strategy and its 2008 review do not mention demographics at all.[4] Instead, the 2008 review lists terrorism and organized crime, energy security, and climate change as the only major threats.[5] More telling, a 2010 draft of internal security strategy also fails to account for the security challenges of plummeting birthrates and poor assimilation among some immigrant populations. Internal challenges identified are limited to terrorism, crime, natural disasters, and traffic accidents.[6] The only mention of population in Europe's strategic planning documents is "exploding population" on Europe's borders[7] and the effect of population growth on climate change.[8] The absence of thoughtful discussion regarding demographic decline should be worrisome to strategic planners.

American strategic planning documents also provide little guidance on how to respond to the coming challenges of global aging. Demographic concerns received honorable mentions in primary defense and security plans in the last few years, and lower-level military and intelligence documents offered some policy guidance, but substantive policy is lacking.[9] U.S. strategic goals focus mainly on protecting the United States from physical attack, thereby protecting its economic strength and control of the seas, affording control of the trade of the world's goods if desired.[10] Along with these fundamental aims, successive U.S. presidents have adopted interventionist postures and ensconced them in their national security and military strategies.

Given its healthy fertility rate and relatively positive population prospects, it is not surprising that, far from projecting a retreat from the world, U.S. strategic documents call for more robust capabilities than ever, including proficiency in manpower-intensive operations such as counterinsurgency and stabilization operations.[11] The Obama administration asserts that the nation must prepare to face "two capable nation-state aggressors," and will be "plausibly challenged by a range of threats that extend far beyond the familiar 'major regional conflicts' that have dominated U.S. planning since the Cold War."[12] Meeting this new obligation would require an increase in American end strength.[13]

As promising as the United States' military advantage seems to be, a fundamental question has yet to be answered: can and will the United States pay for it? The American case shows that in democratic societies, major military systems and important research and development initiatives are prime targets during fiscal crises because they compete with popular social programs. Even a nation with relatively high fertility and immigration may make unwise force planning decisions based not on strategic priorities but on domestic political pressures. This is the question Americans must answer today.

How will all this affect the powers' ability to keep the peace in the rest of the world? The United States is the leading troop contributor to peacekeeping operations, primarily to the NATO mission to rebuild an Afghan state. France, Pakistan, the United Kingdom, and Bangladesh follow, making up the bulk of UN troop contributors in 2008.[14] Pakistan and Bangladesh are the sixth and seventh most populous countries in the world respectively.[15] Nigeria, the world's ninth most populous country is the next largest contributor from the developing world, just behind the aging armies of Italy, Britain, France, and Germany. As European militaries curtail contributions due to demographic and economic constraints, the world will see a significant change in the capability of its peacekeepers. This will be especially true of UN operations, where the United States is not a primary contributor, leading to a growing mismatch between the falling capabilities of, and rising expectations for, UN peacekeepers.[16] It is notable that China has shown willingness to fill the gap in places where it has strategic interests such as Sudan. While not now among major troop contributors, China's surplus of recruitable men will allow it to fill the gap left by the United States and Europe, provided political conditions are met.

Technology: Magic Bullet or Costly Chimera?

One of the reasons little research has been conducted on population and war is the common belief that technology trumps people. Experts in modern warfare warn that this bias can be dangerous and shows a general lack of understanding about war, especially about the strategy and tactics of labor-intensive military organizations.[17] Such faith in technology encompasses a wide array of social, economic, and political problems. One only has to look at international development campaigns whose popularity soar despite the fact that development experts widely criticize them for placing too much confidence in technological solutions while ignoring difficult but essential human behavior and political factors.[18]

Our analysis finds that technology can bode well or ill for a nation's population-power calculus, and can be either a stabilizing or destabilizing influence regionally and globally. Technological advancement can quickly render decades of expensive investment in military training, equipment, and technology obsolete. Technology can also be a "game changer" in a positive way. Payoffs from American investment in the 1970s in the global positioning system (GPS), precision strike weapons, information technology and miniaturization, to name a few projects, were already evident by the early 1990s in the first Gulf War. No one knows the benefits that can be reaped from today's research and development, but the lesson from the 1970s, when the American demographic picture looked bleaker than it does today, is that more, and not less, should be invested today.

Technology could also interact with population trends in unfavorable ways. For example, Russia's fire sale of its top-line weaponry in the 1990s to China coincided with the population implosion in the Russian Far East. The financial windfall gave way to larger strategic challenges. Moscow had inadvertently armed the Chinese with the power projection capabilities to fill the vacuum left behind by the Russian citizenry. While a Sino-Russian conflict or an outright Chinese invasion is farfetched, the borderlands are historically sensitive territories that the Chinese ceded to the tsars during the "century of humiliation." The power imbalance, aggravated by the demographic realities, is clearly a phenomenon of strategic import.

From 1992 to 2007, Russia provided China $20–30 billion in fighter aircraft, ships, tanks, and missiles.[19] Russia now fears China has reverse engineered the technology and is selling it abroad, even to Russia's competitors.[20] Hedging against technological advancements is an expensive enterprise, made costlier by an aging society without the prospects of economic growth and technical innovation afforded by a large working-age population. Training troops to fight with new technology and retiring old systems and soldiers trained with it is also expensive. Economic constraints in the coming decades will tempt nations to curtail costly investments in research and development, and it will likely increase the incentive to borrow or steal technology.

As Toshi Yoshihara demonstrates in his chapter on Japan, unmanned systems can be a welcome alternative to training and equipping troops, especially when each service member is made more costly and more difficult to replace due to fertility decline. Whereas it costs a lot to train and equip a naval aviator, it is relatively cheap to buy and fly unmanned aerial vehicles (UAVs). Beyond cost savings, unmanned systems could benefit crisis stability and escalation control. Without human life at stake, nations may not feel compelled to react or overreact to the loss in case of either hostile action or accident. The recent past confirms that countries go to great lengths to recover downed pilots, either dead or alive. The unmanned aircraft promises to obviate such risks. Indeed, one wonders what might have happened had the collision with a Chinese fighter in April 2001 involved an American UAV rather than an EP-3 reconnaissance aircraft. Absent the subsequent fallout from the detention of U.S. pilots and crew, the incident may not have spiraled into a Sino-American showdown. Nations armed with UAVs may thus find it easier to walk away from an aerial encounter that went badly.

Such technology can also increase national power by its ability to consolidate alliances. Unmanned technology combined with intelligence, surveillance, and reconnaissance give a common operating picture, which increases trust among allies and allows more effective joint operations. Given the high-profile use of UAVs in U.S. operations in the war on terror, it is likely that America's friends and foes will seek out this asset. The UAVs could become a strategic leveler since their proliferation will allow all advanced nations to have the same operating picture.

On the other hand, UAVs could make nations less risk averse and thus make the security environment less stable. If Japan lost even one soldier in combat it would be a national tragedy, but to lose several UAVs in risky reconnaissance operations would be relatively uneventful. One can imagine Japan sending UAVs to monitor disputed territory with the Chinese and ending up violating Chinese sovereignty, evoking an armed response. The 2010 case of a Chinese merchant vessel colliding with a Japanese Self-Defense Forces ship at sea, and Japan's backing down from prosecuting the Chinese captain, shows that such seemingly minor events have strategic implications. In the case of the collision at sea, it showed China will use such incidents to test Japan's power and prestige. As Japan's aging population becomes less willing to inflame tensions with its rising neighbor, such incidents could accelerate international perception of Japan's decline.

While history provides exceptional cases of inferior forces defeating stronger ones, a nation cannot project sustained power without having redundancy in large-scale systems such as ships and aircraft. Mass still matters. Attempts to operate and maintain large, complex weapons systems with fewer personnel have operational implications. For example, when the U.S. Navy implemented its idea of "smart ships" manned with fewer sailors and more advanced technology, it felt the effects of having fewer people to cover the myriad duties that keep ships at peak readiness. Alternatively, responding to costlier manpower by downsizing the fleet has strategic effects. It is quite possible that the real and relative cuts in U.S. Navy spending on capital ships in the next few years will have adverse effects on America's ability to pursue its foreign policy goals, especially in the Pacific.[21]

An increase in operational risk in a potential conflict such as Taiwan is one possibility. Even if such a conflict were not to arise, the cuts could affect the choices Asian countries make about whether to ally themselves with the United States or China. These choices, in turn, could affect the political evolution of the Pacific, vis-à-vis America's more limited ability to pursue its broad foreign policy goals in the region and elsewhere.[22] Such a limitation comes at a time when demographic decline seems to be fostering a turn to neo-authoritarianism that could be hostile to democratic nations and policies in the future.[23]

The ultimate defense technology is nuclear weapons. A major question is whether dwindling populations available for large armies will increase the likelihood of using them. Russia provides a sobering example. There are too few troops available in the Russian Far East to stop a serious Chinese army invasion, and so there are plans to use tactical nuclear weapons if such an invasion cannot be stopped or slowed down using brigade elements. According to one report, several nuclear land mines were notionally exploded during a 2010 exercise called Vostok-2010 at which two Tochka-U (SS-21) missiles, which can carry tactical nuclear warheads, were also launched.[24]

Along with the question of using nuclear weapons is the question of whether population changes will induce more nations to acquire them. Nuclear weapons can elevate a power's status irrespective of its population size or state of development. Pakistan and India's acquisition of the technology in the late 1990s demonstrate the way nuclear weapons enhance international prestige, and the case of Israel emphasizes their role as a military and strategic leveler for smaller countries. The pursuit of nuclear weapons in the cases of Iran and North Korea shows that rogue states, no matter their size or state of development, can destabilize a region and create havoc among the powers. Proliferation of weapons of mass destruction to Al Qaeda and other international terrorist organizations further raises the specter of detonation of nuclear weapons for the first time in almost seventy years. With no counterforce or countervalue targets, these organizations are nearly impervious to nuclear deterrence. At the same time, the end of great power equipoise based on the nuclear standoff has become thinkable again due to the recent nuclear reduction agreement between the United States and Russia. If the Global Zero campaign that fostered the New Start Treaty is successful, then complete nuclear disarmament among the powers by 2030 will ensue. Newly disarmed great powers will become vulnerable to first strikes, especially by rogue states, nonstate actors, and those nations who use their residual capability to threaten the great powers.[25] In any case, nuclear disarmament makes demographics far more important in calculations of military and strategic power. The negative effects of aging on national power become even greater.

Another important aspect of the demographic-nuclear calculus is less tangible. Does the fact that India will soon surpass China in total population somehow change the nuclear power balance? As Lisa Curtis and Gordon Chang have demonstrated in their chapters, strategic decision makers in Delhi and Beijing anticipate the population power shift as a psychological shift. Will Delhi feel more secure and, if so, more emboldened or less? Will Beijing feel more vulnerable and take more risks, or fewer? These are essentially part of the larger normative debate surrounding population and security.

Normative Factors: Social Cohesion vs. Houses Divided

Is it enough for a nation to think it is exceptional? What effect does this have on the way a nation projects or fails to project power? Demographic exceptionalism comes in various forms. The United States is the youngest of the developed nations, with a relatively high fertility rate. China is the world's most populous country, but this is not sustainable. As Gordon Chang concludes in his chapter, "Demography, once China's best friend, will soon become a foe," which will create a "mood of long-term pessimism." India will overtake China's population around the year 2025, but it is already exceptional as the world's largest democracy. Japan leads the world in aging and absolute population decline. Russia is exceptional among the powers for the high mortality that accompanies low fertility. Europe is exceptional in the totality of its fertility demise: thirty European countries are "dying," in the words of sociologist Gunnar Heinsohn.[26]

Francis Sempa reminds us in his chapter that in addition to geography and natural resources, size of population, and military and economic strength, traditional measures of power, we must consider normative factors such as the degree of social cohesion, national character, and type of government. Lack of national cohesion not only diminishes national power, but can lead to violent conflict. Wars in the former Yugoslavia, Somalia, and Rwanda provided global audiences violent images throughout the 1990s. In the Iraq War, insurgency inflamed grudges between Sunni and Shia Muslims unhinged the American victory in 2003, prolonging the war for the rest of the decade. In Russia, Slavic nationalism on one hand and more pro-Muslim foreign policies on the other undermine national cohesion. In India, Hindu nationalism is on the rise. Demographic factors alone were not the cause of these conflicts, but diverging fertility among ethnic and religious groups fanned the flames.

All of the powers we examined face challenges of social cohesion due to divergences in fertility and immigration. Whereas the bifurcation is north-south in India, it is heartland-periphery in China, which divides ethnic Chinese and non-Han minorities. In Europe the divide is native-immigrant and is worsened by spotty assimilation and political backlash against immigration. In the United States a "red-blue" divide, characterized by a polarized political climate between conservative, higher fertility states in the heartland and liberal, lower fertility Northeastern states. Samuel Huntington's 2004 article about "the browning of America" sparked controversy for critiquing the decreasing level of assimilation among ethnic groups in the United States, warning that policymakers ignored it "at their peril."[27] In Japan, there is a striking difference between the child-friendly atmosphere of Tokyo's Sakura City suburb and the hectic anti-family atmosphere of downtown Tokyo. Even within nations, policy corrections may be contentious in the years ahead between regions, but that national leaders must make the tough decisions just the same.

Phil Longman has noted the way that these cleavages are not only taking place between groups, but within them. The more orthodox or conservative members of any given religious group tend to have higher fertility. Others have built upon Longman's work, examining the way this divergence may cause competition inside states for diverging social and economic policies. Some believe the demographic advantage of conservative and religious groups will lead to a rise of a sort of religiosity that will threaten liberal secular societies.[28] Additionally, the rising sex imbalance, owing to sex-selective abortion and infanticide of baby girls, will cause intractable economic and social dilemmas in China. While the trend toward son preference is global, China and India alone account for some 160 million missing girls, more than all the females now living in the United States.[29] Only sub-Saharan Africa has escaped the scourge, due to their relatively high fertility rates, which bode well for the survival of second or third daughters.

While societal divisions from diverging fertility patterns appear to be a global phenomenon, some countries are better poised to manage them. Given their historical track record and the openness of the political debate surrounding the issue, the prospects of the United States for better assimilation of immigrants are far better than for the Europeans. Emblematic of the violent nature of the European troubles, France averages forty thousand automobiles burned annually in ethnic protests, and its national anthem elicits boos and jeers at international soccer matches from French-born-and-raised ethnic minorities.[30] Russia, China, and India have even worse prospects of quelling dissent, due to the widespread nature and the level of violence.

Innovation Freefall or Elegant Decline?

Social mood is a key factor in determining the effects of aging and population decline on foreign policy, and demography can transform the temperament of society.[31] Over the long term, this mood can affect national purpose and strategic posture. As Phillip Longman notes in his chapter, older societies are less willing to invest in increasing worker productivity and may resort to easier ways of fixing fiscal problems. Japan has been accused of taking a "beggar thy neighbor" approach to its economic problems by seeking to devalue its currency, while South Korea seeks instead to improve the productivity of its workers.[32]

What is the connection between Japan's taking the cheaper way out and the overall social mood? Some say that as nations age they become less innovative. The average age of Nobel Prize recipients shows that scientists do their best work before their mid-fifties.[33] Frank Murtha and Richard Peters have demonstrated that the vitality of a nation's stock market is tied to individual market psychology, which grows more risk averse with age.[34] Developed nations may be more likely in the future to count on quick fixes to structural economic problems, which will slow economic recovery and constrict defense dollars for keeping the peace. That said, medical and psychological innovations may someday help the elderly overcome insecurities that lead to risk-averse market psychology. This may challenge the belief that older societies are less adventuresome in foreign policy, which leads to another observation regarding population and power more generally: the quality of a workforce, and not just its size, translates into economic power. An indication of worker quality and innovation is the number of a country's per capita patent applications. Nicholas Eberstadt has demonstrated that aging societies are still very innovative in this regard. After the United States, the nations of Japan, Taiwan, Republic of Korea, Hong Kong, and Singapore were above the world average of patent applications in 2008. Japan, Korea, the United States, and Singapore all beat the world average for patents applied for out of country. Eberstadt found statistical significance in the relationship between gross national product (GDP) and per capita patent applications. India and China fall far behind the world average, and even behind Russia in patent applications, despite their younger populations.[35] It seems that GDP per capita, then, may be a major determinant of a nation's competitiveness in the future. An annual study of global entrepreneurship likewise found a positive correlation between per capita GDP entrepreneurship among young workers (ages twenty-five to thirty-four), but found that cultural and institutional factors also play a role.[36]

And so while Japan's society is the world's oldest with a median age of forty-four, it may not be old enough to have lost innovation momentum.[37] This suggests that there might be a crossover point at which aging begins to swamp innovation and productivity. What age brings on the tipping point is unknown. Another explanation is that a nation's "national morale" produces different patterns of decline. European leaders are trying different ways to foster "active aging," and organizers of Europe's third Demographic Forum in 2010 chose a Japanese scholar to give the keynote address. President of Keio University, Atsushi Seike, told European policymakers to encourage baby boomers to lead by example by continuing to work into their old age. His optimistic remarks contained pessimistic realities. Whereas men ages sixty to sixty-four produce a labor force participation rate of 75 percent in Japan, in Germany the rate is just above 40 percent. In France it is around 20 percent. A Credit Suisse report found that after sixty-five, workforce participation dropped to just over 4 percent in Germany and 7.7 percent in Britain, while remaining at almost 19 percent in Japan, the United States, and China.[38] "Of course, you should not force people to work against their will if they want to retire," Seike concluded.[39] Indeed, riots erupted in the fall of 2010 when France attempted to raise the retirement age by just two years, from sixty to sixty-two. Thus, managing an elegant decline is a challenge when social and cultural norms are at odds with societal health.

How deeply held the norms of leisurely old age have become in Europe remains to be seen. As Doug Sylva found in his analysis of European fertility decline, societal norms can be difficult to reverse. Japan has deeply held beliefs not only in industrious old age, but also in filial piety and respect for the elderly, which facilitates technical acumen among the older generation.

An additional benefit of these values is that they can blunt the negative social effects of fertility decline. The same is true in China, where children and wide social networks have traditionally supported the aged, but that nation lacks Japan's state-sponsored social safety net. Experts warn that the present situation—where only one child supports two parents and four grandparents in China—will severely diminish older people's quality of life, health, and productivity. This in turn has prompted such normative initiatives as the advancement of new human rights for the elderly in the hopes of imposing new obligations on sovereign states to protect the aged.[40] Human rights experts warn that women, who generally outlive men and enjoy fewer benefits from employers or the government, will be the hardest hit. But as admirable as the motives for such efforts may be, they have little prospect of reversing circumstances for the present generation of elderly, nor deterring their aggregate adverse effects on national power.

America Alone or New Security Partners?

When America's European allies began balking at some of the military roles in Afghanistan several years ago, the U.S. vice president took French and German leaders to task for reneging on their duties during a NATO summit.[41] President Obama has avoided such confrontation, but tensions remain. European casualty aversion has led some to claim that there is a two-tier NATO, and the economic slowdown will no doubt exacerbate the problem. Contrast this situation with Europe's ambitious planning documents, and one finds a mismatch. The European Security Strategy calls the transatlantic partnership "an irreplaceable foundation," and proposes NATO and the EU "deepen their strategic partnership for better cooperation in crisis management." It further calls for more costly investment in "strategic airlift, helicopters, space assets, and maritime surveillance," to be "supported by a competitive and robust defense industry across Europe, with greater investment in research and development."[42] As rancor over the Iraq War demonstrated, normative changes in Europe also constrain the use of force. Military intervention to pursue the "national interest" is anathema. Henry Kissinger suggests that for most Europeans, "Military missions and foreign interventions are defined as a form of social work."[43]

The current European monetary crisis—beginning with Greece, and spreading to Spain and Ireland—also leaves the realization of Europe's stated strategic plans in doubt. Indeed, Britain slashed its defense budget, abandoned its carrier fleet in 2010, and announced its plans to share an aircraft carrier with France, all of which suggests the end of the special relationship between Britain and the United States. The rising costs of each serviceman in rapidly aging countries will make rebuilding European militaries much more difficult.[44]

In any case, Europe's parsimonious attitude is contrasted by the relative generosity in peacekeeping troop contributions from African and South Asian nations with burgeoning populations. Rather than taking allies to task when they do not live up to expectations, the United States should court a new set of prospective partners who can take on additional security obligations.

New American security partners should share democratic values, bullish population prospects, and capable military infrastructures. An alliance between the world's largest democracy, India, and the world's oldest democracy, the United States, could have unprecedented effects on the balance of power and also the character of foreign policies.[45] India's naval ambitions and strategic position as a balancer against a rising China in the Indian Ocean are further reasons to develop the partnership. Prospective partners in other regions might include Brazil in Latin America, Indonesia in Southeast Asia, and Nigeria and Uganda in Africa, where both are compliant troop contributors to regional UN peacekeeping. In the Middle East, a democratic and prospering Iraq would be a likely partner in the long term.

Cultivating new partners to share the burden of manpower-intensive missions will be increasingly important, given escalating defense costs associated with mandatory medical and retirement spending. After identifying key partners, the United States should redouble efforts to support the modernization and security architectures and better align other areas of foreign policy, such as international development, to national security interests. This means, for starters, fully addressing the crisis in global health with a focus on reducing mortality rates. While African nations provide the bulk of troops for operations other than war on their continent, they have fourteen of the twenty highest death rates in the world.

In addition to peacekeeping roles, America's new security partners must rescue collective security from the current situation in which rogue states use negotiations to buy time to pursue malign interests. North Korea's use of the Six-Party Talks and Iran's use of international weapons inspections are key examples.

Looking Ahead

This study finds that a very important factor in the population-security calculus is the normative one. Scholars find it difficult to identify a direct causal relationship between population and security, but as these cases have all shown, there appears to be a very clear correlation between population decline and rising strategic pessimism. Eroding demographic prospects have changed the national mood in Japan, China, and throughout Europe, shaping worldviews. Another finding is that it is very difficult for policymakers to respond to these massive but subtle shifts in demographics and social mood precisely because many of the changes are intangible.

We can nonetheless characterize the future by some broad themes. First, global threats do not necessarily unite the world. Whereas the Soviet threat united the West, the specter of terrorism, adverse effects of climate change, and even the proliferation of WMD have not created solidarity to the same extent witnessed in the Cold War. Demographic decline will cause societies to further revert to state-centric approaches.

Second, since the centrality of the sovereign state is reinforced by demographic decline, nations are wise to invest in national strategic solutions rather than betting on international organizations to bail them out. International bodies such as the United Nations can be valuable for sharing and comparing problems and prospects, for example, but solutions are a national undertaking. Third, solving long-term problems is limited by short-term solutions. National policymaking is a three- to five-year enterprise, whereas global demographic trends require policymakers to look beyond a decade and even more. In order to address the instability that global aging and population decline present, policymakers will need to take the long view.

There is virtually no doubt that a reordering of great power politics is coming in the next two decades. India will overtake China as the world's largest nation around 2020,[46] Japan and Russia will drop below 100 million in population around the middle of the twenty-first century,[47] and while lack of data precludes knowing just when, a significant proportion of Europe's population will soon be nonnative, causing radical social changes and shifts in foreign policy. These are near certainties. Even so, a certain sobriety is in order. This study has attempted to question conventional wisdom about the relationship between population and power and population and security. Despite the certainties, it is important to emphasize the fact that demographers and social scientists have gotten it wrong in the past. We accept that our own assertions could be flawed.

There could be unknowable circumstances or wild cards that change the game. For example, circumstances could arise in which the caps on military spending in Europe and Japan at 1 or 2 percent of GDP could be lifted and they could take on larger share of the global security burden. It is possible that, despite its aging population and fallout from the recent earthquake and tsunami, Japan could be provoked to be more assertive on the global security stage by a conflict of a certain magnitude, such as China going to war over Taiwan, Chinese disintegration into chaos, or a massive earthquake devastating Tokyo. Such events could change the social mood, exacerbating Japan's self-perception as a small country surrounded by hostile states. On a global scale, policymakers may reverse course from any number of events that may cause sudden population devastation and panic, such as a nuclear armed attack by Iran against Israel, a similar exchange between Pakistan and India, massive chemical or biological warfare against European or Japanese cities, or a pandemic causing death on the scale of the black plague, such as an uncontrolled version of avian flu.

If circumstances led U.S. foreign policy into isolationism, this would most certainly diminish its credibility as a reliable ally, perhaps causing the Japanese to acquire nuclear weapons. American isolationism could tilt Chinese foreign policy either way: giving Beijing the "breathing space" to delay war with Taiwan, or emboldening it to assert itself more quickly and aggressively than it would otherwise have done. Swings in U.S. defense and security posture abroad could have similar effects upon Russian foreign policy.

Barring these wild card scenarios, our analysis concludes that the graying of the great powers will bring about more turbulent relations in the coming decades. Population size is not a sufficient factor in measuring national power, but it is a necessary one. Global aging will only accentuate this fact. Nor will nations be able to completely replace dwindling manpower with technological solutions. That said, shared technology can be a strategic leveler and can build trust among allies. The "demographic transition" such as it is will not lead to a demographic peace, nor will "geriatric peace" descend upon the powers in the next few decades. On the contrary, the coming decades will be marked by turbulence within, and perhaps among, alliances as aging and economic decline close windows of opportunity to pursue important but destabilizing foreign policy goals (as in the case of China) and cause European nations to retreat from their global role.

Normative changes attendant to aging and diverging fertility patterns will increase tensions within states that may further hinder global peacekeeping duties. Nations may be able to manage an "elegant decline" and prolong competitiveness through longer work lives, but this will not likely translate into past great powers, Russia and Japan, regaining former status. Nor will social initiatives to reverse fertility decline stave off slippage of Europe or China's military power projection in the medium term. While the United States may have to "go it alone" as its allies retreat from the world stage, it does not have to bear the burden indefinitely if it pursues a set of relatively young and democratic regional security partners in the near term. This will require American strategic planners to be more attentive to demographic concerns than they are now, invest in research and technology that will capitalize on American demographic health, and to resist the temptation to allow American demographic exceptionalism delay the tough fiscal choices today that will ensure sustained military and political power for future generations.

Nations cannot reverse the course of global aging in the near term. No public program can bring back citizens who were never born. But leaders can better protect and defend the children of this generation before passing them the torch and placing upon their shoulders the burden of keeping peaceable relations among nations.

NOTES

Introduction

1. United Nations Population Division, Department of Economic and Social Affairs, *World Population Prospects: The 2010 Revision*, CD-ROM version (New York: 2011), http://esa.un.org/unpd/wpp/Excel-Data/fertility.htm.
2. United Nations Population Division, Department of Economic and Social Affairs, *World Population Ageing 2010* (New York: 2010), 13.
3. Ibid., 27.
4. Ibid., 24.
5. United Nations Population Division, Department of Economic and Social Affairs, *World Population Ageing 2007*, 5.
6. Matthew Connelly shows that ten countries in the developing world had nearly identical fertility rate patterns, despite the fact that half of them had population programs and half did not. Matthew Connelly, *Fatal Misconception: The Struggle to Control World Population* (Cambridge, MA: Harvard Belknap Press, 2008), 374.
7. Lant Pritchett, "Desired Fertility and the Impact of Population Policies," *Population and Development Review* 20, no. 1 (March 1994): 1–55.
8. John Bongaarts, a leading demographer at the Population Council, posits that fertility decline takes place in two phases. In the first phase the distribution of contraception alone pushes down the birthrate. The second phase, driven by economic development and education for women, is much harder to achieve and has not yet taken hold in sub-Saharan Africa and other high-fertility nations. But this does not explain why fertility remains relatively high in more developed states like Egypt. To explain that, experts look to cultural and religious reasons that couples choose to have more than two children. Richard Jackson and Neil Howe conclude that in many societies, "the cultural conditions may not exist for fertility to fall to replacement—much less below." Richard Jackson and Neil Howe, *Graying of the Great Powers: Demography*

and Geopolitics in the 21st Century (Washington: Center for Strategic and International Studies, 2008), 134–35.

9. Richard Cincotta, Robert Engelman, and Daniele Anastasion, *The Security Demographic: Population and Civil Conflict after the Cold War*, Population Action International report, August 1, 2003, http://www.populationaction .org/Publications/Reports/The_Security_Demographic/Summary.shtml.

10. Mara Hvistendahl, *Unnatural Selection: Choosing Boys Over Girls and the Consequences of a World Full of Men* (New York: Public Affairs, 2011), 123–37.

11. During the Vietnam War, "population control" was the term used for establishing constabulary forces and identification card systems to counter the communist insurgency. Connelly, *Fatal Misconception*, 312.

12. Jackson and Howe, *Graying of the Great Powers*, 2.

13. Ibid., 112–13. Emphasis in the original.

14. Ibid., 128.

15. Nicholas Eberstadt, "Four Surprises in Global Demography," *Watch on the West*, July 2004, http://www.aei.org/docLib/20040823_17233Eberstadtgraph ics.pdf.

16. Jack A. Goldstone, "Population and Security: How Demographic Change Can Lead to Violent Conflict," *Journal of International Affairs* 56, no. 1 (fall 2002): 12.

17. Richard Jackson, in telephone interview with Susan Yoshihara, March 2008.

18. Ashley J. Tellis, Janice Bially, Christopher Layne, and Melissa McPherson, *Measuring Power in the Postindustrial Age* (Santa Monica: RAND, 2000), iii.

19. Jason Richards et al., *Russia: Demographic Trends and the Projection of Military Power*, conference paper presented at the 50th Annual Meeting of the International Studies Association, New York, June 9, 2008, http://www.all academic.com/meta/p312179_index.html.

20. See Jackson and Howe, *The Graying of the Great Powers*.

21. See European Security Strategy, *A Secure Europe in a Better World: Security Strategy of the European Union*, Brussels, December 12, 2003, http://www .consilium.europa.eu/uedocs/cmsUpload/78367.pdf.

22. The book uses the most reliable demographic figures available from national and international sources. The latest UN report, *World Population Prospects: The 2010 Revision*, assumes that all nations will achieve the same fertility, replacement fertility of 2.1 children per woman, by 2100. We find it unlikely that all nations will converge at the same fertility, and see no evidence substantiating the belief that every country will reach replacement fertility at any point in the future. Even with its optimistic fertility projections, the latest UN report shows a marked increase in aging from its last analysis in 2009 among the countries studied in this book.

Chapter 1. The Geopolitical Implications of Global Aging

1. Unless otherwise noted, all population projections come from the UN, "medium variant." See Population Division of the Department of Economic and Social Affairs of the United Nations Secretariat, *World Population Prospects: The 2008 Revision*, http://esa.un.org/unpp (accessed January 10, 2011).

2.   Jeremy J. Siegel, "Impact of an Aging Population on the Global Economy," *CFA Institute Conference Proceedings Quarterly* 24, no. 3 (September 2007): 4.
3.   *Controlling the World Obesity Epidemic*, World Health Organization, http://www.who.int/nutrition/topics/obesity/en/index.html.
4.   For a slightly dated but still useful survey of pension reform efforts around the world, see: James C. Capretta, *Sustainability of Public Pension Systems: An Assessment of Reform Efforts in Twelve Developed Countries*, (Washington, DC: Center for Strategic & International Studies, January 2007).
5.   John Maynard Keynes quoted in Richard Jackson and Neil Howe, *Graying of the Great Powers: Demography and Geopolitics in the 21st Century* (Washington, DC: Center for Strategic & International Studies, 2008), 94.
6.   Jackson and Howe, *Graying of the Great Powers*.
7.   Total fertility rates by residence and social group-India: 2001 (table), "Fertility Tables: F-9, F-9 SC, F-9 ST AND F-10," Census of India, statement 3, http://censusindia.gov.in/Data_Products/Data_Highlights/Data_Highlights_link/data_highlights_F9_F10.pdf.
8.   Figures at a glance, India 2003 (table), "Vital Statistics," Census of India, http://www.censusindia.gov.in/vital_statistics/Vital_Rates/Vital_rates.aspx.
9.   Robert W. Fogel, "Longer Lives and Lower Health Costs in 2040: Business Class," Bloomberg.com, July 21, 2011, http://www.bloomberg.com/news/2011-07-21/business-class-longer-lives-and-lower-health-costs.html.
10.   Wolfgang Lutz et al., "The End of World Population Growth," *Nature* 412 (August 2, 2001): 543–45.
11.   Alaka Malwade Basu, *On the Prospects for Endless Fertility Decline in South Asia*, United Nations Population Division (March 2003), http://www.un.org/esa/population/publications/complettingfertility/BASUpaper.pdf.

Chapter 2. Strategic Effects of Demographic Shocks: The Classical Precedent

1.   Carl von Clausewitz, *On War*, ed., trans. Michael Howard and Peter Paret (Princeton: Princeton University Press, 1976), 77.
2.   Alfred Thayer Mahan, *The Influence of Sea Power upon History, 1660–1783* (New York: Dover, 1987), 44–50.
3.   Robert B. Strassler, ed., Richard Crawley, trans., *The Landmark Thucydides* (New York: Touchstone, 1998), 16.
4.   Clausewitz, *On War*, 127.
5.   See, for instance, Strassler, *Landmark Thucydides*, 81–85.
6.   Mogens Herman Hansen, *Studies in the Population of Aigina, Athens and Eretria*, Historisk-filosofiske Meddelelser 94 (Copenhagen: Royal Danish Academy of Sciences and Letters, 2006), 19.
7.   Strassler, *Landmark Thucydides*, 16.
8.   As memorably retold by Herodotus in Book Seven of his *History*. Robert B. Strassler, ed., Andrea L. Purvis, trans., *The Landmark Herodotus* (New York: Pantheon, 2007).
9.   Donald Kagan, *The Outbreak of the Peloponnesian War* (Ithaca: Cornell University Press, 1969), 77–78.

10. Thomas J. Figueira, "Population Patterns in Late Archaic and Classical Sparta," *Transactions of the American Philological Association* 116 (1986): 173, 175.
11. Figueira, "Population Patterns in Late Archaic and Classical Sparta," 210.
12. Figueira, "Population Patterns in Late Archaic and Classical Sparta," 169.
13. Aristotle, *The Politics*, trans. Carnes Lord (Chicago: University of Chicago Press, 1984), 75.
14. G. L. Cawkwell, "The Decline of Sparta," *Classical Quarterly* 33, no. 2 (1983): 393.
15. Strassler, *Landmark Herodotus*, 595; Figueira, "Population Patterns in Late Archaic and Classical Sparta," 167.
16. Strassler, *Landmark Herodotus*, 669.
17. Aristotle, *Politics*, 132.
18. Ibid., 232.
19. Ibid., 76. Figueira agrees that such policies were only marginally effective at boosting the birthrate. Figueira, "Population Patterns in Late Archaic and Classical Sparta," 182.
20. Figueira, "Population Patterns in Late Archaic and Classical Sparta," 184.
21. Aristotle, *Politics*, 76.
22. Ibid., 75–76. Emphasis added.
23. Figueira, "Population Patterns in Late Archaic and Classical Sparta," 166.
24. Cawkwell, "Decline of Sparta," 385, 399–400. On the eventual fall of Sparta, see Robert B. Strassler, ed., John Marincola, trans., *The Landmark Xenophon's Hellenika* (New York: Pantheon, 2009), especially Book Six.
25. Kagan, *Outbreak of the Peloponnesian War*, 47.
26. N. G. L. Hammond, *A History of Greece to 322 B.C.*, 3rd ed. (Oxford: Oxford University Press, 1986), 290.
27. Plutarch, *The Rise and Fall of Athens: Nine Greek Lives* (London: Penguin, 1960), 158–159; see also Strassler, *Landmark Thucydides*, 54–55.
28. Figueira, "Population Patterns in Late Archaic and Classical Sparta," 178.
29. Cawkwell, "The Decline of Sparta," 390.
30. Figueira, "Population Patterns in Late Archaic and Classical Sparta," 178.
31. Nigel Guy Wilson, ed., *Encyclopedia of Ancient Greece* (New York: Routledge, 2006), 215–16.
32. Hammond, *History of Greece*, 290.
33. Figueira, "Population Patterns in Late Archaic and Classical Sparta," 178.
34. Hammond, *History of Greece*, 291.
35. Paul Cartledge, *The Spartans: The World of the Warrior-Heroes of Ancient Greece, from Utopia to Crisis and Collapse* (Woodstock and New York: Overlook, 2003), 34.
36. Kagan, *Outbreak of the Peloponnesian War*, 379–80.
37. Figueira, "Population Patterns in Late Archaic and Classical Sparta," 170.
38. Strassler, *Landmark Thucydides*, 224–46.
39. Figueira, "Population Patterns in Late Archaic and Classical Sparta," 185–86, 210.
40. Strassler, *Landmark Thucydides*, 244.

41. Ibid., 39.
42. Ibid.
43. Ibid., 47.
44. Figueira, "Population Patterns in Late Archaic and Classical Sparta," 181.
45. Hammond, *History of Greece*, 404.
46. Figueira, "Population Patterns in Late Archaic and Classical Sparta," 178.
47. Ibid., 177–78.
48. Ibid., 197.
49. Cawkwell, "The Decline of Sparta," 394–95.
50. Ibid., 392–95.
51. Figueira, "Population Patterns in Late Archaic and Classical Sparta," 184–87, 197–98.
52. Ibid., 186–87.
53. Ibid., 198.
54. Cawkwell, "The Decline of Sparta," 399.
55. Strassler, *Landmark Herodotus*, 411.
56. Wilson, *Encyclopedia of Ancient Greece*, 215–16. Bret Mulligan and Robert Germany put the peak population at 43,000 but agree that the total dropped by over half by the end of the war, to 18,500. See Bret Mulligan and Robert Germany, "The Population of Athens during the War," Haverford College website, October 22, 2009, http://iris.haverford.edu/athens/2009/10/22/population-of-athens-during-the-war. For some excerpts from the lively and somewhat arcane debate over Athenian demographics, see A. W. Gomme, *The Population of Athens in the Fifth and Fourth Centuries B.C.* (Oxford: Blackwell, 1933); A. W. Gomme, "The Slave Population of Athens," *Journal of Hellenic Studies* 66 (1946): 127–29; A. W. Gomme, "The Population of Athens Again," *Journal of Hellenic Studies* 79 (1959): 61–68.
57. Strassler, *Landmark Thucydides*, 40.
58. John R. Hale, *Lords of the Sea: The Epic Story of the Athenian Navy and the Birth of Democracy* (New York: Viking, 2009), 3–42.
59. Strassler, *Landmark Thucydides*, 40.
60. Ibid., 118–20.
61. Victor Davis Hanson, *A War Like No Other*, 65.
62. Mulligan and Germany, "The Population of Athens during the War."
63. Strassler, *Landmark Thucydides*, 120.
64. Ibid., 118.
65. Ibid., 120.
66. Ibid., 111–18.
67. Ibid., 121.
68. Hanson, *A War Like No Other*, 77–78.
69. It bears mentioning that Thucydides seems to generalize the effects wrought by natural disasters to manmade upheavals like revolutions and civil wars. He writes about a civil war that convulsed the city-state of Corcyra in much the same terms he uses to describe the Athenian plague. In both case, a calamity gave rise to a moral inversion in which virtue became weakness—or worse.

Civilized practices, suggests the great historian, are little more than a thin overlay over savagery. Strassler, *Landmark Thucydides*, 198–202.

70. Hanson, *A War Like No Other*, 76.
71. Hale, *Lords of the Sea*, 225–32.
72. Ibid., 231–32.
73. Victor Davis Hanson, "Introduction," in Strassler, *Landmark Thucydides*, xix.
74. Plutarch, *Rise and Fall of Athens*, 173–77; Strassler, *Landmark Thucydides*, 127–28.
75. Donald Kagan, *The Peloponnesian War* (New York: Viking, 2003), 78–79.
76. For more on the Greek resistance to Persia, see Strassler, *Landmark Herodotus*, especially Book Seven.
77. Ibid., 128.
78. Ibid., 427–78.
79. Ibid., 83–84, 123–27.
80. Clausewitz, *On War*, 585–86.

Chapter 3. Population in the Study of Geopolitics

1. Saul B. Cohen, *Geography and Politics in a World Divided* (New York: Oxford University Press, 1975), 29.
2. Frank W. Notestein, "Fundamentals of Population Change in Europe and the Soviet Union," in Hans Weigert and Vilhjalmur Stefansson, ed., *Compass of the World: A Symposium on Political Geography* (New York: Macmillan, 1944), 430.
3. Halford J. Mackinder, "The Geographical Pivot of History," in *Democratic Ideals and Reality*, Halford J. Mackinder, ed. (New York: W. W. Norton, 1962), 263.
4. Ibid., 262.
5. Ibid., 32.
6. Ibid., 94.
7. Ibid.
8. Ibid., 111–12.
9. Ibid., 140.
10. Ibid.
11. Ibid.
12. Ibid., 68.
13. Ibid., 70.
14. Ibid., 149–50.
15. Halford Mackinder, "The Round World and the Winning of the Peace," in *Democratic Ideals and Reality*, Halford J. Mackinder, ed. (New York: W. W. Norton, 1962), 273.
16. Alfred Thayer Mahan, *The Influence of Sea Power upon History, 1660–1783* (London: University Paperbacks, 1965), 44–58. First published in 1890 by Little, Brown.
17. Mahan, "Hawaii and Our Future Sea Power," in *The Interest of America in Sea Power Present and Future* (London: Sampson Low, Marston, 1898) 31.
18. Ibid., 123.
19. Ibid., 243.

20. Mahan, *The Problem of Asia: Its Effect upon International Politics* (New Brunswick, NJ: Transaction Publishers, 2003), 98.
21. Mahan, *The Interest of America in International Conditions* (New Brunswick, NJ: Transaction Publishers, 2003), 73.
22. Karl Haushofer, "Power and Space," and G. Seiffert, "Masters of Space," in Andreas Dorpalen, *The World of General Haushofer* (Port Washington, NY: Kennikat Press, 1942), 89–92, 98–101.
23. Nicholas Spykman, *America's Strategy in World Politics: The United States and the Balance of Power* (New Brunswick, NJ: Transaction Publishers, 2007), first published in 1942; Nicholas Spykman, *The Geography of the Peace* (New York: Harcourt, Brace, 1944).
24. Spykman, *The Geography of the Peace*, 29.
25. Ibid.
26. George F. Kennan, *Realities of American Foreign Policy* (New York: W. W. Norton, 1966), 63–64. First published in 1954 by Princeton University Press.
27. Harold and Margaret Sprout, *Foundations of National Power* (Princeton, NJ: Princeton University Press, 1945), 29.
28. Ibid., 30.
29. Raymond Aron, *The Century of Total War* (Boston: Beacon Press, 1955), 111.
30. James Burnham, *Containment or Liberation?* (New York: John Day, 1952), 251–52. A similar warning to the West regarding the manpower aggregation of the Soviet Empire even before the alliance with China, appeared in William C. Bullitt's *The Great Globe Itself: A Preface to World Affairs* (New Brunswick, NJ: Transaction Publishers, 2005), 84–87. First published in 1946 by Charles Scribner.
31. Two other instances of nations defeating more populous countries during that time were Japan's victories over China in 1894–1895, and over Russia in 1904–1905.
32. Walter Russell Mead, *God and Gold: Britain, America, and the Making of the Modern World* (New York: Alfred A. Knopf, 2007).
33. Samuel P. Huntington, *The Clash of Civilizations and the Remaking of World Order* (New York: Simon & Schuster, 1996), 116–17.
34. Ibid., 117.
35. Ibid., 119.
36. Ibid., 216.
37. George Weigel, *The Cube and the Cathedral: Europe, America, and Politics Without God* (New York: Basic Books, 2005), 21.
38. Niall Ferguson, "Eurabia," *New York Times Magazine*, April 4, 2004.
39. United Nations Secretariat, Department of Economic and Social Affairs, Population Division, *World Population Prospects: The 1998 Revision, Vol. 1: Comprehensive Tables*, November 24, 1998, 100, 118, 152, 158, 164, 182, 202, 224, 240, 258, 268, 338, 350, 352, 366, 368, 376; and Patrick J. Buchanan, *The Death of the West: How Dying Populations and Immigrant Invasions Imperil Our Country and Civilization* (New York: St. Martin's Press, 2002), 12–13.
40. Buchanan, *Death of the West*, 13.

41. Richard Jackson and Neil Howe, with Rebecca Strauss and Keisuke Na-kashima, "Major Findings of the Report," *The Graying of the Great Powers: Demography and Geopolitics in the 21st Century* (Washington, DC: Center for Strategic and International Studies, 2008), 1–6, http://www.csis.org/media/csis/pubs/080630_gai_majorfindings.pdf.

42. Weigel, *Cube and Cathedral*, 132–34.

43. Robert Kagan, *Of Paradise and Power: America and Europe in the New World Order* (New York: Alfred A. Knopf, 2003).

44. Ibid., 3.

45. Ibid., 37.

46. Henry Kissinger, *Does America Need a Foreign Policy? Toward a Diplomacy for the 21st Century* (New York: Simon & Schuster, 2001), 112.

47. Zbigniew Brzezinski, *The Choice: Global Domination or Global Leadership* (New York: Basic Books, 2004), 107.

48. Robert D. Kaplan, "Lost at Sea," *New York Times*, September 21, 2007, http://www.nytimes.com/2007/09/21/opinion/21kaplan.html.

49. Tony Corn, "Perils and Promises of a Global NATO," *Policy Review*, August 15, 2007, http://www.hoover.org/publications/policyreview/9179587.html.

Chapter 4. Population and Health Constraints on the Russian Military

1. United Nations Population Division, Department of Economic and Social Affairs, *World Population Prospects: The 2010 Revision*, CD-ROM version (New York: 2011), http://esa.un.org/unpd/wpp/Excel-Data/fertility.htm.

2. *Krasnaya Zvezda*, December 9, 2004, no. 232, quoted in A. Khomyakov, "Prestupnost' voyennosluzhashchikh est' otrazheniye nashego obshchestva," *Morskoy sbornik*, no. 8 (August 2006): 23; Rod Thornton, *Military Modernization and the Russian Ground Forces*, Carlisle Barracks, Pennsylvania, Strategic Studies Institute, June, 2011, 53, note 94.

3. United Nations Program on HIV/AIDS (UNAIDS), http://www.unaids.org/en/regionscountries/countries/russianfederation/.

4. Joint United Nations Program on HIV/AIDS (UNAIDS), *AIDS Info Country Fact Sheet: Russian Federation*, http://www.unaids.org/en/dataanalysis/tools/aidsinfo/countryfactsheets/.

5. United States Administration for International Development (USAID), *Russia: HIV/AIDS Health Profile*, http://www.usaid.gov/our_work/global_health/aids/Countries/eande/russia_profile.pdf.

6. Ibid.

7. United Nations Population Division, Department of Economic and Social Affairs, *World Population Prospects: The 2010 Revision*.

8. For example, in July 2011, President Medvedev signed into law a measure intended to restrict and stigmatize abortion in order to decrease Russia's high abortion rate. See "Russia: Abortion Restrictions Signed," *New York Times*, July 15, 2011, http://www.nytimes.com/2011/07/16/world/europe/16briefs-Russia.html?_r=1.

9.   "Russian Chief Auditor Calls for Urgent Measures to Halt Population De-
     cline," *BBC Worldwide Monitoring*, March 10, 2007, http://w3.nexis.com/.
10. Federal'naya sluzhba gosudarstvennoy statistiki (FSGS), *Predpolozhitel'naya
     chislennost' naseleniya Rossiyskoy Federatsii do 2025 goda. Statisticheskiy byul-
     leten'*, Moscow, 2005, 7; Population Division of the Department of Economic
     and Social Affairs of the United Nations Secretariat, *Revision* (New York:
     United Nations, 2007); and United Nations Population Division, Department
     of Economic and Social Affairs, *World Population Prospects: The 2010 Revi-
     sion*, CD-ROM version (constant fertility).
11. See Figure 3: Number of Females, Ages 20–24, 25–29, and 20–29, Russia:
     2000–2037, in Murray Feshbach, *Russia's Health and Demographic Crises:
     Policy Implications and Consequences*, Washington, DC: The Chemical and
     Biological Arms Control Institute, 2003, 100. Additional information on these
     numbers until 2025 indicates no revival beyond 8 million.
12. United Nations Population Division, Department of Economic and Social Af-
     fairs, *World Population Prospects: The 2010 Revision*, CD-ROM version. See
     also Feshbach, *Russia's Health and Demographic Crisis*, 2003, 15–19, and also
     figure 5, 101.
13. FSGS, *Predpolozhitel'naya chislennost'*, 2005, 106.
14. For the 2006 Russian estimates see: Ministerstvo zdravookhraneniya i
     sotsial'nogo razvitiya Rossiyskoy Federatsii, *Analiticheskaya informatsiya. Ob
     osnovnykh pokazatelyakh razvitiya zdravookhraneniya i sotsial'no-trudovoy
     sfery v yanvare-marte 2007 goda*, http://www.mzsrfr.ru/analit_inform/653
     .html, downloaded May 12, 2007.
15. See T. Yefremenko, "Proizvoditel'nost' v podderzhku 'demografii'," *Rossiys-
     kaya gazeta*, February 15, 2007, 2.
16. I am informally told that my paper—with Cristina Galvin, *HIV/AIDS in
     Russia—An Analysis of Statistics*, Washington, DC, Woodrow Wilson Inter-
     national Center for Scholars (January 2005)—was reviewed at one of their
     meetings. In addition, my paper, *HIV/AIDS in the Russian Military*, prepared
     for a UNAIDS meeting in Copenhagen, was utilized by two leading Russian
     military medical service generals at the Joint U.S./Russian meetings on HIV/
     AIDS in the militaries in August 2004 and September 2005. I do not have the
     full set of papers from the September 2006 meeting.
17. The Russian title is *Doklad o sostoyanii zdorov'ya detey v Rossiskoy Federat-
     sii (po itogam Vserossiyskoy dispanserizatsii 2002 goda)*, Moscow, 2003. Only
     about five pages of summary text was published in the media. The report was
     handed to Putin in April of 2003.
18. Ibid., 31.
19. Ibid., 33; see also Viktor Baranets, "Prizraki na kontrakte," *Komsomol'skaya
     Pravda*, no. 112, August 6, 2007.
20. "Women in the Russian Federation's Armed Forces Today," *Russian Military
     Review*, no. 3 (March 2007): 66; see also D. Litovkin, "Girls will be Converted
     into Officers," *Defense and Security*, July 4, 2007, translated from *Izvestiya*,
     July 2, 2007.

21. "Health Worsening in Russia's Armed Forces," *Associated Press Wordstream*, June 4, 1999.

22. "It is estimated that thousands of potential conscripts fake psychological and physical sickness to escape conscription into the Russian army." Quoted from "We Don't Want You: Soldiers with 'Diseases' not Welcome," *Russian Life* 46, no. 3 (May 1, 2003): 10.

23. Andrey Andreyev, "Medical Notes Cause 'Depletion' of Army Numbers," *Izvestiya*, December 16, 2005, http://toolkit.dialog.com/.

24. "Moscow Prosecutor Reviews Violations of Draft Law by Military Commissariats," *BBC Worldwide Monitoring*, April 4, 2007, http://w3.nexis.com/.

25. See "Postanovleniye pravitel'stva Rossiyskoy Federatsii ot 25 fevralya 2003 g. N. 1243 ob utverzhdenii polozheniya o voyenno-vrachebnoy ekspertize," *Armeyskiy sbornik*, June 30, 2003, 60–69, especially paragraph 17, about the five grades of readiness for active duty service. The five letter (English equivalent) categories are: A. Ready for military service; B. Ready for military service with insignificant limitations; C. Limited readiness for military service; D. Temporarily not ready for military service, and E. Not ready/acceptable for military service.

26. Ibid.

27. See Keir Giles, *Where Have All the Soldiers Gone? Russia's Military Plans Versus Demographic Reality*, Conflict Studies Research Centre, Defence Academy of the United Kingdom, October 12, 2006, 3. A detailed breakdown of the estimated change in numbers available because of the changes in deferments is based on materials provided by Major General V. Kozhushko, of the Main Organization and Mobilization Directorate of the Ministry of Defense, as follows: "1. Children of Invalids and Pensioners: 3,000; 2. Fathers of children under three years of age: 18,000; 3. Young males whose wives are over twenty-six weeks pregnant: 4,500; 4. Rural teachers: up to 1,000; 5. Rural physicians: 90 persons; 6. Males working in government state organizations: 3,000; 7. Students of educational institutions, fire-fighting service, MVD, correctional institutions, customs organizations: 14,000; 8. Those who have completed primary and secondary vocations school education if they have completed secondary education: 45,000; and 9. Talented musicians, artists, sportsmen, who had received deferments by presidential decree: up to 2,000, for a total slightly above 91,000." From V. Oleshchuk, "Sluzhba po 'prizivu'—vopros ukreplenniya oboronosposobnosti strany," *Voyennyy zheleznodorozhnik*, no. 20 (May 22, 2006): 6.

28. *Komsomol'skaya Pravda*, 2006.

29. Thornton, *Military Modernization and the Russian Ground Forces*, 53.

30. Nikolay Prokhorov, "Sluzhba dlya izbrannykh," *Voyenno-promyshlennyy kur'er*, no. 28 (July 25, 2007).

31. Olga Bozhyeva, "Prizyv v armiyu vyrastet vdvoye," *Moskovskiy komsomolets*, no. 153 (July 13, 2007).

32. For example, the rate fell from 32.7 percent in 1988 to 67.6 percent in 2006. P. Titov, "Bolevaya tochka. Poschitali po oseni," *Nezavisimoye voyennoye oboz-*

reniye, no. 2 (January 25, 2002): 3; Ministerstvo Oborony, "Press-konfcrcntsiya nachal'nika Glavnogo organizatsionno-mobilizatsionnogo upravleniya General'nogo Shtaba VS RF General-polkovnika Vasiliya Smirnova," October 2, 2006, Federal News Service (Russian version).

33. V. Litovkin, "Nedozrevshiy prizyvnik," *Nezavisimoye voyennoye obozreniye*, no. 21 (July 6, 2007): 3.

34. First, a methodological problem must be addressed. It is important to note that it is more than likely that all Russian health statistics are undercounted. To put a positive light on this methodology, it may not be deliberate obfuscation per se, but the result of a clear statement that the numbers reflect only "the first time in life" that a person has been diagnosed with the given illness. For present purposes, it is particularly important for statistics on tuberculosis. Second, the official numbers for total prevalence of those with HIV/AIDS has long been estimated to be some three, five, seven, or ten times higher than the official numbers published in Moscow. UNAIDS has long calculated a range of some three to five times higher than the Russian official figure. What has changed is that not only Pokrovskiy, but also others in the Ministry of Health and even Medvedev are using numbers close to the UNAIDS high estimate. At least as important, there appears to be a debate going on among the senior staff of the Military Medical Service whether the number as reported is correct or is as Generals Bykov and Kulikov note that the numbers are the proverbial "tip of the iceberg." More attention to pre-conscription health status also is the subject of debate and disagreement between those who need to fill quotas and those who worry about the quality, not only the quantity, of new recruits. See United Nations Program on HIV/AIDS (UNAIDS), http://www.unaids.org/en/regionscountries/countries/russianfederation/.

35. From AIDS Foundation East-West, based on data from the Russian Federal AIDS Center, http://afew.org, and Joint United Nations Program on HIV/AIDS (UN AIDS), *Epidemiological Fact Sheet: Russian Federation*, http://www.unaids.org/en/regionscountries/countries/russianfederation/.

36. See Col. Jeffrey Holachek, *Russia's Shrinking Population and the Russian Military's HIV/AIDS Problem*, Occasional Paper prepared for the U.S. Atlantic Council, September 2006, 14; and troop strengths through 2004, in Murray Feshbach, *HIV/AIDS in the Russian Military—Update*, prepared for UNAIDS Meeting in Copenhagen, Denmark, February 22–23, 2005, 4.

37. Colonel-General Vasily Smirnov is cited in V. Khudoleyev, "The Military and Society. 29,000 Draftees Already March," *Krasnaya Zvezda*, June 2, 2006, translated in *Defence & Security*, June 5, 2006.

38. O. Yelenskiy, "Ne tol'ko meditsinskaya problema," *Nezavisimoye voyennoye obozreniye* (February 6, 2004): 1.

39. V. Gavrilov, "Armiya voyuyet so spidom," *Trud*, September 1, 2004.

40. "AIDS: Russian Army Takes on Board American Experience," *RIA Novosti*, October 6, 2005, http://w3.nexis.com/.

41. M. V. Shilova, *Tuberkulez v Rossii v 2005 godu*, Voronezh, BGPU, 2006, 14. See also World Health Organization, *Global Tuberculosis Control: Surveillance, Planning, Financing*, Geneva, 2010.

42.   See: Giles *Where Have All the Soldiers Gone*, October 12, 2006, footnote 98 on page 22, which cites BBC Monitoring of the Military News Agency of March 22, 2006.

43.   See my article in the online Johnson's Russia List, of January 29, 2007, item 8, entitled "XDR-TB in Russia," for estimates of extensively or extremely drug-resistant tuberculosis for Russia.

44.   Dr. Margarita Shilova's latest compendium of data and analysis, *Tuberkulez v Rossii v 2005 godu*, 116, contains a chart with data on the proportion of the ex-prison population who go for treatment after release between 1998 and 2005. The share ranged from 60.4 percent in 1998 to a high of 69.6 percent in 2001, and declined to 57.6 percent in 2005; in other words, about 42 percent did not continue treatment in 2005. See also World Health Organization, *Health Ministers to Accelerate Efforts Against Drug-resistant TB*, April 2, 2009, http://www.who.int/mediacentre/news/releases/2009/tuberculosis_drug_resistant_20090402/en/.

45.   See R. D. Muchaidze et al., "Epidemiologiya i infektsionnyye bolezni. O 'tuberkuleze' u voyennosluzhaschikh zapasa, prizvannykh na voyennyye sbory," *Voyenno-meditsinskiy zhurnal*, no. 4 (April 30, 2006): 37–39. The authors cite a previously unknown handbook—but not unexpected—source for these data. The statistical book on health in the military is entitled *Pokazateli sostoyaniya zdorov'ya voyennosluzhashchikh Vooruzhennykh Sil Rossiyskoy Federatsii, a takzhe deyatel'nosti voyenno-meditsinskikh podrazdeleniy, chastey i uchrezhdeniy v 2004*, Moscow, 2005.

46.   World Health Organization, *Health Ministers to Accelerate Efforts Against Drug-resistant TB*, April 2, 2009, http://www.who.int/mediacentre/news/releases/2009/tuberculosis_drug_resistant_20090402/en/.

47.   World Health Organization, *Tuberculosis: MDR-TB & XDR-TB 2011 Progress Report*, March 23, 2011, and World Health Organization, World Health Organization, *Global Tuberculosis Control Epidemiology, Strategy, Financing*, 2009, http://www.who.int/tb/publications/global_report/2009/pdf/report_without_annexes.pdf; Stop TB Partnership, *The Global MDR-TB & XDR-TB Response Plan 2007–2008*, WHO/HTM/TB/2007.387, Geneva, World Health Organization, 2007, 19 and 31.

48.   "Russian Chief Auditor Calls for Urgent Measures to Halt Population Decline," *BBC Worldwide Monitoring*, March 10, 2007, http://w3.nexis.com/.

49.   Dmitry Gorenberg, "The Russian Military's Manpower Problem: Tracking Developments in the Russian Military," *Russian Military Reform* (blog), July 29, 2011, http://russiamil.wordpress.com/2011/07/29/the-russian-militarys-manpower-problem/.

50.   Ibid.

Chapter 5. Europe's Strategic Future and the Need for Large-Family Pronatalism: A Normative Study of Demographic Decline

1.   United Nations Population Division, Economic & Social Affairs, "Future Expectations for Below-Replacement Fertility," *Population Bulletin of the United Nations*, Special Issue 40/41 (1999): 140.

2. See Mark Haas, "A Geriatric Peace? The Future of U.S. Power in a World of Aging Populations," *International Security* 32, no. 1 (2007): 112–47; and Nicholas Eberstadt and Hans Groth, "Europe's Coming Demographic Challenge, Unlocking the Value of Health," the AEI Press, 2007.

3. United Nations Population Division, Economic & Social Affairs, *World Population Prospects: The 2010 Revision.*

4. Ibid.

5. United Nations Population Division, *Future Expectations*, 140, http://esa .un.org/wpp/unpp/panel_population.htm.

6. Wolfgang Lutz, Vegard Skirbekk, and Maria Rita Testa, *The Low Fertility Trap Hypothesis: Forces That May Lead to Further Postponement and Fewer Births in Europe*, Vienna Yearbook of Population Research, 2006, 9.

7. Ibid., 9.

8. Ibid., 5.

9. Ibid., 7.

10. European Parliament Committee on Employment and Social Affairs, *Draft Report on the Demographic Future of Europe*, (2007/2156 [INI]), November 10, 2007, 4.

11. Joseph Chamie, "Fewer Babies Pose Difficult Challenges for Europe," *Yale Global Online*, October 8, 2007.

12. See Eberstadt and Groth, "Europe's Coming Demographic Challenge."

13. Haas, "Geriatric Peace," 112–47.

14. Henry Chu, "European Allies to Slash Military Spending," *Los Angeles Times*, December 26, 2010.

15. Haas, "Geriatric Peace," 112–47.

16. European Defence Agency, *An Initial Long-Term Vision for European Defence Capability and Capacity Needs*, October 3, 2006, 6.

17. Jeffrey Simon, "NATO's Uncertain Future: Is Demography Destiny?" *Strategic Forum*, Institute for National Strategic Studies, October 2008, 4.

18. Clark Whelton, "A Demographic Theory of War, Population, Power and the 'Slightly Weird' Ideas of Gunnar Heinsohn," *Weekly Standard*, October 5, 2007.

19. European Defence Agency, *Initial Long-Term Vision*, 2.

20. European Parliament Committee on Employment and Social Affairs, *Draft Report*, 4.

21. Chamie, "Fewer Babies," 4.

22. Dimiter Philipov and Caroline Berghammer, *Religion and Fertility Ideals, Intentions and Behavior: a Comparative Study of European Countries*, Vienna Yearbook of Population Research, 2007.

23. See *Report on the Evolution of the Family in Europe 2008*, Institute for Family Policies, 2008.

24. Tony Fahey and Zsolt Spéder, *Fertility and Family Issues in an Enlarged Europe,*" *European Foundation for the Improvement of Living and Working Conditions*, 2004, 1.

25. Chamie, "Fewer Babies," 3.

26. European Parliament Committee on Employment and Social Affairs, *Draft Report*, 4.

27. European Commission, *Confronting Demographic Change: A New Solidarity Between Generations*, Green Paper, 2005, 5.

28. Chamie, "Fewer Babies," 4.

29. European Commission, *Confronting Demographic Change*, 5.

30. Joop de Beer, *An Assessment of the Tempo Effect for Future Fertility in the European Union*, European Commission, May 2006, 8.

31. Lutz, "Low Fertility Trap Hypothesis," 16.

32. Wolfgang Lutz, *Adaptation versus Mitigation Policies on Demographic Change in Europe*, Vienna Yearbook of Population Research, 2007, 20.

33. United Nations Population Division, *Replacement Migration: Is It a Solution to Declining and Ageing Populations*, ST/ESA/SER.A/206, 2001, 11.

34. Joshua Goldstein, Wolfgang Lutz, and Rita Maria Testa, "The Emergence of Sub-Replacement Family Size Ideals in Europe," *Population Research and Policy Review*, 2003.

35. Fahey and Spéder, *Fertility and Family Issues*, 26–27.

36. Maria Rita Testa and Leonardo Grilli, *The Influence of Childbearing Regional Contexts on Ideal Family Size in Europe*, Institut National d'Etudes Demographiques, 2006.

37. Lutz, "Low Fertility Trap Hypothesis," 13.

38. Lutz, "Adaptation versus Mitigation Policies," 2007, 20.

39. See *Report on the Evolution of the Family in Europe, 2008*.

40. European Parliament Committee on Employment and Social Affairs, *Draft Report*, 4.

41. "Europe in Figures," *Eurostat Yearbook 2006–2007*, 75.

42. United Nations Population Division, *Replacement Migration*, 24.

43. Chamie, "Fewer Babies," 2.

44. David Coleman, *Demographic Diversity and the Ethnic Consequences of Immigration—Key Issues that the Commission's Report Left Out*, Vienna Yearbook of Population Research, 2007, 10.

45. Mary Kent, *Do Muslims Have More Children Than Other Women in Western Europe?* Population Reference Bureau, 2008, 1.

46. Esther Pan, *Europe: Integrating Islam*, Council on Foreign Relations, July 13, 2005.

47. Benita Ferrero-Waldner, "The EU's Role in Protecting Europe's Security," speech delivered May 30, 2006, 2.

48. European Security Strategy, *A Secure Europe in a Better World*, Brussels, December 12, 2003, 9.

49. Ibid., 3.

50. European Defence Agency, *Initial Long-Term Vision*, 10.

51. Ibid., 13.

52. Ibid.

53. John Van Oudenaren, "Sources of Conflict in Europe and the Former Soviet Union," *Sources of Conflict in the 21st Century: Regional Futures and US Strategy*, Zalmay M. Khalilzad and Ian O. Lesser, eds. (Santa Monica: RAND, 1998).

54. Craig Romm, "Will NATO Be Defeated By Demography?" *San Diego Union-Tribune*, October 4, 2002.

55. Richard Cincotta, Robert Engleman, and Daniele Anastasion, *The Security Demographic, Population and Civil Conflict After the Cold War*, Population Action International report, August 1, 2003, 13–14.

56. Poul Nielson, European Commissioner for Development and Humanitarian Aid, speech given at European Population Forum–UNECE UNFPA (Geneva), January 12, 2004.

57. Whelton, "A Demographic Theory of War, Population, Power."

58. Agnese Vitali, Francesco Billari, Alexia Prskawetz, and Maria Rita Testa, *Preference Theory and Low Fertility: A Comparative Perspective*, European Demographic Research Papers, 6.

59. Ibid., 22.

60. Ibid.

61. Fahey and Spéder, "Fertility and Family Issues," 21.

62. Vitali, "Preference Theory," 8–9.

Chapter 6. American Demographic Exceptionalism and the Future of U.S. Military Power

1. Charles Krauthammer coined the term "unipolar moment" in 1990 to refute those who predicted a multipolar world order after the end of the Cold War. Krauthammer argued, correctly, that American popular consensus favored interventionism over isolationism, and that the threat of great power war had greatly diminished with the Soviet collapse. See Charles Krauthammer, "The Unipolar Moment: America and the World," *Foreign Affairs* (1990–1991).

2. Mark L. Haas, "A Geriatric Peace? The Future of U.S. Power in a World of Aging Populations," *International Security* 32, No. 1 (summer 2007), 114.

3. The competitive economic advantages of American demographic trends are increasingly noted by financial institutions. See, for example, Amlan Roy et al., *U.S. Demographics—Favorably Poised For the Future*, Credit Suisse report, Geneva, May 5, 2010.

4. Phillip Longman, *The Empty Cradle: How Falling Birthrates Threaten World Prosperity (And What To Do About It)* (New York: Basic Books, 2004); Ben J. Wattenberg, *How the New Demography of Depopulation Will Shape Our Future* (Chicago: Evan R. Dee, 2004).

5. CIA World Factbook 2009, https://www.cia.gov/library/publications/the-world-factbook/geos/us.html.

6. U.S. Department of Defense, *A Cooperative Strategy for 21st Century Seapower*, October 2007. See also STRATFOR, *Net Assessment of the United States 2005–2015*, http://www.stratfor.com/analysis/net_assessment_united_states.

7. U.S. Air Force, *Building the 21st Century Air Force: Top 10 Questions*, http://www.alamoafa.org/docs/AF21%20Top%2010Question061606.ppt#745,3,USAF Priorities.

8. Baker Spring, *Defense FY2008 Budget Analysis: Four Percent for Freedom*, Heritage Foundation, March 5, 2007.

9.   Craig Whitlock and Greg Jaffe, "Gates Wants to Drop $14 Billion Marine Landing-craft Program," *Washington Post*, January 6, 2011, http://www.washingtonpost.com/wp-dyn/content/article/2011/01/05/AR2011010506374.html?hpid=topnews.

10. The proposed fiscal year 2010 budget was $712 billion and 4.8 percent of the gross domestic product. *Budget of the U.S. Government: Fiscal Year 2010*, Office of Management and Budget, 55, http://www.whitehouse.gov/omb/budget/fy2010/assets/hist.pdf.

11. Stephen J. Hadley, William J. Perry, et al., *The QDR in Perspective: Meeting America's National Security Needs In the 21st Century:The Final Report of the Quadrennial Defense Review Independent Panel* (Washington, DC: United States Institute of Peace, 2010), iv.

12. Rob Stein, "US Fertility Rate Hits 35-year High, Stabilizing Population," *Washington Post*, December 21, 2007.

13. *World Population Prospects: The 2008 Revision*, vol. 1 (New York: UN Department of Economic and Social Affairs, 2009), 484. This analysis uses the medium variant statistics.

14. The UN's 2010 forecast predicts that the U.S. total fertility rate will remain at 2.09, with its lowest estimate 1.59 in 2050, and its highest estimate 2.59 in that same period. The probabilistic model used to make the 2010 UN fertility estimates remains controversial. This chapter therefore relies on the more conservative forecasts made in the UN's 2008 estimates. United Nations Population Division, Department of Economic and Social Affairs, *World Population Prospects: The 2010 Revision*, CD-ROM version (New York: 2011), http://esa.un.org/unpd/wpp/Excel-Data/fertility.htm.

15. U.S. Census Bureau, *U.S. Census 2010*, Washington, DC: Department of Commerce, http://2010.census.gov/2010census/data/.

16. *World Population Prospects: The 2008 Revision*, vol. 2 (New York: UN Department of Economic and Social Affairs, 2009), 922–23.

17. Ibid., 485.

18. *World Population Ageing 2009* (New York: UN Department of Economic and Social Affairs, 2010), 72. The median age is the age that divides the nation. Half of Americans are older, and half younger, than thirty-six and a half.

19. *World Population Ageing 2007* (New York: UN Department of Economic and Social Affairs, 2008), 496.

20. Jeffrey S. Passel and D'Vera Cohn, *U.S. Population Projections: 2005–2050* (Washington, DC: Pew Research Center, 2008), 11.

21. Passel and *U.S. Population Projections: 2005–2050*, 22.

22. The economic impact of an aging America is evident in the changing mix of the dependency ratio—the number of dependent old and young per one hundred workers ages sixteen to sixty-five—which is divided into youth and old age dependency ratios. The U.S. youth dependency ratio fell from 41.7 in 1950 to 30.5 in 2007, and is expected to fall to 27.8 by 2050. Meanwhile, the old age ratio rose from 12.8 to 18.5 from 1950 to 2007, and is expected to reach 33.3 by 2050, at which time the dependent old will outnumber the dependent

young. With 11 million very old people (age eighty or over), the United States is one of five countries that are home to half the world's very old persons, and Americans will remain in this group for the foreseeable future. The number of U.S. eighty-plus-year-olds is expected to rise to 29 million by mid-century. As percentage of all the aged, the over-eighty category has risen to 3.6 percent from 1 percent in 1950, and is expected to reach 7.3 percent by 2050. Passel and Cohn, *U.S. Population Projections: 2005–2050*, 28.

23. Nicholas Eberstadt, "Global Demographic Outlook to 2025" (speech, Economic Conference on Demography, Growth and Wellbeing, Zurich, November 30, 2006), available at http://www.aei.org.

24. Phillip Longman, "The Liberal Baby Bust," *USA Today*, March 13, 2006.

25. Ibid.

26. Kate Connolly, "Nine Months On, World Cup Scorers Spark German Baby Boom," *Guardian*, April 28, 2007.

27. Michael Bloomberg, New York City Mayor's Office Press Release of December 12, 2006, available at http://www.nyc.gov.

28. Ibid.

29. Robert Kagan, *Dangerous Nation: America's Foreign Policy From Its Earliest Days to the Dawn of the Twentieth Century* (New York: Vintage, 2006), 3.

30. A. J. B., "Population Trends and Power," *International Affairs* 21, no. 1 (1945): 79–86.

31. Ibid.

32. STRATFOR, *Net Assessment of the United States*.

33. Ibid.

34. Passel and Cohn, *U.S. Population Projections: 2005–2050*, 1.

35. While the rate of growth of U.S. immigrant population has increased from 0.6 immigrants per 1,000 people in the 1920s to 2.2 in the 1960s, to a high of 6.4 in the 1990s and 5.2 today, the current rates pale in comparison to the 1850s rate of 12.1, the 1880s rate of 10.5, and the first decade of the 1900s rate of 11.0.

36. Max Boot and Michael O'Hanlon, "A Military Path to Citizenship," *Washington Post*, October 19, 2006.

37. Bryan Bender, "Military Considers Recruiting Foreigners, Expedited Citizenship Would Be an Incentive," *Boston Globe*, December 26, 2006.

38. Quester reminds military planners that during the American Civil War "the Union Army extensively recruited recent immigrants, most particularly from Ireland and Germany, allowing them to serve in segregated regiments where all their comrades would be of the same ethnicity, with a great number of these enlistees not yet being American citizens." George H. Quester, "Demographic Trends and Military Recruitment: Surprising Possibilities," *Parameters*, spring 2005, 31.

39. Donna Miles, "Officials Hope to Rekindle Interest in Immigration Bill Provision," *American Forces Press Service*, June 11, 2007.

40. New England Army National Guard recruiters, in written responses to author, October 4, 2010.

41. Quester, "Demographic Trends and Military Recruitment," 33. This is corroborated by anecdotal data from military recruiters. The U.S. Department of Defense does not collect data on the number of siblings of new recruits from all the services.

42. Longman, "The Liberal Baby Bust."

43. Ibid.

44. Taking advantage of unique American media savvy, the Army hired nine Madison Avenue firms for their recruiting campaign, including individual firms exclusively hired to target the growing American Hispanic and Asian demographics. Stuart Elliot, "Army's New Battle Cry Aims At Potential Recruits," *New York Times*, November 9, 2006. See also http://www.goarmy.com/for_parents/index.jsp?hmref=tn?bl=.

45. Tim Kane, *Who Bears the Burden? Demographic Characteristics of U.S. Military Recruits Before and After 9/11*, Center for Data Analysis, Heritage Foundation, November 7, 2005.

46. U.S. Census Bureau, *2010 Census*; see also U.S. Census Bureau, *Population Projections for States, by Age, Sex, Race, and Hispanic Origin: 1995 to 2025*, Population Paper Listing 47 (Washington, DC: U.S. Department of Commerce, 1996), http://www.census.gov/population/www/projections/ppl47.html.

47. Recruit-to-population ratios from Kane, *Who Bears the Burden?* Population growth rates are from U.S. Census Bureau, *Population Projections for States, by Age, Sex, Race, and Hispanic Origin: 1995 to 2025*.

48. Leadership expert Gen. Walter Ulmer described this as the vision of "a thousand leaders, alone with their units on a thousand hills." Ulmer was commanding general of U.S. Army III Corps, Fort Hood, Texas, from 1982 to 1985.

49. "Rangel Calls for Reinstating Military Draft," Associated Press, November 20, 2006. Rep. Charles Rangel (D-NY) justified his demand on the grounds that it would give a more balanced representation of ethnic groups to the forces risking their lives in the Iraq war.

50. The All-Volunteer Force cost approximately $10 billion more per year (in 2006 dollars) than the draft army did in 1974. Reversion to a draft would not entirely eliminate the need for recruiting and bonuses since volunteers would still be necessary. Congressional Budget Office, *The All Volunteer Military: Issues and Performance* (Washington: Congressional Budget Office, 2007), viii, 35–36.

51. Office of the Under Secretary of Defense (Military Community and Family Policy), *Demographics 2008: Profile of the Military* (Washington: Department of Defense, 2008).

52. Ibid., 28.

53. Ibid., 31.

54. Ibid., 20.

55. Ibid., 15.

56. Capt. Kenneth Barrett, U.S. Navy, senior military recruiter, in interview with the author, March 2008.

57. New England National Guard recruiters, in interview with the author, October 4, 2010.

58. Ibid.

59. A Vermont recruiter said that one typical example was when a women's group restricted his access to their constituents despite the fact that the military fulfilled their mission of giving women economic independence. Maj. Greg Knight, Vermont National Guard, in interview with the author, October 2010.

60. The program requires two years of service for every year on sabbatical without pay but with medical and dental benefits. Twenty enlisted and twenty officers inaugurated the pilot program. Capt. Ken Barrett, in interview with the author, March 2008.

61. Hadley, Perry, et al., *The QDR in Perspective*, iv.

62. Ibid., xiv.

63. Capt. Ronald Ratcliff, U.S. Navy (Ret.), U.S. Naval War College, in interview with the author, June 23, 2010.

64. Robert M. Gates (speech, Navy League Sea-Air-Space-Exposition, May 3, 2010).

65. John Cawley and Johanna Catherine Maclean, *Unfit for Service: The Implications of Rising Obesity for U.S. Military Service* (Washington, DC: National Bureau of Economic Research, 2010), http://www.nber.org/papers/w16408.

66. Ibid.

67. David Ochmanek, Deputy Assistant Secretary of Defense for Force Development, in e-mail interview with the author.

68. Seth Cropsey, "Anchors Away: American Sea Power in Dry Dock," *Foreign Affairs* (January-February 2011).

69. Hadley, Perry, et al., *The QDR in Perspective*, 55.

70. Ibid.

71. Ibid., 25.

72. Ibid.

73. Ibid.

74. Anthony Cordesman, "A Poisoned Chalice? The Flaws in the FY2008 Defense Program," Center for Strategic and International Security, July 3, 2007, http://csis.org/files/media/csis/pubs/080630_fy2009_poisoned_chalice.pdf.

75. Ibid.

76. Congressional Budget Office, *Federal Debt and the Risk of a Fiscal Crisis*, July 27, 2010, 3–4, http://www.cbo.gov/ftpdocs/116xx/doc11659/07-27_Debt_FiscalCrisis_Brief.pdf.

77. Ibid. See also Congressional Budget Office projections, http://www.cbo.gov/publications/collections/health.cfm.

78. Ibid. These estimates were made before the 2010 health-care reform legislation.

79. Douglas Holtz-Eakin, "Obama Report Card: It's Worse Than We Thought," *National Review Online*, October 27, 2010, http://www.nationalreview.com/corner/251158/obamacare-report-card-its-worse-we-thought-douglas-holtz-eakin#.

80. Twenty-six states filed lawsuits to block the enactment of the health-care law's requirement that all Americans carry health insurance or be subject to fines.

In August 2011 a federal appeals court sided with those states and struck down the requirement.

81. Jagdeesh Gokhale, *Social Security: A Fresh Look at Policy Alternatives* (Chicago: University of Chicago Press, 2010).

82. Jagdeesh Gokhale, in interview with the author, November 9, 2010.

83. Gokhale, *Social Security.*

84. Jagdeesh Gokhale, in interview with the author, November 9, 2010.

85. Kata Fustos, *Marriage and Partnership Turnover for American Families*, Population Reference Bureau, June 2010, http://www.prb.org/Articles/2010/usmarriagepolicyseminar.aspx.

86. Ibid.

87. U.S. Government Accounting Office, *Defense Acquisitions: Assessment of Selected Weapons Programs*, March 2007, cited in Cordesman, "A Poisoned Chalice?," 53.

88. Ibid.

89. Robert M. Gates, speech.

90. Hans Ulrich Kaeser and Anthony H. Cordesman, "Abandon Ships: The Costly Illusion of Unaffordable Transformation," Center for Strategic and International Studies, August 19, 2008, 18, http://csis.org/publication/abandon-ships.

91. Ibid., 22.

92. Mark Arena et al., *Why Has the Cost of Navy Ships Risen? A Macroscopic Examination of the Trends in U.S. Naval Ship Costs Over the Past Several Decades* (Santa Monica: RAND, 2006).

93. Congressional Budget Office, *An Analysis of the Navy's Fiscal Year 2011 Shipbuilding Plan*, May 2010, 1.

94. Kaeser and Cordesman, "Abandon Ships," 27.

95. Ibid., 28.

96. Capt. George Fink, U.S. Navy (Ret.), in interview with the author, November 19, 2010.

97. Robert M. Gates, speech.

98. Ibid.

99. U.S. Department of Defense, *Fiscal Year 2011 Budget Request Overview*, February 2010, 6, http://comptroller.defense.gov/defbudget/fy2011/FY2011_Budget_Request_Overview_Book.pdf.

100. Congressional Budget Office, *Federal Debt and the Risk of a Fiscal Crisis*, July 27, 2010, 4.

101. Anthony H. Cordesman, "Cleansing the Poisoned Chalice? The Obama Administration and the Challenge of National Security Planning, Programming, and Budgeting," 23.

102. Ibid.

103. Jagdeesh Gokhale and Kent Smetters, "Bailout-Mania," *Forbes.com*, September 17, 2008.

104. Jagdeesh Gokhale, "Point of No Return Approaching for U.S. Debt," podcast of July 14, 2010, http://www.cato.org/dailypodcast/podcast-archive.php?podcast_id=1195.

105. Paul Kennedy, "The Relative Decline of America," *Atlantic*, August 1997.
106. Michael Cox, "Is the United States in Decline—Again? An Essay," *International Affairs* 83, no. 4 (July 2007): 643–53.
107. Mark L. Haas, "A Geriatric Peace?," 145.
108. Samuel P. Huntington, "The U.S.—Decline or Renewal?" *Foreign Affairs*, winter 1988–1989.
109. For example, two classified strategic planning documents, *Guidance for Employment of the Force* and *Guidance for the Development of the Force*, if more fully integrated into strategic and force planning, may help planners seize the demographic advantages afforded by American society and tailor decisions to strategic interests. Jason Sherman, "Gates Signs Planning Documents to Guide Investments, Operations," *Inside the Pentagon*, May 15, 2008, http://www.military-quotes.com/forum/gates-signs-planning-documents-guide-t62194.html.
110. Passel and Cohn, *U.S. Population Projections: 2005–2050*.

Chapter 7. The Setting Sun? Strategic Implications of Japan's Demographic Transition

1. See "The Demographic Dilemma: Japan's Aging Society," *Asia Program Special Report*, Woodrow Wilson International Center for Scholars, no. 107 (January 2003): 1–23; K. S. Seetharam, "Population, Society, and Power: East Asia's Future," *Georgetown Journal of International Affairs* 4, no. 2 (summer 2003): 27–34; and David J. Staley, "Japan's Uncertain Future: Key Trends and Scenarios," *The Futurist*, March-April 2002, 48–53.
2. Richard Jackson and Neil Howe, *The Graying of the Great Powers: Demography and Geopolitics in the 21st Century* (Washington, DC: CSIS, 2008), 36.
3. For total fertility figures, see United Nations Population Division, Economic & Social Affairs, *World Population Prospects: The 2008 Revision, Volume I: Comprehensive Tables*, 2009, 622–23.
4. United Nations Population Division, Economic & Social Affairs, *World Population Ageing, 2007*, 2007, 6.
5. United Nations Population Division, Economic & Social Affairs, *World Population Ageing, 2009*, 2010, 72 and 70.
6. United Nations Population Division, Economic and Social Affairs, *World Population Ageing, The 2010 Revision*, 2011, http://esa.un.org/unpd/wpp/index.htm.
7. Ibid.
8. United Nations Population Division, *World Population Prospects: The 2008 Revision*, volume 1, 292–93.
9. *Population Projections for Japan: 2001–2050*, National Institute of Population and Social Security Research, January 2002, 12.
10. For a summary of findings from the 2006 report, see Ryuichi Kaneko, Akira Ishikawa, et al., "Population Projections for Japan: 2006–2055—Outline of Results, Methods, and Assumptions," *Japanese Journal of Population* 6, no. 1 (March 2008): 76–83.
11. *Long-Term Forecast of Global Economy and Population 2006–2050: Demographic*

Change and the Asian Economy, Japan Center for Economic Research (JCER), March 2007, 22.

12. *Japan's Visions for Future Security and Defense Capabilities*, Council on Security and Defense Capabilities, October 2004, 13.

13. The first National Defense Program Outlines document was published in 1976, the second in 1995.

14. Government of Japan, *National Defense Program Guideline: Approved by the Security Council and the Cabinet on December 10, 2004*, 4, http://www.kantei .go.jp/foreign/policy/2004/1210taikou_e.html.

15. Ibid., 7.

16. *Japan's Visions for Future Security and Defense Capabilities in the New Era: Toward a Peace-Creating Japan*, The Council on Security and Defense Capabilities in the New Era, August 2010, 2.

17. Ibid. 13.

18. Government of Japan, *National Defense Program Guidelines for FY 2011 and beyond: Approved by the Security Council and the Cabinet on December 17, 2010*, 17.

19. Japan Ministry of Defense, *Defense of Japan 2005*, 81.

20. National Institute of Population and Social Security Research, *Population Statistics of Japan 2008*, September 2008, 10.

21. United Nations Population Division, Economic & Social Affairs, *World Population Prospects: The 2008 Revision, Volume II: Sex and Age Distribution of the World Population*, 2009, 538.

22. Japan Ministry of Defense, *Defense of Japan 2009*, 343.

23. U.S. Census Bureau, *Population Projections of the United States by Age, Race, Sex, and Hispanic Origin: 1995–2050* (Washington, DC: U.S. Department of Commerce, 1996), 9

24. *Population Statistics of Japan 2008*, 11.

25. The analytical framework for this section is drawn from Brian Nichiporuk, *The Security Dynamics of Demographic Factors* (Santa Monica, CA: RAND, 2000), 26–34.

26. For details on the stopping power of water, see John J. Mearsheimer, *The Tragedy of Great Power Politics* (New York: W. W. Norton, 2001), 114–28.

27. See Michael O'Hanlon, "Why China Cannot Conquer Taiwan," *International Security* 25, no. 2 (fall 2000): 51–86.

28. Andrew C. Winner and Toshi Yoshihara, "India and Pakistan at the Edge," *Survival* 44, no. 3 (fall 2002): 69–86.

29. See Eliot A. Cohen, Michael J. Eisenstadt, and Andrew J. Bacevich, *Knives, Tanks, and Missiles: Israel's Security Revolution* (Washington, DC: Washington Institute for Near East Policy, 1998).

30. See John Wilson Lewis and Xue Litai, *China Builds the Bomb* (Stanford, CA: Stanford University Press, 1991), 212.

31. Peter G. Peterson, "The Shape of Things to Come: Global Aging in the Twenty-first Century," *Journal of International Affairs* 56, no. 1 (fall 2002), 205.

32. George H. Quester, "Demographic Trends and Military Recruitment: Suprising Possiblities," *Parameters* 35, no. 1 (spring 2005): 38–39.

33. Peter G. Peterson, "Gray Dawn: The Global Aging Crisis," *Foreign Affairs* 78, no. 1 (January-February 1999), 50.

34. *Japan's Visions for Future Security and Defense Capabilities in the New Era*, 2010, 4.

35. Ibid., 41.

36. Ibid., 14-21.

37. Ibid., 25.

38. National Defense Program Guidelines, 2010, 2.

39. Ibid., 12.

40. U.S.-Japan Security Consultative Committee, "Joint Statement," Washington, DC, February 19, 2005.

41. U.S.-Japan Security Consultative Committee, "Joint Statement: Transformation and Realignment for the Future," Tokyo, October 29, 2005.

42. U.S.-Japan Security Consultative Committee, "Joint Statement: Alliance Transformation: Advancing United States-Japan Security and Defense Cooperation," Washington, DC, May 1, 2007.

43. U.S.-Japan Security Consultative Committee, "Joint Statement: Toward a Deeper and Broader U.S.-Japan Alliance: Building on 50 Years of Partnership," Washington, DC, June 21, 2011.

44. Ratios of active-duty personnel to population are drawn from the annual series by International Institute for Strategic Studies, *The Military Balance* (London: Routledge, 1997–2007).

45. *Defense of Japan, 2009*, 495.

46. "One-Star General, Senior Sergeant to Be Created As New Ranks," *Asagumo*, July 5, 2007, 1.

47. *Japan's Visions for Future Security and Defense Capabilities in the New Era*, 2010, 43.

48. General Joji Higuchi, "Will Japan Be Able to Survive the New East Asian Cold War?" *Seiron*, May 1, 2007, 88–95.

49. "Can the SDF Protect Japan?" *Sapio*, July 22, 2009, 9.

50. "Japan's Marine Defense in Abnormal Situation With 1 Escort Flotilla at Home," *Tokyo Shimbun*, July 20, 2002; and Shigeru Handa, "Is There a Need for Escort Ships to Protect Fueling Operations?" *Tokyo Shimbun*, February 23, 2003.

51. "Laws Stretch Resources of MSDF to the Limit," *Yomiuri Shimbun*, September 22, 2004.

52. "The Self-Defense Forces Have No Means to Take Necessary Action," *Shukan Bunshun*, July 20, 2006, 32–35.

53. Koichi Furusho, "Present and Future of JMSDF," *Sekai no Kansen*, July 2009, 147.

54. "Major Items of the 2010 Defense Budget Request," *Asagumo*, September 3, 2009.

55. The newest *Aegis* destroyer to join the MSDF cost $1.4 billion. See "Japan Deploys Sixth High-tech Aegis Destroyer," *AFP*, March 13, 2008, http://www.spacewar.com/reports/Japan_deploys_sixth_high-tech_Aegis_destroyer_999.html.

56. *Japan's Visions for Future Security and Defense Capabilities in the New Era*, 2010, 40.
57. Japan Ministry of Defense, *Defense of Japan 2006*, 382.
58. "Fiscal Health 'Will Need 27 Trillion Yen in Cuts,'" *Daily Yomiuri*, March 26, 2006.
59. Japan Defense Agency, *Info-RMA: Study on Info-RMA and the Future of the Self-Defense Forces*, December 2000, 9.
60. For more recent Japanese views of the RMA, or "defense transformation" in current parlance, see Sugio Takahashi, "The Japanese Perception of the Information Technology-Revolution in Military Affairs: Toward A Defensive Information-Based Transformation," in *The Information Revolution in Military Affairs in Asia*, Emily O. Goldman and Thomas G. Mahnken, eds. (New York: Palgrave, 2004), 81–95; and Noboru Yamaguchi, "US Defence Transformation and Japan Defence Policy," *RUSI Journal*, August 2006, 62–67.
61. *Defense of Japan 2007*, 119.
62. *Japan's Visions for Future Security and Defense Capabilities*, 2004, 13.
63. *National Defense Program Guideline*, 2004, 4.
64. Western analysts anticipate that this transition to a technology-intensive defense posture will be a key pillar of Japanese military strategy. See United States Joint Forces Command, *Joint Operating Environment 2008: Challenges and Implications for the Future Joint Force*, November 25, 2008, 10; and Jackson and Howe, *The Graying of the Great Powers*, 171.
65. "Indigenously Developed UAV," *Asagumo*, December 24, 2009.
66. Japan's Ministry of Defense, *Defense Programs and Budget of Japan: Overview of FY2010 Budget*, April 2010, 7.
67. Nisohachi Hyodo, *The SDF's Unmanned Plan* (Tokyo: PHP, 2009), 96–116.
68. National Defense Committee of the Liberal Democratic Party, *A Framework for the New National Defense Policy Guideline*, June 9, 2009, 12.
69. One U.S. analyst argues that for the United States military to meet current demands, it will need "an additional percent of GDP per year or more" and "an expansion of at least 200,000 or so active duty solders and Marines." See Frederick W. Kagan, *Finding the Target: The Transformation of American Military Policy* (New York: Encounter Books, 2006), 386–87.
70. *Info-RMA*, 4.
71. National Institute for Defense Studies, *East Asian Strategic Review 2009* (Tokyo: NIDS, 2010), 281.
72. Fumitaka Susami, "Gates Backs Idea of Permanent Law for SDF Dispatch Abroad," *Kyodo World Service*, November 9, 2007.
73. Tomoko Tsunoda and Brad Glosserman, "The Guillotine: Japan's Demographic Transformation and its Security Implications," *Issues and Insights* 9, no. 10 (June 2009): 36.
74. The Ministry of Defense plans to colocate key command centers with U.S. headquarters in Japan in order to facilitate interoperability between the two militaries. See "Ceremony Held for relocation of Defense Force Function to Yokota Base," *Kyodo World Service*, Feburary 15, 2008.

75. National Intelligence Council, *Global Trends 2025: A Transformed World*, November 2008, 97.

76. Shigeru Ishiba, "If Japan and China Fought Against Each Other, Which Would Win?" *Bungei Shunju*, May 1, 2006, 138–42. Ishiba was the former director general of Japan's Defense Agency.

77. Emma Chanlett-Avery and Mary Beth Nikitin, *Japan's Nuclear Future: Policy Debate, Prospects, and U.S. Interests*, CRS Report RL 34487, Washington, DC: Congressional Research Service, February 19, 2009, 7.

78. Ito Kan, "China's Nuclear Power Will Control the World by 2020," *Shokun*, January 1, 2006, 34–45. Emphasis added.

79. Mark L. Haas, "A Geriatric Peace? The Future of U.S. Power in a World of Aging Populations," *International Security* 32, no. 1 (summer 2008): 113.

Chapter 8. The Geopolitical Consequences of China's Demographic Turmoil

1.   China's population was 1.34 billion as of November 1, 2010 according to the latest national census. See National Bureau of Statistics, "Press Release on Major Figures of the 2010 National Population Census," April 28, 2011, http://www.stats.gov.cn/english/newsandcomingevents/t20110428_402722237.htm. The country's people have undoubtedly been undercounted in the various censuses because, among other reasons, families have hidden children to avoid punishment for violating Beijing's one-child policy.

2.   Baidu, *Knowledge* forum, http://zhidao.baidu.com/question/124727995 (response of "Xiao Ao Zhang Wu").

3.   Blogchina, "The True Power of China's Rise Is a Powerful Reproductive Force," http://vibokee.com/20080718574689.html.

4.   Hongbin Li, Junsen Zhang, and Yi Zhu, *The Effect of the One-Child Policy on Fertility in China: Identification Based on the Differences-in-Differences*, Discussion Paper 00019, Chinese University of Hong Kong, August 11, 2005, http://ideas.repec.org/p/chk/cuhkdc/00019.html.

5.   See CIA World Factbook, https://www.cia.gov/library/publications/the-world-factbook/geos/ch.html. The official Xinhua News Agency reports China's fertility rate was 1.2 in 2007. See "China to Maintain Low Birthrate: Vice Premier," *People's Daily*, January 20, 2010, http://english.peopledaily.com.cn/90001/90776/90785/6873409.html. Beijing's reporting of its rate has been inconsistent, at times claiming a stable rate of about 1.8. See "Minister: Chinese Population Would Be 1.7 bln Without Family Planning," *People's Daily*, April 1, 2009, http://english.peopledaily.com.cn/90001/90776/90785/6627190.html.

6.   See Tian Ying and Guo Likun, "China Focus: China's One Child Policy Pressurized by Aging Population," Xinhua News Agency, August 12, 2009, http://news.xinhuanet.com/english/2009–08/12/content_11867131.htm. Officials also maintain that the one-child policy saves 1.83 billion tons of carbon dioxide emissions a year. See "China's Population Policy Helps Slow Global Warming, Says Official," Xinhua News Agency, December 10, 2009, http://news.xinhuanet.com/english/2009–12/10/content_12624315.htm.

7.   Nicholas Eberstadt, "China's Family Planning Goes Awry," *Far Eastern Economic Review*, December 2009, 24.

8.   See Wei Xing Zhu, Li Lu, and Therese Hesketh, "China's Excess Males, Sex Selective Abortion, and One Child Policy: Analysis of Data from 2005 National Intercensus Survey," *BMJ* (2009), 338: b1211, April 9, 2009, http://www.bmj.com/cgi/reprint/338/apr09_2/b1211. China's abnormal ratios are unfortunately part of a worldwide trend. See Nicholas Eberstadt, "The Global War Against Baby Girls" (speech, United Nations General Assembly Third Committee, New York, December 6, 2006), http://www.aei.org/speech/25399.

9.   See He Dan and Cang Wei, "China Becoming Even More Male," *China Daily*, August 10, 2011, http://www.chinadaily.com.cn/china/2011-08/10/content _13081440.htm. Chinese authorities reported more credibly that the sex ratio at birth was 119.45 in 2009. See National Population and Family Planning Commission of China, *Main Population Data in 2009, China*, February 26, 2010, http://www.npfpc.gov.cn/en/detail.aspx?articleid=100226103318203294.

10.   See Zhu, Lu, and Hesketh, "China's Excess Males, Sex Selective Abortion, and One Child Policy."

11.   See United Nations, *World Population Prospects: The 2010 Revision*. The CIA believes there were 40.8 million more men than women in 2011. See CIA World Factbook online.

12.   There was much attention paid in the middle of 2009 to Shanghai officials encouraging certain couples to have two children. The move was not a relaxation of the policy, however. The Shanghai government was merely reminding people of the policy's exceptions. A couple is permitted, under the policy, to have a second child if both spouses are only children. For more information on the Shanghai initiative, see Will Clem, Lilian Zhang, and Anna Zhang, "The One-Child Enforcers Who Are Pushing for Two," *South China Morning Post* (Hong Kong), July 24, 2009.

13.   The temporary measure also permitted a second child in those cases where an only child was severely injured or disabled in that earthquake. See "Family Planning Policy Revised for Quake Areas," *China Daily*, May 27, 2008, http://www.chinadaily.com.cn/china/2008-05/27/content_6714891.htm.

14.   See Lan Tian, "Experts Urge Switch from One Child Policy," *China Daily*, November 27, 2009, http://www2.chinadaily.com.cn/china/2009-11/27/content_9067869.htm. In September 2010, a Guangdong population official said couples will be allowed to have two children by 2030. See Zheng Caixiong, "Guangdong to Relax Family Policy by 2030," *China Daily*, September 25, 2010, http://www.chinadaily.com.cn/china/2010-09/25/content_11342254 .htm.

15.   See "Sex-Ratio Imbalance Not a Result of Family Planning Policy: Official," *People's Daily*, January 23, 2007, http://english.people.com.cn/200701/23/ eng20070123_343899.html (comments of Zhang Weiqing). Chinese population officials are prone to setting overly ambitious targets. In July 2004, for instance, Beijing announced the goal of achieving a normal sex ratio by 2010. See "China Bans Selective Abortion to Fix Imbalance," *China Daily*,

July 16, 2004, http://www.chinadaily.com.cn/english/doc/2004–07/16/content _349051.htm (comments of Zhao Baige).

16. See Xin Dingding and Wang Huazhong, "Craving for a Second Child? Govt Will Dent Your Pockets," *China Daily*, March 26, 2009, http://www.chinadaily.com.cn/china/2009–03/26/content_7618314.htm.

17. Despite hints of relaxation, central government officials confirm that the nation's one-child policy will remain in place. See Shan Juan, "Family-Planning Policy Stays Put," *China Daily*, September 27, 2010, http://www.chinadaily.com.cn/china/2010–09/27/content_11350778.htm (comments of Li Bin).

18. The UN's *World Population Prospects, the 2010 Revision* estimates that fertility rates around the world will converge around 2.1. There is nothing at the moment to indicate that China's rate—which could be as low as 1.2—will increase dramatically in the near or far future. Moreover, for the rate to increase to 2.1, the Chinese central government would have to abandon its one-child policy, and there is virtually no indication that central officials are planning to do that.

19. Eberstadt, "China's Family Planning Goes Awry."

20. Some graying societies, such as Germany in the 1930s and Serbia in the 1990s, have nonetheless been particularly violent and aggressive. See Nicholas Eberstadt, "Critical Cross-Cutting Issues Facing Northeast Asia: Regional Demographic Trends and Prospects," *Asia Policy*, no. 3 (2007): 54.

21. Demographers disagree as to when China's population will peak. The earliest estimate is 2025. See Li Jianxin, *The Structure of Chinese Population* (Beijing: Social Sciences Academic Press, 2009), 34. The UN figures, Beijing's numbers with minor adjustments, show Chinese population falling off after 2025. See United Nations, *World Population Prospects: The 2010 Revision*. Nonetheless, the country's population growth is slowing faster than predicted, so the peak may be reached well before 2025. See note 57.

22. Valerie M. Hudson and Andrea M. den Boer, *Bare Branches: Security Implications of Asia's Surplus Male Population* (Cambridge, MA: MIT Press, 2004), 263.

23. Christian G. Mesquida and Neil I. Wiener, "Human Collective Aggression: A Behavioral Ecology Perspective," *Ethology and Sociobiology* 17 (1996): 258 (citation omitted).

24. Jiang Zhenghua and Mi Hong, *Population Security* (Hangzhou: Zhejiang University Press, 2008), 39.

25. Li, *The Structure of Chinese Population*, 91.

26. Chinese officials have linked the nation's skewed sex ratio to social instability. See "Rising Sex-Ratio Imbalance 'A Danger,' " *China Daily*, January 23, 2007, http://www2.chinadaily.com.cn/china/2007–01/23/content_789821.htm.

27. Hudson and den Boer, *Bare Branches*, 212.

28. Ibid., 202.

29. Ibid., 263.

30. Li, *The Structure of Chinese Population*, 118. Chinese officials have suggested that single children are one of the causes of a juvenile crime wave. See Xie Zhuanjiao, "Juvenile Criminal Cases Rising," *China Daily*, December 5, 2007,

http://www.chinadaily.com.cn/china/2007–12/05/content_6298758.htm (comments of Shang Xiuyun).

31. Mutant Palm, *America's Bare Branches?* October 26, 2008, http://www.mutant palm.org/2008/10/26/americas-bare-branches.html.

32. For a discussion of the intolerance of casualties, see Edward N. Luttwak, "Toward Post-Heroic Warfare," *Foreign Affairs*, May 1995, 109, 115.

33. Most observers believe the one-child policy has given rise to a self-centered generation of children. See Fiona Tam, "One-Child Policy Gives Birth to a Selfish Generation," *South China Morning Post* (Hong Kong), October 8, 2009.

34. For more on the West's trend toward peace, see James J. Sheehan, *Where Have All the Soldiers Gone? The Transformation of Modern Europe* (Boston: Houghton Mifflin, 2008); and Michael Mandelbaum, *The Ideas That Conquered the World: Peace, Democracy, and Free Markets in the Twenty-First Century* (New York: Public Affairs, 2002), 122–28.

35. "Japan's Former PM Says China Seeking 'Lebensraum,'" AFP, October 18, 2010, http://news.yahoo.com/s/afp/20101018/wl_asia_afp/japanchinadiplomacy disputeusabe (comments of Shinzo Abe).

36. Beijing, adding in areas covered by its various claims, maintains that China is the world's third largest nation.

37. "Kazakhs Protest Alleged Chinese Plan to Rent Farmland," Radio Free Europe/ Radio Liberty, December 11, 2009, http://www.rferl.org/content/Kazakhs_ Protest_Alleged_Chinese_Plan_To_Rent_Farmland/1903278.html (comments of Murat Auezov). Rumors of Beijing's plan to rent farmland has created further unrest in Kazakhstan. See Birgit Brauer, "Rumors of Secret Land Lease to China Causes Unease in Kazakhstan," Eurasia Daily Monitor, March 14, 2011, http://www.jamestown.org/programs/edm/single/?tx_ttnews[tt_news] =37645&cHash=29594cf51b9c25b4074f697b039a2533.

38. Kenjali Tinibai, "China and Kazakhstan: A Two-Way Street," *BusinessWeek*, May 28, 2010, http://www.businessweek.com/globalbiz/content/may2010/ gb20100528_168520.htm (comments of Murat Auezov).

39. See Paul Goble, "Chinatowns Emerging in Post-Soviet Central Asia But Not Near the Chinese Border," *Window on Eurasia* (blog), May 18, 2010, http:// windowoneurasia.blogspot.com/2010/05/window-on-eurasia-chinatowns- emerging.html.

40. See Andrew Higgins, "As China Finds Bigger Place in World Affairs, Its Wealth Breeds Hostility," *Washington Post*, September 8, 2010, http://www.washington post.com/wp-dyn/content/article/2010/09/07/AR2010090707448.html.

41. Greg Shtraks, "Russian Exaggeration of the 'Chinese Invasion,'" *Jamestown Foundation* (blog), January 15, 2010, http://jamestownfoundation.blogspot .com/2010/01/russian-exaggeration-of-chinese.html.

42. The Chinese believe they have the power to assimilate others. They can always live in peace with other ethnicities and "finally become one," writes Li Jianxin, the demographer. Li, *The Structure of Chinese Population*, 165.

43. Mikhail A. Alexseev and C. Richard Hofstetter, "Russia, China, and the Im-

migration Security Dilemma," *Political Science Quarterly* 121 (2006): 1 (comments of Vitalii Poluyanov).

44. "Eventually, all those things we build will be ours," temporary Chinese construction workers told political scientist Mikhail Alexseev about a decade ago. Alexseev and Hofstetter, "Russia, China, and the Immigration Security Dilemma," 13.

45. The number of illegal Chinese workers in Mongolia is in much dispute. Some analysts believe they could even outnumber the legal Chinese workers there. See John Garnaut, "Second Wave of Chinese Invasion," *Sydney Morning Herald*, August 13, 2007, http://www.smh.com.au/news/business/second-wave-of-chinese-invasion/2007/08/12/1186857347594.html?page=fullpage#contentSwap1 (comments of Tuvshintsegel).

46. "Focus: Anti-Chinese Sentiment Swelling in Mongolia," Kyodo News International, April 11, 2005, http://findarticles.com/p/articles/mi_m0WDP/is_2005_April_11/ai_n13601320/.

47. For a discussion of Mongolians' views on China, see Peter Stein, "China Casts Its Shadow on Mongolia," *Wall Street Journal*, December 14, 2009, http://online.wsj.com/article/SB10001424052748703954904574595651461527632.html.

48. "Feature: Chinese Spouses Demand Right to Work in Taiwan," *Taipei Times*, October 29, 2009, http://www.taipcitimes.com/News/taiwan/archives/2009/10/29/2003457147.

49. Ko Shu-ling, "ECFA Threat to Middle Class: Think Tank," *Taipei Times*, April 11, 2010, http://www.taipeitimes.com/News/front/archives/2010/04/11/2003470290.

50. Eliot A. Cohen, "Isolate or Liberate?" *Wall Street Journal*, October 4, 2004, http://online.wsj.com/article/0,,SB109684407036834817,00.html?mod=opinion%5Fmain%5Fcommentaries.

51. Beijing, among other claims, declares as its own the following locations: Taiwan, the Senkakus controlled by Japan, and parts of India. China, incredibly, appears to be contesting the claims to the Arctic of the five Arctic states, and it is establishing, by promoting its version of the history of the Korean people, the justification for the annexation of a large portion of North Korea.

52. Beijing claims the continental shelves of all the countries bordering the South China Sea. The Chinese government issues maps showing sovereignty over virtually all of that body of water and has tried to deny access to the South China and Yellow Seas.

53. Willy Lam, "Beijing Seeks Paradigm Shift in Geopolitics," China Brief, March 5, 2010, http://www.jamestown.org/programs/chinabrief/single/?tx_ttnews[tt_news]=36120&tx_ttnews[backPid]=25&cHash=a9b9a1117e (comments of Yuan Peng).

54. Liu Mingfu, *The China Dream: Big Power Thinking and Strategic Positioning in a Post-American Era* (Beijing: China Friendship Publishing, 2009), 25.

55. See Eberstadt, "Critical Cross-Cutting Issues Facing Northeast Asia: Regional Demographic Trends and Prospects."

56. "China's Aging Population Hits 167 Million," Xinhua News Agency, July 14, 2010, http://news.xinhuanet.com/english2010/china/2010–07/14/c _13399044.htm.

57. UN estimates show this group going from 12.3 percent of the population in 2010 to 24.4 percent in 2030. See United Nations, *World Population Prospects: The 2010 Revision*. Beijing's actual statistics for 2009 indicate that the 2010 estimate, released in 2008, was far too low. As noted in the text, the sixty-and-older cohort reached 12.5 percent of the population in 2009. See "China's Aging Population Hits 167 Million," Xinhua News Agency. For a demographer's perspective on China aging faster than expected, see Li, *The Structure of Chinese Population*, 34.

58. See Tian and Guo, "China Focus."

59. See Zhao Huanxin, "Working-Age Population Set to Decline," *China Daily*, September 1, 2006, http://www.chinadaily.com.cn/china/2006–09/01/content _678901.htm.

60. Most Chinese retire at fifty-five (not sixty-four), thereby making China's age problem even worse than commonly used statistics indicate.

61. Beijing's statisticians believe that China's workforce in 2016 will be larger than the combined workforces of the developed world. See National Population and Family Planning Commission of China, *Research Report on National Population Development Strategy*, May 19, 2009, http://www.chinapop.gov.cn/ fzgh/sewgh/200905/t20090519_171063.htm.

62. Li, *The Structure of Chinese Population*, 52–53. The UN estimates that the workforce will fall from 72.7 percent of the population in 2015 to 60.9 percent in 2050. See United Nations, *World Population Prospects: The 2010 Revision*.

63. See "China's 'Demographic Dividend' to Come to an End in 2010: World Bank," *People's Daily*, March 25, 2007, http://english.peopledaily.com.cn/200703/25/ eng20070325_360808.html.

64. See Sim Chi Yin, "China's Labor Crunch: End to One-Child Policy?" *Straits Times* (Singapore), March 20, 2010. For detail on Cai's views on the effect of China's demography on its future economic prospects, see Ingrid Nielsen and Cai Fang, "Demographic Shift and Projected Labor Shortage in China," *Economic Papers* 26 (September 2007): 231.

65. Li Jianxin believes the high speed of China's economic growth in the last twenty years is due to population dividends. See Li, *The Structure of Chinese Population*, 51. Chinese officials these days seem to be concerned by the ending of the demographic dividend. See "China's 'Demographic Dividend' to Decline in 2015," *Global Times* (Beijing), September 9, 2010, http://china.global times.cn/society/2010–09/571766.html.

66. George Gilder, "Let a Billion Flowers Bloom," *Cato Journal* (winter 1989): 669.

67. See Eberstadt, "China's Family Planning Goes Awry."

68. The statement in the text is based on estimated 2009 statistics from the CIA World Factbook online. The figures are calculated using the purchasing power parity method.

69. Zhou Jiangong, "Getting Rich Before Getting Old," *Forbes.com*, September 28, 2009, http://www.forbes.com/2009/09/25/zhou-jiangong-china-pensions -leadership-jiangong.html.

70. Gunnar Heinsohn, "Babies Win Wars," *Wall Street Journal*, March 6, 2006, http://online.wsj.com/article/SB114159651882789812.html?mod=opinion& ojcontent=otep. Incidentally, Heinsohn, a professor of sociology at Bremen University, makes the case that excess males were largely responsible for European conquest from the late fifteenth century onward. "The original population bomb was a weapon made in Europe," he writes.

71. "1,100 Apply to Collect Night Soil," *South China Morning Post* (Hong Kong), June 25, 2010.

72. There is debate as to when India will surpass China to become the world's most populous country. The U.S. Census Bureau believes that will happen in 2025. See U.S. Census Bureau, *China's Population to Peak at 1.4 Billion Around 2026*, December 15, 2009, http://www.census.gov/newsroom/releases/ archives/international_population/cb09–191.html. UN data indicate this event will occur sometime between 2020 and 2025. See United Nations, *World Population Prospects: The 2010 Revision.*

73. See Amitendu Palit, "Is China or India Aging Better?" *Forbes.com*, June 30, 2010, http://www.forbes.com/2010/06/30/population-india-china-markets- economy-economic-growth.html?boxes=marketschannelnews. According to the UN, China's population will peak around 2025 while India's will peak about 2060. See United Nations, *World Population Prospects: The 2010 Revision.*

74. See Tian and Guo, "China Focus" (comments of Zeng Yi).

75. Xue Yong, "India Surpassing China, No Longer Alarmism," *Southern Metropolis Weekly*, October 19, 2010, http://www.nbweekly.com/Print/Article/ 11320_0.shtml.

76. In the eighteenth and nineteenth centuries, the rapid population growth in the West "added wings to the tiger," allowing it to dominate the world. Li, *The Structure of Chinese Population*, 166.

77. Ibid, 198.

78. Ibid, 194.

79. Yao Yang, interview by Hu Yihu, *Tiger Talk*, Phoenix Television, October 17, 2009, http://www.youtube.com/watch?v=8mNoH6TUQMs&feature=related.

80. For a discussion of Chinese views, see Mohan Malik, "War Talk: Perceptual Gaps in 'Chindia' Relations," China Brief, October 7, 2009, http://www .jamestown.org/programs/chinabrief/single/?tx_ttnews[tt_news]=35589 &tx_ttnews[backPid]=25&cHash=127f567fb8; and D. S. Rajan, *China: Strategic Experts Talk About a "Partial" Sino-Indian War*, South Asia Analysis Group Paper 2939, November 24, 2008, http://www.southasiaanalysis.org/%5 Cpapers30%5Cpaper2939.html. The anti-India views of analysts have seeped into popular discourse due to official media. See Zhu Shanshan, "90% in Online Poll Believe India Threatens China's Security," *Global Times* (Beijing), June 11, 2009, http://china.globaltimes.cn/top-photo/2009–06/436320 .html.

81. See "Indian PM's Visit a Provocative Move," *Global Times* (Beijing), October 14, 2009, http://opinion.globaltimes.cn/editorial/2009–10/476836.html.

82. Beijing supplies anti-India terrorists with equipment and training. More important, the Chinese have continually blocked UN sanctions against them. See Gordon G. Chang, "India's China Problem," *Forbes.com*, August 14, 2009, http://www.forbes.com/2009/08/13/india-china-relations-population -opinions-columnists-gordon-chang.html.

83. See "Nervous China May Attack India by 2012: Expert," *Times of India* (Mumbai), July 12, 2009, http://timesofindia.indiatimes.com/NEWS-India-Nervous -China-may-attack-India-by-2012-Expert/articleshow/4769593.cms.

84. Yan Hao, "PLA Kicks Off Largest Long-Range Tactical Military Exercise," Xinhua News Agency, August 11, 2009, http://news.xinhuanet.com/english /2009-08/11/content_11863847.htm.

85. Countries have been particularly unsuccessful in changing their demographic profiles in the long run. Even if China could, it would take decades for increased births to have a beneficial effect. In the interim, a boomlet of newborns would only worsen the country's dependency ratio and further strain the Chinese economy.

86. Yao Yang, interview by Hu Yihu, *Tiger Talk*, Phoenix Television, October 17, 2009.

87. Neil Howe and Richard Jackson, "The World Won't Be Aging Gracefully. Just the Opposite," *Washington Post*, January 4, 2009, http://www.washingtonpost .com/wp-dyn/content/article/2009/01/02/AR2009010202231.html.

88. Li, *The Structure of Chinese Population*, 173.

Chapter 9. India's Demographic Trends and Implications for the Asian Strategic Landscape

1. Tushar Poddar and Pragyan Deb, *India's Rising Labour Force*, Global Economics Paper 201, Goldman Sachs Global Economics, Commodities and Strategy Research, July 28, 2010, http://www.scribd.com/doc/35055286/Goldman Sachs-Global-Economics-Paper-20100728.

2. Naxalism refers to the leftist radical insurgency that plagues parts of central and eastern India. The Naxalite movement, inspired by Maoist Communist ideology, first broke out in the village of Naxalbari in the state of West Bengal in the late 1960s. In recent years the movement has spread into underdeveloped rural areas of states like Chhattisgarh, Orissa, and Andra Pradesh.

3. Nandan Nilekani, *Imagining India* (New York: The Penguin Group, 2009), 43.

4. V. R. Krishna Iyer, "Population Policy and Legal Prescriptions," *The Hindu*, August 13, 2008.

5. P. K. Chaubey, *Population Policy of India: Perspectives, Issues and Challenges* (New Delhi: Kanishka Publishers, 2001), 55.

6. Ibid., 86, 88.

7. Ibid., 62.

8. Ibid., 123–24. Replacement fertility is the total fertility rate at which newborn girls would give birth to an average of one daughter over their lifetimes. In other words, women have just enough babies to replace themselves.

9.   National Commission on Population, Government of India, accessed December 22, 2010, http://populationcommission.nic.in/facts1.htm.

10. For a thorough analysis of these issues, see Derek Scissors and Michelle Kaffenberger, "U.S.-India Relations: Ensuring Indian Prosperity in the Coming Demographic Boom," *Heritage Backgrounder* 2274, May 15, 2009, http://www.heritage.org/Research/Reports/2009/05/US-India-Relations-Ensuring-Indian-Prosperity-in-the-Coming-Demographic-Boom.

11. Nilekani, *Imagining India*, 176.

12. Derek Scissors and Michelle Kaffenberger, *India's Future in the Balance*, Heritage WebMemo 2586, August 13, 2009, http://www.heritage.org/Research/Reports/2009/08/Indias-Future-in-the-Balance.

13. Nilekani, *Imagining India*, 194.

14. Ibid., 191.

15. P. Vaidyanathan Iyer, "Going for the Skill," *Indianexpress.com*, August 16, 2010, http://www.indianexpress.com/news/going-for-the-skill/660788/0.

16. Mira Kamdar, *Planet India* (New York: Scribner, 2007), 161.

17. Peter Wonacott, "Deadly Labor Wars Hinder India's Rise," *Wall Street Journal*, November 20, 2009.

18. Nilekani, *Imagining India*, 298–99.

19. Ibid., 198–203.

20. Richard Dobbs and Shirish Sankhe,"India's Urban Awakening," *Forbes.com*, April 29, 2010.

21. Christophe Jaffrelot, "India, an Emerging Power, But How Far?," in Christophe Jaffrelot, ed., *Emerging States: The Wellspring of a New World Order* (New York: Columbia University Press, 2009), 87.

22. William Magioncalda, "A Modern Insurgency: India's Evolving Naxalite Problem," *CSIS South Asia Monitor*, no. 140, April 8, 2010, http://csis.org/publication/modern-insurgency-india's-evolving-naxalite-problem-0.

23. Animesh Roul, "100 More Terrorist Groups Banned in India: What are India's Counterterrorism Priorities?," *Terrorism Monitor* VIII, no. 22 (June 5, 2010), http://www.jamestown.org/single/?no_cache=1&tx_ttnews%5Btt_news%5D=36451.

24. Magioncalda, "A Modern Insurgency."

25. *Navigating the Near: Non-Traditional Security Threats to India 2022*, Observer Research Foundation, July 2010.

26. Ibid.

27. Sidney B. Westley and Minja Kim Choe, "How Does Son Preference Affect Populations in Asia?" *Analysis from the East-West Center*, no. 84, September 2007.

28. The "bare branches" phenomenon refers to a Chinese term for the branches of a family tree that will never bear fruit, but which may be used as "bare sticks," or clubs. Valerie Hudson and Andrea den Boer write about this phenomenon and its link to national security and foreign policy in *Bare Branches: Security Implications of Asia's Surplus Male Population* (Cambridge, MA: MIT Press, 2004).

29. Meeta Singh and Vasu Mohan, "The Rise of Sex Selection in India," *Democracy at Large* 2, no. 1 (2005), http://www.ifes.org/Content/Publications/Feature-Stories/2007/Jun/The-Rise-of-Sex-Selection-in-India.aspx.

30. *Human Trafficking*, Center for Social Research Web Site, http://www.csrindia.org/index.php/human-trafficking, accessed December 22, 2010.

31. Stephanie Nolen, "Land of the Rising Son," *Globe and Mail*, September 19, 2009.

32. Nilekani, *Imagining India*, 54.

33. "Increase in Muslim Population a Threat: BJP," *The Hindu*, September 9, 2004, http://www.hindu.com/2004/09/09/stories/2004090907080500.htm.

34. Anuj Nadadur, "The 'Muslim Threat' and the Bharatiya Janata Party's Rise to Power," *Peace and Democracy in South Asia* 2, nos. 1 and 2 (2006).

35. Carin Zissis, *Demographic Insecurity: Hindu-Muslim Tensions*, Council on Foreign Relations, June 22, 2007, http://www.cfr.org/publication/13659/indias_muslim_population.html.

36. *Navigating the Near*, Observer Research Foundation, 66.

37. Lisa Curtis, "After Mumbai: Time to Strengthen U.S.-India Counterterrorism Cooperation," *Heritage Backgrounder* 2217, December 9, 2008, http://www.heritage.org/Research/Reports/2008/12/After-Mumbai-Time-to-Strengthen-US-India-Counterterrorism-Cooperation.

38. Curtis, "After Mumbai."

39. C. Christine Fair, "Students Islamic Movement of India and the Indian Mujahideen: An Assessment," *Asia Policy*, no. 9 (January 2010): 104–5.

40. Poddar and Deb, *India's Rising Labour Force*.

41. Geoff Hiscock, "India Likely to Grow Faster than China Next year," *The Australian*, July 26, 2010, http://www.theaustralian.com.au/business/in-depth/india-likely-to-grow-faster-than-china-next-year/story-e6frgaho-1225896897344.

42. OECD Stat Extracts, http://stats.oecd.org/Index.aspx, accessed January 3, 2011.

43. World Intellectual Property Organization, July 1, 2010, http://www.wipo.int/export/sites/www/ipstats/en/statistics/patents/x/s/xls/wipo_pat_grant_by_office_origin_table.xls.

44. Gaurie Mishra, "India Lags in Number of IT Patents," *Rediff India Abroad*, January 5, 2006.

45. "Patenting Landscape in India 2009," *Evaluserve White Paper*, October 2009.

46. Amitendu Palit, "Is China or India Aging Better?" *Forbes.com*, June 30, 2010, http://www.forbes.com/2010/06/30/population-india-china-markets-economy-economic-growth.html.

47. Kamdar, *Planet India*, 163.

48. Lisa Curtis, "U.S.-India Relations: The China Factor," *Heritage Backgrounder* 2209, November 25, 2008, http://www.heritage.org/research/reports/2008/11/us-india-relations-the-china-factor.

49. Aziz Haniffa, "India-US: After the Euphoria, Skepticism," *Rediff.com*, August 12, 2010, http://news.rediff.com/report/2010/aug/11/notes-from-the-unofficial-indo-us-strategic-dialogue-at-brookings.htm.

50. P. K. Mehra, "Future Shape, Size, and Role of Indian Air Force," *Air Power Journal* 4, no. 1 (spring 2009), 30.

51. "India Mulls Deploying Missiles near Border in North-East," *Press Trust of India*, August 24, 2010, http://www.hindustantimes.com/India-mulls-deploying-missiles-near-border-in-North-East/Article1–591252.aspx.

52. Lisa Curtis and Nicholas Hamisevicz, *U.S. Should Block China-Pakistan Nuclear Deal*, Heritage WebMemo 2910, May 20, 2010, http://www.heritage.org/research/reports/2010/05/us-should-block-china-pakistan-nuclear-reactor-deal.

53. The Nuclear Suppliers Group is a forty-six-nation grouping that seeks to control nuclear proliferation through rules that limit the export and retransfer of nuclear weapons materials. NSG members are prohibited from transferring civil nuclear technology to states that have not joined the Nuclear Nonproliferation Treaty (NPT). Neither India nor Pakistan have joined the NPT, but India received a special exemption from the NSG to receive civilian nuclear technology and fuel in September 2008.

54. Lisa Curtis, "China's Military and Security Relationship with Pakistan," testimony before the U.S.-China Economic and Security Review Commission, May 20, 2009, http://www.heritage.org/Research/Testimony/Chinas-Military-and-Security-Relationship-with-Pakistan.

55. "India, Japan Likely to Seal Trade Pact in October: Anand Sharma," *The Hindu*, August 26, 2010, http://www.thehindu.com/business/Economy/article596016.ece.

56. Rajeev Sharma, "Indo-Japan Ties Poised for Great Leap Forward," *Eurasia Review*, August 18, 2010, http://www.eurasiareview.com/201008187148/indo-japan-ties-poised-for-great-leap-forward.html.

57. Robert D. Kaplan, "The Geography of Chinese Power: How Far Can Beijing Reach on Land and at Sea?" *Foreign Affairs*, May–June 2010, http://www.foreignaffairs.com/articles/66205/robert-d-kaplan/the-geography-of-chinese-power.

58. Dean Cheng, *China's View of South Asia and the Indian Ocean*," Heritage Lecture 1163, August 31, 2010.

59. Walter Ladwig, "India Sets Sail for Leadership," *Wall Street Journal*, June 9, 2010, http://online.wsj.com/article/NA_WSJ_PUB:SB10001424052748703302604575295773533377334.html; Sikander Rehman, "India's Future Aircraft Carrier Force and the Need for Strategic Flexibility," *Institute for Defense Studies and Analysis Comment*, June 1, 2010, http://www.idsa.in/idsacomments/IndiasFutureAircraftCarrierForceandtheNeedforStrategicFlexibility_irehman_010610.

60. Gunnar Heinsohn, "Babies Win Wars," *Wall Street Journal*, March 6, 2006.

61. World Bank, *India*, at http://siteresources.worldbank.org/EXTHNPSTATS/Resources/3237117–1208547350942/IND_POP.XLS, accessed January 3, 2011.

62. Mark L. Haas, "A Geriatric Peace? The Future of U.S. Power in a World of Aging Populations," *International Security* 32, no. 1 (summer 2007): 112–47.

63. Laxman K. Behera, "India's Defense Budget 2011–12," *IDSA Comment*, March 7, 2011, http://www.idsa.in/idsacomments/IndiasDefenceBudget2011-12_lk behera_070311.

64. Brian Nichiporuk, *The Security Dynamics of Demographic Factors* (Santa Monica, CA: RAND, 2000).

65. Ibid., 32.

66. C. Raja Mohan, "Sino-American Rivalry: Failure and Opportunity for Indian Military Diplomacy," *Indianexpress.com*, August 10, 2010, http://www.indianexpress.com/news/Sino-American-rivalry--Failure---opportunity-for-Indian-military-diplomacy/658535.

67. Mehra, "Future Shape, Size, and Role of Indian Air Force," 31.

68. Sandeep Dikshit, "India, U.S. Review Defence Cooperation," *The Hindu*, August 11, 2010, http://www.thehindu.com/todays-paper/tp-national/article563490.ece.

69. "India's Foreign Policy and Future India-US Relations" (remarks by former Indian Foreign Minister, now Finance Minister, Pranab Mukherjee at the Council on Foreign Relations, New York City), October 1, 2007.

70. Ashley Tellis, *Measuring National Power in the Postindustrial Age* (Santa Monica, CA: RAND, 2000).

71. George Perkovich, "The Measure of India: What Makes Greatness?" (remarks at a symposium on the Emerging World Order), September 2003, http://www.indiaseminar.com/2003/529/529 george perkovich.htm.

72. Kamdar, *Planet India*, 87.

73. "India to Be Net Provider of Security in Indian Ocean, Beyond," *Rediff.com*, February 2, 2010, http://news.rediff.com/interview/2010/feb/02/pentagon-report-hails-growth-of-indian-military.htm.

Conclusion: Population, Power, and Purpose

1. See Nicholas Eberstadt, "Critical Cross-Cutting Issues Facing Northeast Asia: Regional Demographic Trends and Prospects," *Asia Policy*, no. 3 (2007): 54

2. Mark L. Haas, "A Geriatric Peace? The Future of U.S. Power in a World of Aging Populations," *International Security* 32, no. 1 (summer 2008): 113.

3. Government of Japan, *National Defense Program Guidelines, Approved by the Security Council and the Cabinet*, December 10, 2004, 4.

4. See European Security Strategy, *A Secure Europe in a Better World*, Brussels, December 12, 2003, http://www.consilium.europa.eu/uedocs/cmsUpload/78367.pdf; Council of the European Union, *Report on the Implementation of the European Security Strategy: Providing Security in a Changing World*, Brussels, December 11, 2008, http://www.consilium.europa.eu/ueDocs/cms_Data/docs/pressdata/EN/reports/104630.pdf.

5. European Security Strategy, *A Secure Europe in a Better World*, 4.

6. European Security Strategy, *Draft Internal Security Strategy of the European Union*, February 23, 2010, 6, http://register.consilium.europa.eu/pdf/en/10/st05/st05842-re02.en10.pdf.

7. Ibid., 7.

8.   Council of the European Union, *Report on the Implementation of the European Security Strategy*, 5.

9.   See U.S. Department of Defense, *National Defense Strategy*, June 2008; United States Joint Forces Command, *Joint Operating Environment 2008: Challenges and Implications for the Future Joint Force*, November 2008; National Intelligence Council, *Global Trends 2025: A Transformed World*, November 2008. For an assessment of the degree to which the U.S. Department of Defense has integrated demographic concerns into its policy planning, see Jennifer Dabbs Sciubba, *The Future Faces of War: Population and National Security* (Santa Barbara, CA: Praeger, 2010).

10.   Robert Kaplan has recently argued that in the current economic and strategic climate, control of the seas should be America's primary military-strategic goal. See Robert Kaplan, *Monsoon: The Indian Ocean and the Future of American Power* (New York: Random House, 2010), and Robert Kaplan, "Center Stage for the Twenty-first Century: Power Plays in the Indian Ocean," *Foreign Affairs*, March-April 2009, http://www.foreignaffairs.org/20090301faessay88203/robert-d-kaplan/center-stage-for-the-twenty-first-century.html. See also STRATFOR, www.stratfor.com/decade_forecast_2005_2015.

11.   Department of Defense, *Quadrennial Defense Review*, February 3, 2006.

12.   Department of Defense, *2010 Quadrennial Defense Review*, 42.

13.   The end strengths of the U.S. military were previously set at around 482,000 active duty and 533,000 reserves for the U.S. Army, and 175,000 active duty and 39,000 reserve Marines for fiscal year 2011, with a drawdown of the U.S. Navy and Air Force to 322,000 and 316,000, respectively.

14.   Center on International Cooperation at New York University, *Annual Review of Global Peace Operations*, 2009, http://www.cic.nyu.edu/peace_ssr/docs/GPO_2009.pdf.

15.   CIA's World Factbook online.

16.   This trend is evident in UN Security Council approval of more mission in the recent past, UN establishment of the UN Peacebuilding Commission, world leaders' accepting new language concerning a "responsibility to protect" (R2P) in the World Summit Document in 2005, and the creation of attendant peacekeeping bureaucracies.

17.   Monica Duffy Toft, *The State of the Field: Demography and War*, ECSP Report 11 (Washington, DC: Wilson Center, 2005): 25–7.

18.   For example, William Easterly has criticized United Nations programs that are top-down driven and almost exclusively technological. One example is the "Nothing but Nets" anti-malaria campaign.

19.   Jeremy Page, "China Clones, Sells Russian Fighter Jets," *Wall Street Journal*, December 5, 2010, http://online.wsj.com/article/SB10001424052748704679204575646472655698844.html?mod=WSJ_hp_LEFTTopStories.

20.   Ibid.

21.   Ron O'Rourke, "Programs vs. Resources: Some Options for the Navy," *Naval War College Review* 63, no. 4 (fall 2010): 29.

22.   Ibid.

23. Richard Jackson and Neil Howe, *Graying of the Great Powers: Demography and Geopolitics in the 21st Century* (Washington: Center for Strategic and International Studies, 2008), 1–2.

24. Roger McDermott, "Russian Military Prepares for Vostok 2010," *The Jamestown Foundation Eurasia Daily Monitor* 7, no. 106 (June 2, 2010), cited in Rod Thornton, *Military Modernization and the Russian Ground Forces*, Carlisle Barracks, Pennsylvania, Strategic Studies Institute, June 2011, 29.

25. Josef Joffe and James W. Davis, "Less than Zero," *Foreign Affairs* 90, no. 1 (January-February 2011): 11.

26. Gunnar Heinsohn, "Babies Win Wars," *Wall Street Journal*, March 6, 2006, http://online.wsj.com/article/SB114159651882789812.html?mod=opinion&ojcontent=otep.

27. See Samuel Huntington, "The Hispanic Challenge," *Foreign Policy*, March 1, 2004, http://www.foreignpolicy.com/articles/2004/03/01/the_hispanic_challenge.

28. See Eric Kaufmann, *Shall the Religious Inherit the Earth: Demography and Politics in the Twenty-first Century* (London: Profile Books, 2010).

29. Son preference, the pervasiveness of ultrasound technology, and easy access to abortion have amounted to what Nicholas Eberstadt calls "the global war against baby girls." Latest figures show that while there are normally 105 boys born for every 100 girls, today there are 120 boys for every 100 girls in some regions. This is projected to lead to some 30 million "missing brides" by 2020 in China and another 30 million unmarriageable men in India at the same time. This will exacerbate the problem of caring for the increasing number of elderly in these nations where extended families, women in particular, are the primary source of dependent care. Sociologists have also projected increased social unrest due to the glut of males unable to marry and settle down with families. See Nicholas Eberstadt, "The Global War Against Baby Girls," testimony before the United Nations Third Committee, New York, December 6, 2006, http://www.aei.org/speech/25399; and Mara Hvistendahl, *Unnatural Selection: Choosing Boys Over Girls and the Consequences of a World Full of Men* (New York: Public Affairs, 2011).

30. Joseph A. Hariss, "In Search of Lost Identity," *American Spectator*, March 2010, 45.

31. Jackson and Howe, *The Graying of the Great Powers*, 9.

32. Richard Katz, "Flying Geese No More," *PacNet* 56, at http://www.orientaleconomist.com.

33. John Baffes and Athanasios Vamvakidis, *Are You Too Young For the Nobel Prize*, World Bank and International Monetary Fund, September 18, 2008, http://papers.ssrn.com/sol3/papers.cfm?abstract_id=1270231. Particularly: "Despite public perceptions, not all Nobel winners were old. Physicists are, on average, the youngest recipients (54 years of age), followed by chemists (56), physicians (57), peace advocates (63), writers and poets (64), and economists (67). Almost 60 percent of Nobel recipients were between the ages of 45 and 65; 20 recipients were younger than 35; while 24 recipients were older than 80."

34. See Richard Peters and Frank Murtha, *Market Psych: How to Manage Fear and Build Your Investor Identity* (Hoboken: Wiley, 2010).

35. Nicholas Eberstadt, *Russia's Peacetime Demographic Crisis* (Washington, DC: National Bureau of Asian Research, 2010).

36. *The 2010 Global Entrepreneurship Monitor Report*, a joint project of Babson College and the London School of Business, http://www3.babson.edu/News room/Releases/us-gem-with-julio.cfm.

37. UN Population Division, Economic & Social Council, *World Population Ageing 2007*, 66.

38. Amlan Roy et al., *U.S. Demographics—Favorably Poised For the Future*, Credit Suisse report, Geneva, May 5, 2010, 6.

39. Atsushi Seike, "Towards a Life-Long Active Society" (keynote speech for the Third European Demography Forum, Brussels), November 22, 2010.

40. Ferdous Ara Begum, *Ageing, Discrimination, and Older Women's Human Rights From the Perspective of the CEDAW Convention*, March 2010, 3, http://www.globalaging.org/agingwatch/cedaw/cedaw.pdf.

41. Tabassum Zakaria, "Cheney Visits Afghanistan, Wants More NATO Troops," Reuters, March 21, 2008.

42. Council of the European Union, *Report on the Implementation of the European Security Strategy: Providing Security in a Changing World*, 11.

43. Henry Kissinger, "Power Shifts," *Survival* 52, no. 6 (December 2010–January 2011): 205.

44. Gunnar Heinsohn presents a pessimistic counterfactual to Europe's multilateral strategic posture: "If Europeans had continued to multiply like in its imperialistic prime, the world would still tremble before their armies. . . . In the last century, the Muslim population skyrocketed to 1.4 billion from 140 million. . . . Thus the new clothes of European 'pacifism' and 'soft power' conceal its naked weakness." See Heinsohn, "Babies Win Wars."

45. India, with a 2.9 total fertility rate, is expected to see a 45 percent increase in population by 2050 (from 1.1 billion to 1.6 billion) to become the world's most populous nation. With 60 percent of its population of working age, and only 4 percent aged sixty-five or older, it is a relatively young nation with a diversified and capable military. Population Reference Bureau, *2006 World Population Data Sheet*, 8, at http://www.prb.org.

46. United Nations Population Division, Department of Economic and Social Affairs, *World Population Prospects: The 2010 Revision*, CD-ROM version (New York: 2011). It is important to note that this is five years earlier than previously estimated in the UN's 2008 revision.

47. United Nations Population Division, Department of Economic and Social Affairs, *World Population Prospects: the 2010 Revision*, CD-ROM version, and *World Population Prospects: The 2008 Revision*, volume 1 (New York: 2009), 293 and 407. This estimate uses the constant fertility variant.

SELECTED BIBLIOGRAPHY

Alexseev, Mikhail A., and C. Richard Hofstetter. "Russia, China, and the Immigration Security Dilemma." *Political Science Quarterly* 121, no. 1 (2006): 1–32.

Arena, Mark, et al. *Why Has the Cost of Navy Ships Risen? A Macroscopic Examination of the Trends in U.S. Naval Ship Costs Over the Past Several Decades.* Santa Monica, CA: RAND, 2006.

Aron, Raymond. *The Century of Total War.* Boston: Beacon Press, 1955.

Babson College and the London School of Business. *The 2010 Global Entrepreneurship Monitor Report.* http://www3.babson.edu/Newsroom/Releases/us-gem-with-julio.cfm.

Baffes, John, and Athanasios Vamvakidis. *Are You Too Young For the Nobel Prize.* World Bank and International Monetary Fund, September 18, 2008. http://papers.ssrn.com/sol3/papers.cfm?abstract_id=1270231.

Brzezinski, Zbigniew. *The Choice: Global Domination or Global Leadership.* New York: Basic Books, 2004.

Buchanan, Patrick J. *The Death of the West: How Dying Populations and Immigrant Invasions Imperil Our Country and Civilization.* New York: St. Martin's Press, 2002.

Bulitt, William C. *The Great Globe Itself: A Preface to World Affairs.* New Brunswick, NJ: Transaction Publishers, 2005.

Burnham, James. *Containment or Liberation?* New York: John Day, 1952.

Capretta, James C. *Sustainability of Public Pension Systems: An Assessment of Reform Efforts in Twelve Developed Countries.* Washington, DC: Center for Strategic & International Studies, January 2007.

Cartledge, Paul. *The Spartans: The World of the Warrior-Heroes of Ancient Greece, from Utopia to Crisis and Collapse.* Woodstock and New York: Overlook, 2003.

Cawkwell, G. L. "The Decline of Sparta." *Classical Quarterly* 33, no. 2 (1983): 385–400.

Cawley, John, and Johanna Catherine Maclean. *Unfit for Service: The Implications of Rising Obesity for U.S. Military Service.* Washington: National Bureau of Economic Research, 2010. http://www.nber.org/papers/w16408.

Center on International Cooperation at New York University. "Annual Review of Global Peace Operations," 2009. http://www.cic.nyu.edu/peace_ssr/docs/GPO_2009.pdf.

Chamie, Joseph. "Fewer Babies Pose Difficult Challenges for Europe." *Yale Global Online*, October 8, 2007.

Chang, Gordon G. "India's China Problem." *Forbes.com*, August 14, 2009. http://www.forbes.com/2009/08/13/india-china-relations-population-opinions-columnists-gordon-chang.html.

Chanlett-Avery, Emma, and Mary Beth Nikitin. "Japan's Nuclear Future: Policy Debate, Prospects, and U.S. Interests." Congressional Research Service, February 19, 2009.

Chaubey, P. K. *Population Policy of India: Perspectives, Issues and Challenges.* New Delhi: Kanishka Publishers, 2001.

Cheng, Dean. *China's View of South Asia and the Indian Ocean.* Heritage Lecture 1163. August 31, 2010.

"China's Aging Population Hits 167 Million." Xinhua News Agency, July 14, 2010. http://news.xinhuanet.com/english2010/china/2010-07/14/c_13399044.htm.

"China's 'Demographic Dividend' to Come to an End in 2010: World Bank." *People's Daily*, March 25, 2007. http://english.peopledaily.com.cn/200703/25/eng20070325_360808.html.

"China's 'Demographic Dividend' to Decline in 2015." *Global Times* (Beijing), September 9, 2010. http://china.globaltimes.cn/society/2010-09/571766.html.

"China's Population Policy Helps Slow Global Warming, Says Official." Xinhua News Agency, December 10, 2009. http://news.xinhuanet.com/english/2009-12/10/content_12624315.htm.

"China to Maintain Low Birthrate: Vice Premier." *People's Daily*, January 20, 2010. http://english.peopledaily.com.cn/90001/90776/90785/6873409.html.

Cincotta, Richard, Robert Engleman, and Daniele Anastasion. *The Security Demographic, Population and Civil Conflict After the Cold War.* Population Action International report, August 1, 2003.

Clausewitz, Carl von, Michael Howard and Peter Paret, eds, trans. *On War.* Princeton, NJ: Princeton University Press, 1976.

Cohen, Eliot A. "Isolate or Liberate?" *Wall Street Journal*, October 4, 2004. http://online.wsj.com/article/0,,SB109684407036834817,00.html?mod=opinion%5Fmain%5Fcommentaries.

Cohen, Eliot A., Michael J. Eisenstadt, and Andrew J. Bacevich. *Knives, Tanks, and Missiles: Israel's Security Revolution.* Washington, DC: The Washington Institute for Near East Policy, 1998.

Cohen, Saul B. *Geography and Politics in a World Divided.* New York: Oxford University Press, 1975.

Coleman, David. *Demographic Diversity and the Ethnic Consequences of Immigration—Key Issues that the Commission's Report Left Out.* Vienna Yearbook of Population Research, 2007.

Congressional Budget Office. *An Analysis of the Navy's Fiscal Year 2011 Shipbuilding Plan.* May 2010.

———. *Federal Debt and the Risk of a Fiscal Crisis.* July 27, 2010, 3–4. http://www.cbo.gov/ftpdocs/116xx/doc11659/07-27_Debt_FiscalCrisis_Brief.pdf.

Connelly, Matthew. *Fatal Misconception: The Struggle to Control World Population.* Cambridge, MA: Harvard Belknap Press, 2008.

Connolly, Kate. "Nine Months On, World Cup Scorers Spark German Baby Boom."

Guardian, April 28, 2007. http://www.guardian.co.uk/world/2007/apr/28/germany.football.

Cordesman, Anthony H. "Cleansing the Poisoned Chalice? The Obama Administration and the Challenge of National Security Planning, Programming, and Budgeting." Center for Strategic & International Studies, April 16, 2009. http://www.comw.org/qdr/fulltext/0904cordesman.pdf.

———. "A Poisoned Chalice? The Flaws in the FY2008 Defense Program." Center for Strategic & International Studies, July 3, 2007. http://csis.org/files/media/csis/pubs/080630_fy2009_poisoned_chalice.pdf.

Corn, Tony. "Perils and Promises of a Global NATO." *Policy Review*, August 15, 2007. http://www.hoover.org/publications/policyreview/9179587.html.

Council of the European Union. *Report on the Implementation of the European Security Strategy: Providing Security in a Changing World*. Brussels, December 11, 2008. http://www.consilium.europa.eu/ueDocs/cms_Data/docs/pressdata/EN/reports/104630.pdf.

Council on Security and Defense Capabilities. *Japan's Visions for Future Security and Defense Capabilities in the New Era: Toward a Peace-Creating Japan*. Tokyo, August 2010.

Cox, Michael. "Is the United States in Decline—Again? An Essay." *International Affairs* 83, no. 4 (July 2007): 643–53.

Curtis, Lisa. "After Mumbai: Time to Strengthen U.S.-India Counterterrorism Cooperation." *Heritage Backgrounder* 2217, December 9, 2008. http://www.heritage.org/Research/Reports/2008/12/After-Mumbai-Time-to-Strengthen-US-India-Counterterrorism-Cooperation.

———. "China's Military and Security Relationship with Pakistan." Testimony before the U.S.-China Economic and Security Review Commission, May 20, 2009. http://www.heritage.org/Research/Testimony/Chinas-Military-and-Security-Relationship-with-Pakistan.

———. "U.S.-India Relations: The China Factor." *Heritage Backgrounder* 2209, November 25, 2008. http://www.heritage.org/research/reports/2008/11/us-india-relations-the-china-factor.

Curtis, Lisa, and Nicholas Hamisevicz. "U.S. Should Block China-Pakistan Nuclear Deal." *Heritage Backgrounder* 2910, May 20, 2010. http://www.heritage.org/research/reports/2010/05/us-should-block-china-pakistan-nuclear-reactor-deal.

Dabbs Sciubba, Jennifer. *The Future Faces of War: Population and National Security*. Santa Barbara, CA: Praeger, 2010.

Eberstadt, Nicholas. "China's Family Planning Goes Awry." *Far Eastern Economic Review*, December 2009. http://www.aei.org/article/101389.

———. "Critical Cross-Cutting Issues Facing Northeast Asia: Regional Demographic Trends and Prospects." *Asia Policy*, no. 3 (2007): 48–74.

———. "Four Surprises in Global Demography." *Watch on the West*, July 2004. http://www.aei.org/docLib/20040823_17233Eberstadtgraphics.pdf.

———. "Global Demographic Outlook to 2025." Speech at the Economic Conference on Demography, Growth and Wellbeing, Zurich, November, 30 2006, at http://www.aei.org.

———. "The Global War Against Baby Girls." Speech at the United Nations General Assembly Third Committee, New York, December 6, 2006. http://www.aei.org/speech/25399.

————. *Russia's Peacetime Demographic Crisis.* Washington, DC: National Bureau of Asian Research, 2010.

European Parliament Committee on Employment and Social Affairs. *Draft Report on the Demographic Future of Europe.* 2007/2156 (INI), November 10, 2007.

European Security Strategy. *Draft Internal Security Strategy of the European Union.* February 23, 2010, 6. http://register.consilium.europa.eu/pdf./en/10/st05st 05842-re02.en10.pdf.

————. *A Secure Europe in a Better World.* Brussels, December 12, 2003. http:// www.consilium.europa.eu/uedocs/cmsUpload/78367.pdf.

Eurostat. "Europe in Figures." *Eurostat Yearbook 2006–2007.*

Fair, C. Christin. "Students Islamic Movement of India and the Indian Mujahideen: An Assessment." *Asia Policy*, no. 9 (January2010): 101–19.

Ferguson, Niall. "Eurabia." *New York Times Magazine*, April 4, 2004.

Ferrero-Waldner, Benita. "The EU's Role in Protecting Europe's Security." Speech delivered at "Protecting Europe: Policies for Enhancing Security in the European Union" conference, Brussels, May 30, 2006.

Feshbach, Murray. *Russia's Health and Demographic Crises: Policy Implications and Consequences.* Washington, DC: Chemical and Biological Arms Control Institute, 2003.

Figueira, Thomas J. "Population Patterns in Late Archaic and Classical Sparta." *Transactions of the American Philological Association* 116 (1986): 165–213.

Fustos, Kata. *Marriage and Partnership Turnover for American Families.* Population Reference Bureau, June 2010. http://www.prb.org/Articles/2010/usmarriage-policyseminar.aspx.

Gilder, George. "Let a Billion Flowers Bloom." *Cato Journal*, winter 1989, 669–75.

Giles, Keir. *Where Have All the Soldiers Gone? Russia's Military Plans Versus Demographic Reality.* Conflict Studies Research Centre, Defense Academy of the United Kingdom. October 12, 2006. http://www.isn.ethz.ch/isn/Digital-Library/Publications/Detail/?ots591=0c54e3b3-1e9c-be1e-2c24-a6a8c7060 233&lng=en&id=94460.

Gokhale, Jagadeesh. *Social Security: A Fresh Look at Policy Alternatives.* Chicago: University of Chicago Press, 2010.

Gokhale, Jagadeesh, and Kent Smetters. "Bailout-Mania." *Forbes.com*, September 17, 2008.

Goldstone, Jack. "Population and Security: How Demographic Change Can Lead to Violent Conflict." *Journal of International Affairs* 56, no. 1 (fall 2002): 3–22.

Gomme, A. W. "The Population of Athens Again." *Journal of Hellenic Studies* 79 (1959): 61–68.

————. *The Population of Athens in the Fifth and Fourth Centuries B.C.* Oxford: Blackwell, 1933.

————. "The Slave Population of Athens." *Journal of Hellenic Studies* 66 (1946): 127–29.

Japan's Ministry of Defense. *Defense Programs and Budget of Japan: Overview of FY2010 Budget*, April 2010, 7.

Japan's National Defense Committee of the Liberal Democratic Party. *A Framework for the New National Defense Policy Guideline*, June 9, 2009, 12.

Japan's National Institute for Defense Studies. *East Asian Strategic Review 2006.*

Tokyo: June 2006. http://www.nids.go.jp/english/dissemination/east-asian/pdf/e2007summary.pdf.

———. *East Asian Strategic Review 2009*. Tokyo: 2010.

———. "Executive Summary." *East Asian Strategic Review 2007*. Tokyo: March 2007. http://www.nids.go.jp/english/dissemination/east-asian/pdf/e2007summary.pdf.

Japan's National Institute of Population and Social Security Research. *Population Projections for Japan: 2001–2050*. January 2002.

———. *Population Statistics of Japan 2008*. September 2008.

Haas, Mark. "A Geriatric Peace? The Future of U.S. Power in a World of Aging Populations." *International Security* 32, no. 1 (summer 2007): 112–47.

Hadley, Stephen J., William J. Perry, et al. *The QDR in Perspective: Meeting America's National Security Needs In the 21st Century: The Final Report of the Quadrennial Defense Review Independent Pane*. Washington, DC: United States Institute of Peace, 2010.

Hale, John R. *Lords of the Sea: The Epic Story of the Athenian Navy and the Birth of Democracy*. New York: Viking, 2009.

Hammond, N. G. L. *A History of Greece to 322 B.C.*, 3d ed. Oxford: Oxford University Press, 1986.

Hariss, Joseph A. "In Search of Lost Identity." *The American Spectator*, March 2010, 45.

Haushofer, Karl. "Power and Space." In Andreas Dorpalen. *The World of General Haushofer*. Port Washington, NY: Kennikat Press, 1942.

"Health Worsening in Russia's Armed Forces." *Associated Press Wordstream*, June 4, 1999.

Heinsohn, Gunnar. "Babies Win Wars." *Wall Street Journal*, March 6, 2006. http://online.wsj.com/article/SB114159651882789812.html?mod=opinion&ojcontent=otep.

Higgins, Andrew. "As China Finds Bigger Place in World Affairs, Its Wealth Breeds Hostility." *Washington Post*. September 8, 2010. http://www.washingtonpost.com/wp-dyn/content/article/2010/09/07/AR2010090707448.html.

Holachek, Jeffrey. *Russia's Shrinking Population and the Russian Military's HIV/AIDS Problem*. Occasional Paper prepared for the U.S. Atlantic Council, September 2006.

Holtz-Eakin, Douglas, and Michael Ramlet. "The Fiscal Implications of the Patient Protection and Affordable Care Act." *Health Affairs* 29, no. 6 (June 2010): 1136–41.

Howe, Neil, and Richard Jackson. "The World Won't Be Aging Gracefully. Just the Opposite." *Washington Post*, January 4, 2009. http://www.washingtonpost.com/wp-dyn/content/article/2009/01/02/AR2009010202231.html.

Hudson, Valerie M., and Andrea M. den Boer. *Bare Branches: Security Implications of Asia's Surplus Male Population*. Cambridge, MA: MIT Press, 2004.

Huntington, Samuel P. *The Clash of Civilizations and the Remaking of World Order*. New York: Simon & Schuster, 1996.

———. "The Hispanic Challenge." *Foreign Policy*, March 1, 2004. http://www.foreignpolicy.com/articles/2004/03/01/the_hispanic_challenge.

———. "The U.S.—Decline or Renewal?" *Foreign Affairs*, winter 1988–1989.

http://www.foreignaffairs.com/articles/43988/samuel-p-huntington/the
-us-decline-or-renewal.

Hvistendahl, Mara. *Unnatural Selection: Choosing Boys Over Girls and the Consequences of a World Full of Men*. New York: Public Affairs, 2011.

International Institute for Strategic Studies. *The Military Balance*. London: Routledge, 1997–2007.

Jackson, Richard, and Neil Howe. *Graying of the Great Powers: Demography and
Geopolitics in the 21st Century*. Washington, DC: Center for Strategic & International Studies, 2008.

Jaffrelot, Christophe. "India, an Emerging Power, But How Far?" *Emerging States:
The Wellspring of a New World Order*. New York: Columbia University Press,
2009.

Japan Center for Economic Research (JCER). *Long-Term Forecast of Global Economy and Population 2006–2050: Demographic Change and the Asian Economy*.
Tokyo: JCER, March 2007.

Japan Defense Agency. *Info-RMA: Study on Info-RMA and the Future of the Self-
Defense Forces*, December 2000.

Jenkins, Philip. "The Rise of Global Christianity: A Conversation with Philip Jenkins and David Brooks." Washington, DC: Ethics and Public Policy Center. July
2003.

Jiang Zhenghua and Mi Hong. *Population Security*. Hangzhou: Zhejiang University
Press, 2008.

Joffe, Josef, and James W. Davis. "Less than Zero." *Foreign Affairs* 90, no. 1 (January-
February 2011): 7–13.

Kaeser, Hans Ulrich, and Anthony H. Cordesman. "Abandon Ships: The Costly Illusion of Unaffordable Transformation." Washington: Center for Strategic &
International Studies, August 19, 2008. http://csis.org/publication/abandon-
ships.

Kagan, Donald. *The Outbreak of the Peloponnesian War*. Ithaca, NY: Cornell University Press, 1969.

Kagan, Frederick W. *Finding the Target: The Transformation of American Military
Policy*. New York: Encounter Books, 2006.

Kagan, Robert. *Dangerous Nation: America's Foreign Policy From Its Earliest Days to
the Dawn of the Twentieth Century*. New York: Vintage, 2006.

———. *Of Paradise and Power*. New York: Alfred A. Knopf, 2005.

Kamdar, Mira. *Planet India*. New York: Scribner, 2007.

Kaneko, Ryuichi, Akira Ishikawa, Futoshi Ishii, Tsukasa Sasai, Miho Iwasawa, Fusa-
mi Mita, and Rie Moriizumi. "Population Projections for Japan: 2006–2055—
Outline of Results, Methods, and Assumptions." *The Japanese Journal of Population* 6, no. 1 (March 2008): 76–83.

Kane, Tim. *Who Bears the Burden? Demographic Characteristics of U.S. Military
Recruits Before and After 9/11*. Center for Data Analysis, The Heritage Foundation, November 7, 2005.

Kaplan, Robert. "Center Stage for the Twenty-first Century: Power Plays in the
Indian Ocean." *Foreign Affairs* 88, no. 2 (March-April 2009). http://www.for
eignaffairs.org/20090301faessay88203/robert-d-kaplan/center-stage-for-the
-twenty-first-century.html.

————. "The Geography of Chinese Power: How Far Can Beijing Reach on Land and at Sea?" *Foreign Affairs* 89, no. 3 (May-June 2010). http://www.foreign affairs.com/articles/66205/robert-d-kaplan/the-geography-of-chinese-power.

————. *Monsoon: The Indian Ocean and the Future of American Power.* New York: Random House, 2010.

Kaufmann, Eric. *Shall the Religious Inherit the Earth: Demography and Politics in the Twenty-First Century.* London: Profile Books, 2010.

Kennan, George F. *Realities of American Foreign Policy.* New York: W. W. Norton, 1966.

Kennedy, Paul. "The Relative Decline of America." *Atlantic,* August 1997.

Kissinger, Henry. *Does America Need a Foreign Policy? Toward a Diplomacy for the 21st Century.* New York: Simon & Schuster, 2001.

————. "Power Shifts." *Survival* 52, no. 6 (December 2010–January 2011): 205–12.

Lewis, John Wilson, and Xue Litai. *China Builds the Bomb.* Stanford, CA: Stanford University Press, 1991.

Li Hongbin, Junsen Zhang, and Yi Zhu. *The Effect of the One-Child Policy on Fertility in China: Identification Based on the Differences-in-Differences.* Discussion Paper 00019. Chinese University of Hong Kong, August 11, 2005. http://ideas .repec.org/p/chk/cuhkdc/00019.html.

Li Jianxin. *The Structure of Chinese Population.* Beijing: Social Sciences Academic Press, 2009.

Litovkin, D. "Girls will be Converted into Officers." *Defense and Security,* July 4, 2007.

Liu Mingfu. *The China Dream: Big Power Thinking and Strategic Positioning in a Post-American Era.* Beijing: China Friendship Publishing, 2009.

Longman, Phillip. *The Empty Cradle: How Falling Birthrates Threaten World Prosperity [And What to Do About It].* New York: Basic Books, 2004.

Luttwak, Edward N. "Toward Post-Heroic Warfare." *Foreign Affairs,* May 1995.

Lutz, Wolfgang. *Adaptation Versus Mitigation Policies on Demographic Change in Europe.* Vienna Yearbook of Population Research, 2007.

Lutz, Wolfgang, Vegard Skirbekk, and Maria Rita Testa. *The Low Fertility Trap Hypothesis: Forces that May Lead to Further Postponement and Fewer Births in Europe.* Vienna Yearbook of Population Research, 2006.

Mackinder, Halford J. *Democratic Ideals and Reality.* New York: W. W. Norton, 1962.

Magioncalda, William. "A Modern Insurgency: India's Evolving Naxalite Problem." *CSIS South Asia Monitor,* no. 140, April 8, 2010. http://csis.org/publication/ modern-insurgency-india's-evolving-naxalite-problem-0.

Mahan, Alfred Thayer. *The Influence of Sea Power upon History 1660–1783.* London: University Paperbacks, 1965.

————. *The Interest of America in International Conditions.* New Brunswick, NJ: Transaction Publishers, 2003.

————. *The Problem of Asia: Its Effect upon International Politics.* New Brunswick, NJ: Transaction Publishers, 2003.

Mandelbaum, Michael. *The Ideas That Conquered the World: Peace, Democracy, and Free Markets in the Twenty-First Century.* New York: Public Affairs, 2002.

McNeill, William H. *Population and Politics Since 1750.* Charlottesville: University Press of Virginia, 1990.

Mead, Walter Russell. *God and Gold: Britain, America, and the Making of the Modern World.* New York: Alfred A. Knopf, 2007.

Mearsheimer, John J. *The Tragedy of Great Power Politics*. New York: W. W. Norton, 2001.

Mehra, P. K. "Future Shape, Size, and Role of Indian Air Force." *Air Power Journal* 4, no. 1 (spring 2009): 23–42.

Mesquida, Christian G., and Neil I. Wiener. "Human Collective Aggression: A Behavioral Ecology Perspective." *Ethology and Sociobiology* 17 (1996): 247–62.

Miles, Donna. "Officials Hope to Rekindle Interest in Immigration Bill Provision." *American Forces Press Service*, June 11, 2007.

Nadadur, Anuj. "The 'Muslim Threat' and the Bharatiya Janata Party's Rise to Power." *Peace and Democracy in South Asia* 2, nos. 1 and 2 (2006): 88–110. http://himalaya.socanth.cam.ac.uk/collections/journals/pdsa/pdf/pdsa_02_01_05.pdf.

National Population and Family Planning Commission of China. *Main Population Data in 2009, China*. February 26, 2010. http://www.npfpc.gov.cn/en/detail.aspx?articleid=100226103318203294.

———. *Research Report on National Population Development Strategy*. May 19, 2009. http://www.chinapop.gov.cn/fzgh/sewgh/200905/t20090519_171063.htm.

Nichiporuk, Brian. *The Security Dynamics of Demographic Factors*. Santa Monica, CA: RAND, 2000.

Nichiporuk, Brian, Clifford Grammich, Angel Rabasa, and Julie Da Vanzo. "Demographics and Security in Maritime Southeast Asia." *RAND Labor and Population* (winter-spring 2006): 83–91. http://www.rand.org/pubs/reprints/2006/RAND_RP1219.pdf.

Nielsen, Ingrid, and Cai Fang. "Demographic Shift and Projected Labor Shortage in China." *Economic Papers* 26 (September 2007): 231–36.

Nilekani, Nandani. *Imagining India*. New York: Penguin, 2009.

Nolen, Stephanie. "Land of the Rising Son." *Globe and Mail*, September 19, 2009.

Notestein, Frank W. "Fundamentals of Population Change in Europe and the Soviet Union." Hans Weigert and Vilhjalmur Stefansson, ed. *Compass of the World: A Symposium on Political Geography*. New York: Macmillan, 1944.

O'Hanlon, Michael. "Why China Cannot Conquer Taiwan." *International Security* 25, no. 2 (autumn 2000): 51–86.

O'Rourke, Ron. "Programs vs. Resources: Some Options for the Navy." *Naval War College Review* 63, no. 4 (fall 2010): 25–37.

Page, Jeremy. "China Clones, Sells Russian Fighter Jets." *Wall Street Journal*, December 5, 2010. http://online.wsj.com/article/SB100014240527487046792045756464726565698844.html?mod=WSJ_hp_LEFTTopStories.

Palit, Amitendu. "Is China or India Aging Better?" *Forbes.com*, June 30, 2010. http://www.forbes.com/2010/06/30/population-india-china-markets-economy-economic-growth.html?boxes=marketschannelnews.

Passel, Jeffrey S., and D'Vera Cohn. *U.S. Population Projections: 2005–2050*. Washington, DC: Pew Research Center, 2008.

Peterson, Peter G. "Gray Dawn: The Global Aging Crisis." *Foreign Affairs* 78, no. 1 (January-February 1999): 42–55.

———. "The Shape of Things to Come: Global Aging in the Twenty-first Century." *Journal of International Affairs* 56, no. 1 (fall 2002): 189–210.

Peters, Richard, and Frank Murtha. *Market Psych: How to Manage Fear and Build Your Investor Identity.* Hoboken, NJ: Wiley, 2010.

Philipov, Dimiter, and Berghammer, Caroline. *Religion and Fertility Ideals, Intentions and Behavior: a Comparative Study of European Countries.* Vienna Yearbook of Population Research, 2007.

Plutarch. *The Rise and Fall of Athens: Nine Greek Lives.* London: Penguin, 1960.

Poddar, Tushar, and Pragyan Deb. *India's Rising Labour Force.* Global Economics Paper 201. Goldman Sachs Global Economics, Commodities and Strategy Research, July 28, 2010. http://www.scribd.com/doc/35055286/GoldmanSachs-Global-Economics-Paper-20100728.

Population Reference Bureau. *2006 World Population Data Sheet.* Available at http://www.prb.org.

Pritchett, Lant. "Desired Fertility and the Impact of Population Policies." *Population and Development Review* 20, no. 1 (March 1994): 1–55.

Quester, George H. "Demographic Trends and Military Recruitment: Surprising Possibilities." *Parameters* 35, no. 1 (spring 2005): 27–40. http://www.carlisle.army.mil/USAWC/parameters/Articles/05spring/quester.htm.

Rajan, D. S. *China: Strategic Experts Talk About a "Partial" Sino-Indian War.* South Asia Analysis Group Paper 2939, November 24, 2008. http://www.southasiaanalysis.org/%5Cpapers30%5Cpaper2939.html.

Rehman, Iskander. "India's Future Aircraft Carrier Force and the Need for Strategic Flexibility." *Institute for Defense Studies and Analysis Comment,* June 1, 2010. http://www.idsa.in/idsacomments/IndiasFutureAircraftCarrierForceandtheNeedforStrategicFlexibility_irehman_010610.

Richards, Jason, et al. *Russia: Demographic Trends and the Projection of Military Power.* Conference paper presented at the 50th Annual Meeting of the International Studies Association, New York, June 9, 2008. http://www.allacademic.com/meta/p312179_index.html.

Scissors, Derek, and Michelle Kaffenberger. "India's Future in the Balance." Heritage WebMemo 2586. August 13, 2009. http://www.heritage.org/Research/Reports/2009/08/Indias-Future-in-the-Balance.

———. "U.S.-India Relations: Ensuring Indian Prosperity in the Coming Demographic Boom." *Heritage Backgrounder* 2274, May 15, 2009. http://www.heritage.org/Research/Reports/2009/05/US-India-Relations-Ensuring-Indian-Prosperity-in-the-Coming-Demographic-Boom.

Seetharam, K. S. "Population, Society, and Power: East Asia's Future." *Georgetown Journal of International Affairs* 4, no. 2 (summer-fall 2003): 27–34.

Seiffert, G. "Masters of Space." Andreas Dorpalen, *The World of General Haushofer.* Port Washington, NY: Kennikat Press, 1942.

Sharma, Rajeev. "Indo-Japan Ties Poised for Great Leap Forward." *Eurasia Review,* August 18, 2010. http://www.eurasiareview.com/201008187148/indo-japan-ties-poised-for-great-leap-forward.html.

Sheehan, James J. *Where Have All the Soldiers Gone? The Transformation of Modern Europe.* Boston: Houghton Mifflin, 2008.

Sherman, Jason. "Gates Signs Planning Documents to Guide Investments, Operations." *Inside the Pentagon,* May 15, 2008. http://www.military-quotes.com/forum/gates-signs-planning-documents-guide-t62194.html.

Siegel, Jeremy J. "Impact of an Aging Population on the Global Economy." *CFA Institute Conference Proceedings Quarterly* 24, no. 3 (September 2007): 1–7.

Sim, Chi Yin. "China's Labor Crunch: End to One-Child Policy?" *Straits Times* (Singapore), March 20, 2010.

Singh, Meeta, and Vasu Mohan. "The Rise of Sex Selection in India," *Democracy at Large* 2, no. 1 (2005): 30–32. http://www.ifes.org/Content/Publications/Feature-Stories/2007/Jun/The-Rise-of-Sex-Selection-in-India.aspx.

Spring, Baker. *Defense FY2008 Budget Analysis: Four Percent for Freedom*. The Heritage Foundation, March 5, 2007.

Sprout, Harold and Margaret. *Foundations of National Power*. Princeton, NJ: Princeton University Press, 1945.

Spykman, Nicholas. *America's Strategy in World Politics: The United States and the Balance of Power*. New Brunswick, NJ: Transaction Publishers, 2007.

———. *The Geography of the Peace*. New York: Harcourt, Brace, 1944.

Staley, David J. "Japan's Uncertain Future: Key Trends and Scenarios." *The Futurist* (March-April 2002): 48–53.

Stein, Peter. "China Casts Its Shadow on Mongolia." *Wall Street Journal*, December 14, 2009. http://online.wsj.com/article/SB10001424052748703954904574595651461527632.html.

Stein, Rob. "US Fertility Rate Hits 35-year High, Stabilizing Population." *Washington Post*, December 21, 2007.

Strassler, Robert B., ed., Andrea L. Purvis, trans. *The Landmark Herodotus*. New York: Pantheon, 2007.

Strassler, Robert B., ed., John Marincola, trans. *The Landmark Xenophon's Hellenika*. New York: Pantheon, 2009.

Strassler, Robert B., ed., Richard Crawley, trans. *The Landmark Thucydides*. New York: Touchstone, 1998.

Sugio, Takahashi. "The Japanese Perception of the Information Technology-Revolution in Military Affairs: Toward a Defensive Information-Based Transformation."Emily O. Goldman and Thomas G. Mahnken, eds. *The Information Revolution in Military Affairs in Asia*. New York: Palgrave, 2004: 81–95.

Tellis, Ashley, et al. *Measuring National Power in the Postindustrial Age*. Santa Monica, CA: RAND, 2000.

Testa, Maria Rita, and Leonardo Grilli. "The Influence of Childbearing Regional Contexts on Ideal Family Size in Europe." *Population-E* 61, nos. 1 and 2 (2006): 109–38.

Thornton, Rod. *Military Modernization and the Russian Ground Forces*. Carlisle Barracks, Pennsylvania, Strategic Studies Institute, June 2011.

Toft, Monica Duffy. *The State of the Field: Demography and War*. ECSP Report 11. Washington, DC: Wilson Center, 2005.

Tsunoda, Tomoko, and Brad Glosserman. "The Guillotine: Japan's Demographic Transformation and Its Security Implications." *Issues and Insights* 9, no. 10 (June 2009): 1–52.

United Nations Population Division, Department of Economic and Social Affairs. *World Population Ageing 2007*. New York: 2008.

———. *World Population Ageing 2009*. New York: 2010.

———. *World Population Prospects: The 1998 Revision*, vol. 1: *Comprehensive Tables*. New York: 1998.

———. *World Population Prospects: The 2006 Revision*. New York: 2007.

———. *World Population Prospects: The 2008 Revision*, vol. 1: *Comprehensive Tables*. New York: United Nations, 2009.

———. *World Population Prospects: The 2008 Revision*, vol. 2: *Sex and Age Distribution of the World Population*. New York: United Nations, 2009.

———. *World Population Prospects: The 2010 Revision*, CD-ROM version. New York: 2011.

U.S. Census Bureau. "China's Population to Peak at 1.4 Billion Around 2026." Press release, December 15, 2009. http://www.census.gov/newsroom/releases/archives/international_population/cb09-191.html.

———. *Population Projections for States, by Age, Sex, Race, and Hispanic Origin: 1995 to 2025*. Population Paper Listing 47. Washington, DC: U.S. Department of Commerce, 1996. http://www.census.gov/population/www/projections/ppl47.html.

———. *Population Projections of the United States by Age, Race, Sex, and Hispanic Origin: 1995–2050*. Washington, DC: U.S. Department of Commerce, 1996.

———. *U.S. Census 2010*. Washington, DC: U.S. Department of Commerce. http://2010.census.gov/2010census/data/.

U.S. Department of Defense. *A Cooperative Strategy for 21st Century Seapower*. Washington, DC: October 2007.

———. *Demographics 2008: Profile of the Military*. Washington, DC: 2008.

———. *Fiscal Year 2011 Budget Request Overview*. Washington, DC: February 2010. http://comptroller.defense.gov/defbudget/fy2011/FY2011_Budget_Request_Overview_Book.pdf.

———. *National Defense Strategy*. Washington, DC: June 2008.

———. *Quadrennial Defense Review*. Washington, DC: February 2006.

U.S. Government. *Budget of the U.S. Government: Fiscal Year 2010*. Washington, DC: Office of Management and Budget, 2009. http://www.whitehouse.gov/omb/budget/fy2010/assets/hist.pdf.

U.S. Joint Forces Command. *Joint Operating Environment 2008: Challenges and Implications for the Future Joint Force*. November 2008.

U.S. National Intelligence Council. *Global Trends 2025: A Transformed World*. November 2008.

Van Oudenaren, John. "Sources of Conflict in Europe and the Former Soviet Union." Zalmay M. Khalilzad and Ian O. Lesser, eds. *Sources of Conflict in the 21st Century: Regional Futures and US Strategy*. Santa Monica, CA: RAND, 1998: 231–305.

Wattenber, Ben J. *How the New Demography of Depopulation Will Shape Our Future*. Chicago: Evan R. Dee, 2004.

Weigel, George. *The Cube and the Cathedral: Europe, America, and Politics Without God*. New York: Basic Books, 2005.

Westley, Sidney B., and Minja Kim Choe. "How Does Son Preference Affect Populations in Asia?" *Analysis from the East-West Center*, no. 84 (September 2007): 1–11. http://www.eastwestcenter.org/fileadmin/stored/pdfs/api084.pdf.

Whelton, Clark. "A Demographic Theory of War, Population, Power and the

'Slightly Weird' Ideas of Gunnar Heinsohn." *Weekly Standard*, October 5, 2007. http://www.weeklystandard.com/Content/Public/Articles/000/000/014/185je plm.asp.

Wilson, Nigel Guy, ed. *Encyclopedia of Ancient Greece*. New York: Routledge, 2006.

Winner, Andrew C., and Toshi Yoshihara. "India and Pakistan at the Edge." *Survival* 44, no. 3 (fall 2002): 69–86.

Wolf, Martin. "How to Prevent Old Europe Becoming a Dying Continent." *Financial Times*, March 5, 2003.

"Women in the Russian Federation's Armed Forces Today." *Russian Military Review*, no. 3 (March 2007).

Wonacott, Peter. "Deadly Labor Wars Hinder India's Rise." *Wall Street Journal*, November 20, 2009.

Woodrow Wilson International Center for Scholars. "The Demographic Dilemma: Japan's Aging Society." *Asia Program Special Report*, no. 107 (January 2003): 1–23.

World Health Organization. *The Global MDR-TB & XDR-TB Response Plan 2007–2008*. Geneva: 2007.

———. *Global Tuberculosis Control: Surveillance, Planning, Financing*. Geneva: 2007.

———. *Global Tuberculosis Control: Surveillance, Planning, Financing*. Geneva: 2010.

Xie Zhuanjiao. "Juvenile Criminal Cases Rising." *China Daily*, December 5, 2007. http://www.chinadaily.com.cn/china/2007-12/05/content_6298758.htm.

Xin Dingding and Wang Huazhong. "Craving for a Second Child? Govt Will Dent Your Pockets." *China Daily*, March 26, 2009. http://www.chinadaily.com.cn/china/2009-03/26/content_7618314.htm.

Ying Tian and Guo Likun. "China Focus: China's One Child Policy Pressurized by Aging Population." Xinhua News Agency, August 12, 2009. http://news.xin huanet.com/english/2009-08/12/content_11867131.htm.

Zakaria, Tabassum. "Cheney Visits Afghanistan, Wants More NATO Troops." Reuters, March 21, 2008.

Zhao Huanxin. "Working-Age Population Set to Decline." *China Daily*, September 1, 2006. http://www.chinadaily.com.cn/china/2006-09/01/content_678901.htm.

Zheng Caixiong. "Guangdong to Relax Family Policy by 2030." *China Daily*, September 25, 2010. http://www.chinadaily.com.cn/china/2010-09/25/content _11342254.htm.

Zhou Jiangong. "Getting Rich Before Getting Old." *Forbes.com*, September 28, 2009. http://www.forbes.com/2009/09/25/zhou-jiangong-china-pensions-leadership-jiangong.html.

Zhu Wei Xing, Li Lu, and Therese Hesketh. "China's Excess Males, Sex Selective Abortion, and One Child Policy: Analysis of Data from 2005 National Intercensus Survey." *BMJ*. April 9, 2009. http://www.bmj.com/cgi/reprint/338/apr09_2/b1211.

Zissis, Carin. *Demographic Insecurity: Hindu-Muslim Tensions*. Council on Foreign Relations, June 22, 2007. http://www.cfr.org/publication/13659/indias_muslim _population.html.

INDEX

271

ABOUT THE EDITORS

Susan Yoshihara is senior vice president for research at Catholic Family and Human Rights Institute (C-FAM) and director of the International Organizations Research Group in New York. She previously served on the faculty at the Naval War College, where she taught national security affairs and international relations. In her twenty-year career as a U.S. Navy helicopter pilot, she held the rank of commander, led combat logistics and search-and-rescue units in the Pacific and Persian Gulf, advised the Atlantic Fleet commander, and worked for the Under Secretary of Commerce for International Trade as a White House Fellow. She is a graduate of the U.S. Naval Academy and has received an MA in national security affairs from the Naval Postgraduate School in Monterey, California, and a PhD in international relations from the Fletcher School of Law and Diplomacy, Tufts University. Yoshihara is the author of *Waging War to Make Peace: U.S. Intervention in Global Conflicts* (Praeger, 2010).

Douglas A. Sylva is a senior fellow at C-FAM, where he studies topics related to international social policy and law. He has addressed members of the European Parliament, the British House of Lords, the German Bundestag, and the U.S. Congress. Sylva served on numerous Vatican delegations to the United Nations, including the United Nations Ad Hoc Committee on the Rights and Dignity of Persons with Disabilities (2005–2007). His published research includes analysis of the United Nations Population Fund (UNFPA) and the United Nations Children's Fund (UNICEF). His white paper "Rights by Stealth," coauthored with

Susan Yoshihara, chronicles the misuse of the international legal regime. His writings have appeared in such publications as the *New York Times*, the *Washington Times*, *National Review*, the *Weekly Standard*, and *First Things*. Sylva is also the Chair of Catholic Social Teaching at St. Paul Inside the Wall, the Catholic Center for Evangelization for the Diocese of Paterson, New Jersey. Sylva is a Phi Beta Kappa graduate of Dartmouth College and earned a political science doctorate from Columbia University, where he also taught political philosophy.

ABOUT THE CONTRIBUTORS

Gordon G. Chang is a columnist at *Forbes.com* and the author of *Nuclear Showdown: North Korea Takes On the World* (Random House, 2001) and *The Coming Collapse of China* (Random House, 2006). Chang lived and worked in China and Hong Kong for almost two decades, most recently in Shanghai as counsel to the American law firm Paul Weiss. Prior to that, he was a partner in the international law firm Baker & McKenzie, in Hong Kong. His writings have appeared in the *New York Times*, the *Wall Street Journal*, the *International Herald Tribune*, *Commentary*, the *Weekly Standard*, *National Review*, and *Barron's*. Chang has spoken at Columbia, Cornell, Princeton, Yale, and other universities and at the Heritage Foundation, the Brookings Institution, the Cato Institute, RAND, the American Enterprise Institute, the Council on Foreign Relations, and other institutions. He has given briefings at the National Intelligence Council, the Central Intelligence Agency, the State Department, and the Pentagon. He has also spoken before industry and investor groups, including Bloomberg, Sanford Bernstein, and Credit Lyonnais Securities Asia. Chang has appeared before the U.S.-China Economic and Security Review Commission and has delivered to the Commission a report on the future of China's economy. He has appeared on CNN, Fox News Channel, CNBC, MSNBC, the BBC, and Bloomberg Television. He has also appeared on the *Daily Show with Jon Stewart*. Outside the United States, he has spoken in Beijing, Shanghai, Taipei, Hong Kong, Seoul, Singapore, Tokyo, The Hague, London, Toronto, and Vancouver. He has served two terms as a trustee of Cornell University.

Lisa Curtis is a senior research fellow at the Heritage Foundation, focusing on U.S. security policy toward India, Pakistan, Afghanistan, and the other nations of South Asia. She was a professional staff member of the Senate Foreign Relations Committee; a senior adviser (White House Appointment) in the State Department's South Asia Bureau, where she advised the assistant secretary on India-Pakistan relations; and an analyst for the Central Intelligence Agency. Curtis served in the U.S. Foreign Service, including the U.S. embassies in Pakistan and India in the mid-1990s, and continues to travel frequently to the region. She earned a Meritorious Honor Award from the State Department in 1996 for her role as embassy point-person in a yearlong, four-nation endeavor to free hostages held by militants in Kashmir. Curtis has published op-eds in the *Los Angeles Times*, the *Washington Times*, *National Review Online*, and *Fox News.com*, and has appeared on CNN, CBS, CNBC, PBS, MSNBC, and FOX. She has also testified before Congress on more than a dozen occasions on topics related to Pakistan, India, Afghanistan, and U.S. engagement with Muslim communities abroad. Curtis earned her BA in economics at Indiana University.

Nicholas Eberstadt is a Henry Wendt Scholar in Political Economy at the American Enterprise Institute. A political economist and a demographer by training, Eberstadt is also a senior adviser to the National Board of Asian Research, a member of the Visiting Committee at the Harvard School of Public Health, and a member of the Global Leadership Council at the World Economic Forum. He researches and writes extensively on economic development, foreign aid, global health, demographics, and poverty. He is the author of numerous monographs and articles on North and South Korea, East Asia, and countries of the former Soviet Union. His books range from *The End of North Korea* to *The Poverty of "The Poverty Rate."* Eberstadt is a member of the Global Leadership Council, World Economic Forum, and Key National Indicators Forum. He is senior adviser to the National Board of Asian Research, a member of the U.S. Commission on Helping to Enhance the Livelihood of People and of the Board of Scientific Counselors, National Center for Health Statistics, U.S. Department of Health and Human Services, as well as a visiting fellow at the Center for Population and Developmental Studies, Harvard University, and a consultant to the World Bank, the State Department, the Agency for International Development, and the U.S. Bureau of the Census. Eberstadt holds a PhD in political economy and government from Harvard University; MPA from the Kennedy School of Government, Harvard University; MSc from the London School of Economics; and AB from Harvard University.

Murray Feshbach is a senior scholar at the Woodrow Wilson Center at the Smithsonian Institution in Washington, D.C. He served as chief of the USSR Population, Employment and Research and Development Branch of the Foreign Demographic Analysis Division (now the Center for International Research) of the Census Bureau from 1957 to 1981, receiving the Silver Medal of the Department of Commerce in 1973 for meritorious service. He then served as a fellow at the Kennan Institute from 1979 to 1980. After he retired from government service, he was a research professor at Georgetown University until 2000, when he retired as professor emeritus. At the request of the U.S. Department of State, he served as the first (experimental) Sovietologist-in-Residence, in the Office of the Secretary General of NATO, Lord Peter Carrington, from 1986 to 1987, with an assimilated rank of Assistant Secretary General. His book, *Ecocide in the USSR: Health and Nature Under Siege*, with Alfred Friendly Jr. (Basic Books, 1992) was translated into Russian and published in Moscow in January 1993. He is the author of *Ecological Disaster: Cleaning Up the Hidden Legacy of the Soviet Regime* (Twentieth Century Fund, 1995); the editor in chief of *Environmental and Health Atlas of Russia* (1995), which was simultaneously published in Russian and English in Moscow; and author of *Russia's Health and Demographic Crises* (Chemical and Biological Arms Control Institute, 2003). In May 2004 Feshbach received the Annual Award of the Twelfth International Conference on HIV/AIDS, Cancer and Related Problems, sponsored by the Russian Biomedical Research Center, held at St. Petersburg State University, for his lifetime work on population, environment, and health of the former Soviet Union and Russia. Feshbach is listed in *Who's Who in the World* and *Who's Who in America*. He was born in New York, received his BA in history from Syracuse University, his MA in European diplomatic history from Columbia University, and his PhD in economics from American University.

James R. Holmes is an associate professor of strategy at the Naval War College and a faculty associate at the University of Georgia School of Public and International Affairs. He was a senior research associate and adjunct professor at the University of Georgia School of Public and International Affairs, research associate at the Institute for Foreign Policy Analysis, and a U.S. Navy surface warfare officer, serving in the engineering and weapons departments on board the battleship *Wisconsin*. He is the author of *Theodore Roosevelt and World Order: Police Power in International Relations* (Potomac Books, 2006), and, most recently, coauthor of *Red Star over the Pacific: China's Rise and the Challenge to U.S. Maritime Strategy* (Naval Institute Press, 2010). Holmes holds a PhD and MALD from the Fletcher School of Law and Diplomacy, Tufts University, MA degrees from Salve Regina University and Providence College, graduated from the Naval War College with highest distinction, and is a Phi Beta Kappa graduate of Vanderbilt University.

Phillip Longman is a senior research fellow at the New America Foundation, an editor at the *Washington Monthly*, and an instructor at Johns Hopkins Center for Advanced Governmental Studies. He writes frequently on global aging and related issues, such as health-care delivery system reform and the long-term financing of the welfare state. His books include *Best Care Anywhere*, second edition (Polipoint, 2010), which chronicles the quality transformation of the Veterans Health Administration and applies its lessons to a plan for reforming the U.S. health-care system as a whole. His book *The Empty Cradle: How Falling Birthrates Threaten World Prosperity and What to Do About It* (Basic Books, 2004) explored economic and geopolitical implications of global fertility decline. *Born to Pay: the New Politics of Aging in America* (Houghton Mifflin, 1987) accurately predicted the mounting strains on federal spending and economic growth associated with the aging of the baby boom generation. And *The Return of Thrift: How the Collapse of the Middle Class Welfare State Will Reawaken Values in America* (Free Press, 1997) correctly warned of the consequences excess debt and insufficient savings. His writing on these and other subjects has appeared in such publications as *Foreign Policy*, *Foreign Affairs*, *Harvard Business Review*, and *Fortune*. He is a graduate of Oberlin College, and was also a Knight-Bagehot Fellow at Columbia University.

Francis P. Sempa is Assistant U.S. Attorney for the Middle District of Pennsylvania, and an adjunct professor of political science at Wilkes University. He is the author of *Geopolitics: From the Cold War to the 21st Century* (Transaction,

2007), *America's Global Role: Essays and Reviews on National Security* (University Press of America, 2009), and *Somewhere in France, Somewhere in Germany: A Combat Soldier's Journey Through the Second World War* (forthcoming, Hamilton Books), and has written lengthy introductions to four other books on U.S. foreign policy. He is a contributor to the 1990 volume *The Conduct of American Foreign Policy Debated*. He has written on geopolitics and historical and foreign policy topics for *Strategic Review, American Diplomacy*, the *National Interest, National Review, Human Rights Review, Presidential Studies Quarterly*, the *Washington Times*, and the *International Social Science Review*. Sempa is a contributing editor to the web journal *American Diplomacy*.

Toshi Yoshihara is the John A. van Beuren Chair of Asia-Pacific Studies at the Naval War College in Newport, Rhode Island. Previously, he was a visiting professor in the Strategy Department at the Air War College. Yoshihara has also served as an analyst at the Institute for Foreign Policy Analysis, RAND, and the American Enterprise Institute. He is the coauthor of *Red Star over the Pacific: China's Rise and the Challenge to U.S. Maritime Strategy* (Naval Institute Press, 2010), *Indian Naval Strategy in the Twenty first Century* (Routledge, 2009), and *Chinese Naval Strategy in the Twenty-first Century: The Turn to Mahan* (Routledge, 2008). He is also the coeditor of *Asia Looks Seaward: Power and Maritime Strategy* (Praeger, 2008). Yoshihara holds a PhD from the Fletcher School of Law and Diplomacy, Tufts University.